NEW STATE,
MODERN STATESMAN
HASHIM THAÇI – A BIOGRAPHY

NEW STATE,
MODERN STATESMAN
HASHIM THAÇI – A BIOGRAPHY

ROGER BOYES
AND SUZY JAGGER

Biteback Publishing

First published in Great Britain in 2018 by
Biteback Publishing Ltd
Westminster Tower
3 Albert Embankment
London SE1 7SP

ISBN 978-1-78590-230-7

10 9 8 7 6 5 4 3 2 1

A CIP catalogue record for this book is available from the British Library.

Set in Minion Pro by Adrian McLaughlin

Printed and bound in Great Britain by
CPI Group (UK) Ltd, Croydon CR0 4YY

CONTENTS

FOREWORD BY BOB DOLE

'Thaçi's journey is Kosovo's journey'

My first visit to Kosovo was in the summer of 1990, less than a year after the fall of the Berlin Wall. I was part of a congressional delegation meeting with Serbian authorities who did not seem too excited to see us there, claiming it was too dangerous for us to move around the countryside.

It became apparent during this trip that Kosovars are some of the most pro-American, pro-democracy people in Eastern Europe. It was also clear to me that they were being subjugated by the Belgrade government to the level of second-hand citizens. Evidence began to surface – photos of tortured people and ill-treated communities – indicating that Kosovo was a nation in despair. Our bipartisan delegation witnessed all too clearly the vile nature of Slobodan Milošević's regime and the dangers that escalation of violence in Kosovo posed for the stability of the entire region. This concern extended to the administration of President George H. W. Bush, who within two years of my first visit sent a 'Christmas Warning' to Milošević, informing him that Serbian aggression in Kosovo would bring a unilateral military response by the United States.

As it happened – and rather tragically so – Milošević decided to test the resolve of the United States, and he launched a campaign of genocide and violence that prompted the largest military intervention on European soil since the Second World War. Milošević was ousted, and the entire Western Balkans entered a period of relative peace and stability.

The now independent Kosovo is striving towards becoming a stable democratic country – at peace with neighbours, secular in nature and a staunch ally in the global fight against religious and ethnic extremism. It is a country of young, dynamic people who are fully committed to European Union and NATO accession – progressive people who care deeply about ethnic reconciliation and global interfaith dialogue.

Kosovo has had an incredible journey, and one man critical to the development of this bastion of democracy in the Balkans is President Hashim Thaçi. As a young man barely thirty years old, he headed the Kosovar Albanian delegation at the international conference at Château de Rambouillet in France. Thaçi came to the table as an unknown quantity, but by the conclusion of the conference two weeks later, he was recognised as the voice of reason during a time of severe internal factionalism. The fate of the nation rested on Thaçi's keen ability to convince his fellow fighters to compromise – not an easy task for those in the field who were witnessing the atrocities being committed by the Serbian forces.

When Milošević adamantly opposed any peace agreement and his diabolic plans for ethnic cleansing were stopped by NATO, Thaçi again proved his mettle by enabling the full demilitarisation of Kosovo in less than three months. The ability of Kosovar leadership to pacify and stop the cycle of violence is admirable, especially when we consider recent conflict areas such as Afghanistan, Iraq or Libya. When, in 2000, Thaçi lost his first national election, he accepted the results even though he was the political leader of the KLA, signalling a new era of democratic behaviour among Kosovars.

By 2008, the then recently elected Prime Minister Thaçi declared the independence of Kosovo, establishing the youngest state in Europe and ensuring the democratic freedom of every Kosovar.

Kosovo has had other great 'fathers of the nation' over the past several decades. They tried to organise peaceful resistance. Milošević, however, did not believe in dialogue with Kosovars. It took a new generation of leadership, headed by President Thaçi, to call Kosovo's allies to action.

Thaçi's journey is Kosovo's journey. The United States assisted Kosovo because we recalled our own fight for independence. We saw our own values reflected in Kosovo's dedication to self-determination and pro-tection of human rights. Kosovo is a shining example of success. This is a nation that defies the typical ethnic and religious fault lines in the region. Though a majority Muslim country, the Constitution approved by President Thaçi's government bans any discrimination on the basis of religion, ethnicity or sexual orientation. Kosovo's minority groups are considered integral to the nation's heritage and, along with the country's security services, are strong allies in the renewed fight against ISIS and other terrorist organisations. Kosovo may be a small nation, but its value as a young democratic republic is of global proportions.

I hope this book, written by two of Britain's most renowned journalists – Roger Boyes and Suzy Jagger – will provide an enlightening glimpse into the birth of a republic and a country whose inspiring people I am proud to call my friends.

Robert Joseph Dole served as a US senator from Kansas from 1969 until 1996, also serving as the Senate Majority Leader from 1985 until 1996. He was the Republican nominee for President of the United States in 1996.

HASHIM THAÇI AND THE FIGHT FOR KOSOVO

History is full of guerrilla leaders who die in combat, who fail to topple regimes or whose revolutions go adrift. Few mourn them. Some, those with shrewd political brains, courage, and good instincts, do indeed achieve their goals and become leaders of liberated, independent countries. Nelson Mandela is the name that still carries the most resonance in this regard, but there are many others in South America, Israel, decolonised Africa and Asia who have made this transition from insurgent to head of state.

Yet in modern Europe only one man, Hashim Thaçi, has made such a successful passage. Still in his forties, Thaçi has steered Kosovo from a suppressed colony under the boot of one of Europe's most savage dictators to a vibrant democracy. It has been an extraordinary political journey and it is still not complete: as President of the new country, he is struggling to bring it into NATO and the European Union, to build bridges with Kosovo's enemies. When he and Kosovo have achieved this goal, they will have reshaped the Balkans and turned Europe's historically unstable south-eastern borderlands into a part of a modern community of states.

Thaçi has faced, and is facing, four great battles. All have been a test of leadership on the battlefield and at the negotiating table. Leaving his village in the mountains of western Kosovo, Thaçi studied history and philosophy in the capital, at Pristina University. Appalled by the near-apartheid conditions imposed on ethnic Albanians by the Milošević regime, he began to organise protests. Serb leader Slobodan Milošević reacted to the upheavals of 1989 – the peaceful revolutions that brought communist regimes tumbling down across Eastern Europe – by becoming even more nationalist and trampling on the rights of the Kosovars. As Thaçi shifted into the underground resistance, dodging arrest, he realised that Milošević could not be blocked by passive resistance. This became Thaçi's first major challenge: to convince those Kosovars who followed the intellectual resistance leader Ibrahim Rugova that they were leading the province into a cul-de-sac. Rugova imagined himself to be a kind of Václav Havel: the standard-bearer of the Czech Velvet Revolution. But it would be impossible to win back even a limited amount of autonomy from Milošević without the shedding of blood. Beaten down by years of repression, many Kosovars simply could not picture how it would be possible ever to impose their will on the Serb leader. The only sensible option, it seemed, was to keep one's head down and keep alive, as best one could, the flame of an independent Kosovo. Thaçi's first foe, then, was the defeatism that spread out from Rugova's circle. He understood, and had to communicate that insight, that Milošević was on the road to war, that the whole region was about to be set ablaze. And Kosovo had to be ready. Not to prepare for war, he told his underground cells, would be an act of irresponsibility.

For Thaçi, there has always been a time to fight and a time to strike a deal. Neither stratagem was ever going to be easy. In May 1940, Churchill told Cabinet members: 'We shall go on and we shall fight it out, here or elsewhere, and if at last the long story is to end, it were better it should end, not through surrender, but only when we are rolling senseless on the ground.' Thaçi saw the situation in a similar way: to negotiate with Milošević would betray weakness and the outcome of talks would be worse than if the Kosovars had taken up arms. And, like Churchill, he understood that the war would only be won when the Americans were drawn into the fighting by the pluck and the suffering of the victim-nation.

And that was to be Thaçi's second test of leadership. Having put together the ideology of the Kosovo Liberation Army (KLA/UÇK), its brain and organisational skeleton, he had to find a way of winning a guerrilla war. The answer was clear to him: engage the West. It was US force (backing up the on-the-ground Croatian and Bosnian soldiers) that had ended the war in Bosnia. That meant talking NATO, the world's greatest military alliance, into fighting together with the KLA. Again and again, top US officials warned that NATO could not be used as the air force of the rebels.

Thaçi persuaded them otherwise. In long, tactically ingenious negotiations at the Rambouillet conference in 1999, he outflanked Serbia, and nudged the US towards a war it did not really want to fight. At the time, Thaçi was barely thirty-one years old and suddenly found himself at home with the foreign and defence ministers of NATO and the EU. He had seen the weakness of Kosovo's handgun army and, through a remarkable piece of alchemy, transformed its vulnerability into a position of strength. No other guerrilla movement has leveraged its limited power so successfully. And NATO did not feel duped: their action didn't just loosen Milošević's grip, it also gave the alliance a mission. It discovered that it could conduct limited military interventions without risking its ground troops. Kosovo became alliance shorthand for the projection of power against those who committed atrocities: an answer to all those who had accused the West of passivity in the face of genocide in Rwanda and elsewhere. The success of Kosovo, of liberal interventionism, tempted Western leaders into the morass of Iraq and a long, disastrous involvement with the Middle East. But this did not detract from Thaçi's standing among Western politicians; to this day he is a figure of respect.

Thaçi's third test, the great post-war dilemma, was how to reach an accommodation with the recently defeated enemy. That meant in the first place trying to ensure that Serb residents of Kosovo would not become victims of vendetta after the war. This was difficult, and only patchily successful. However, Thaçi managed to prevent friction and occasional blood-letting turning into an all-out conflagration. And he addressed the broader question of reaching an understanding with Belgrade, the erstwhile occupier and, to many, many Kosovars, the eternal foe. The Serbs did not trust Thaçi – indeed, Serbia still has a warrant out for his arrest – but he managed to talk at least some of the moderate Belgrade politicians into entering a modus vivendi with Kosovo. The carrot offered by Thaçi, and by his ally Baroness Ashton, the representative head of European foreign policy, was that Serbia was more likely to enter the EU if it came closer to recognising Kosovo. Even after a lost war, most Serbs continue to believe that Kosovo is an integral part of their homeland. Other Serbs questioned whether their country should even aspire to become part of the European Union that was home to so many of its former enemies. Russia had never stopped lobbying Serb leaders to stay out of the orbit of the EU. Today, Russian efforts to influence the politics of the region are stronger than ever. Most recently, Russian intelligence operatives are suspected to have organised an assassination attempt against the Montenegrin Prime Minister to derail the country's accession to NATO.

These were powerful opponents for Thaçi, and remain so. At home, meanwhile, he was accused by fellow KLA veterans of appeasing with the enemy, trying to strike compromises with a power that had slaughtered Kosovars and driven them at gunpoint from their homes. For Thaçi, sitting face to face with Serb politicians whom he would once have been ready to kill was an extraordinary challenge but only he could bring it off; it was strategically akin to the anti-communist President Richard Nixon travelling to communist China. Like Nixon, Thaçi had carefully calculated the odds. His record as a war leader made it less likely that Kosovars would reject outright the makings of a deal. Thaçi was counting not so much on the healing power of time as on the rise of a new generation of Serbs with different, more pressing priorities than reclaiming ancient battlefields. All this required resourcefulness, determination and a readiness to swim against the tide. Thaçi's legacy demanded that he present himself as a national unifier: of the ethnic Albanians, of the Kosovan Serbs, and of the Roma. The agreement he reached with Serbia netted him a Nobel Peace Prize nomination by a bipartisan group of US Congressmen and members of the European Parliament. He may yet win it if he succeeds in his aim to bring about the full reconciliation between Kosovo and Serbia.

There have been other, more dangerous scrapes in his life: assassination attempts, the murder of a friend with a screwdriver, the perils of leading a mule laden with weapons across the mountains to arm up his ragamuffin followers. Yet the final challenge, as a freshly elected President, is the most complex. It is about winning recognition for his nation state, building institutions and building trust, harnessing popular energy and fending off more insidious enemies. Kosovo is now recognised by over 110 states but important players, notably Spain (worried that Kosovo's breakaway will encourage Catalonia) and Russia, have dug in their heels.

Thaçi's mission is to convince the world that the scramble for recognition is not attention-seeking, an attempt to keep in the international spotlight. Rather it is about reinventing the whole south-eastern flank of Europe, which since the sixteenth century under the Ottomans has been seen as backward, a region of blood feuds out of sync with the rest of the continent.

Surrounded by a group of young advisors and backed by the West, Thaçi has found a way of changing that image: through encouraging digital diplomacy and tapping Kosovo's remarkable reservoir of entrepreneurial talent. It is, demographically, a young country; effective leadership would mean finding ways of persuading the new generation to stay in the country, or to study abroad and return with new skills. All in the name of reclaiming and rediscovering Balkan space. A bold vision.

The advances made by Kosovo have irritated the Kremlin. If Thaçi accelerates towards prosperity and aligns itself with the EU and NATO, then Moscow believes its sphere of influence in the region will shrink. Serbia, Russia's traditional ally, could, Moscow fears, be drawn in a similar direction. Under Vladimir Putin, the Russian leadership has been determined to show that getting closer to the West brings nothing but chaos and destruction. Kosovo proves otherwise. As a result, Thaçi finds himself pitted against the Kremlin's Dirty Tricks department, which applies pressure and calls in favours to block Kosovo's acceptance by symbolically important organisations such as UNESCO.

These are the new battlefields. Thaçi is clear: it is in the self-interest of Europe and the West as a whole to integrate Kosovo fully into their community. His war against dictatorship and ethnic cleansing was fought at the very end of the last century. Western leaders in the twenty-first century cannot allow Kosovo to inhabit a limbo; to do so would be a surrender of values and demonstrate a failure of resolve. And in Hashim Thaçi the world has a leader who does not easily surrender.

CHAPTER 1

THE WALKER

He's a walker, Hashim Thaçi – a hardy one. As a boy in the Kosovo highlands he hunted pheasant in the early mornings, side by side with his father, and learned to slide noiselessly down the scree. Later, as an insurgent leader, he would don his hiking boots to trek across the mountains to and from Albania, his backpack loaded with ammunition and weapons. 'I must have made the journey thirty times or more,' he says, 'usually together with comrades-in-arms such as Kadri Veseli.' Sometimes it took him three days following the smuggler routes through the passes. In a rush to reach international peace talks outside Paris, blocked from conventional transport by the Serbian government, he took short-cuts through the minefields on the Kosovo–Albania border and managed the journey in six hours flat. 'I could slither my way around the high mountain passes,' says Thaçi. 'My first nickname was The Student, but later my comrades gave me the nickname The Snake.' Snake in the old Albanian folktales is also associated with protecting the household.

Sometimes, though, the longest walks are the shortest. Dodging the Serbian secret police, the history student Thaçi would trudge cautiously through the backstreets of the Kosovan capital Pristina, as treacherous in the days of martial law as any craggy upland. That was in 1989, when elsewhere across Europe communist governments were tumbling. In Poland, a round table deal between the regime and the Solidarity opposition essentially handed power to the dissidents. In Prague, a Velvet Revolution spearheaded by the playwright Václav Havel booted out a thuggish government. In Berlin, the Wall fell. The political landscape was transformed with little blood spilled; it seemed like a blueprint for a future free of ideology.

But not for Kosovo. Although change was in the air, the Serbian communist leader Slobodan Milošević was embarking on a plan to crush the province and make the whole of Yugoslavia, with its patchwork of republics, into a commonwealth centrally steered from Belgrade. The brand of communism that had held Yugoslavia together under Josip Broz Tito was to be replaced by a strident Serbian nationalism. The Yugoslav army was the fourth largest standing army in Europe and its officer corps was overwhelmingly Serb; it stood at Milošević's disposal.

Since 1389, when Ottoman forces of Sultan Murad trounced the Serbian knights of Prince Lazar on the Kosovo plains, it has been regarded as a place worth fighting for. Surrounded by mountains, laced by gurgling rivers, Kosovo has become wrapped up with Serbia's sense of destiny. Lazar had, according to Serbian poems and legends, performed a God-given duty in resisting the encroachment of Islam on Christian Europe. That it failed was immaterial for most Serbs; their victory came from the martyrdom on the Kosovo Polje, the so-called field of blackbirds. That sense of righteous victimhood, coupled with the resentment stored up from more than 600 years of Turkish domination, is still the lifeblood of Serbian nationalism. Kosovo Albanians campaigning for a fully independent, internationally acknowledged state fight to this day against the deep irrationalism of its neighbour.

Milošević understood the Battle of Kosovo as a debt to be settled. On the Kosovo plain 600 years after the battle he told a throng of one million that 'we are again involved in battles, and facing battles. They are not battles with arms but such battles cannot be excluded.' To win, he said, Serbs had to be ready to demonstrate 'decisiveness, courage and sacrifice'.

The old battlefield, in other words, was soon to become a new one. The fierce Balkan wars of the 1990s – that raised so many modern questions about post-communist Europe, about the role of military intervention to prevent massacres, about toxic nationalism – were rooted in ancient hatred and vendettas.

Hashim Thaçi could not in 1989 begin to answer the questions thrown up by the ruthless rise of Milošević. But he could see trouble brewing, and over the coming years entered an almost gladiatorial duel with the Serb strongman. No one in Thaçi's native Drenica Valley had any illusions about Serbian intentions. 'My family was always anti-Yugoslav, anti-communist, against the Serbian state,' he recalls. 'My grandfather had been a fierce opponent of communism and around the kitchen table stories of defiance were passed down through the generations.' Nor was there any doubt that ultimately the Serbs would use force against them. 'My parents sent four of their sons for one year into the Yugoslav army for compulsory military service, though I was exempted as a student,' says Thaçi. 'But while conscription was a moment for celebration elsewhere in Yugoslavia, for Kosovo Albanians it was a sombre and fearful moment.' Albanians were bullied by Serb officers, given the most demeaning tasks; few were ever promoted. Almost 100 Kosovo Albanian soldiers in the Yugoslav army would return home in coffins. Their families were not allowed to open their coffins and were forced to bury their sons without seeing their bodies one last time. Thus, the first military uniform he wore was not a Yugoslav one but that of the Kosovo Liberation Army in late 1996.

Milošević manipulated the Yugoslav army into declaring martial law in Pristina. It turned out later that he was more talented at orchestrating the start of a war than running one. Kosovo, so much under the thumb of his secret police and with a big Yugoslav army presence, did not, however, seem to present a significant military challenge to Milošević in 1989. It was, despite its immense symbolic importance to Serbian nationalists, merely an unruly province that had to be subjugated. Two years earlier, as a mid-level communist apparatchik, he had started to beat the war drums at a Pristina rally of Kosovo Serbs. When the police, made up of ethnic Albanians, tried to disperse the crowd, Milošević exploded: 'They will never do this to you again! No one will ever have the right to beat you!' And, in a chilling prophecy, he declared: 'This is your country, these are your houses, your fields and gardens, your memories... Yugoslavia doesn't exist without Kosovo! Yugoslavia would disintegrate without Kosovo! Yugoslavia and Serbia are not going to give up Kosovo!'

Those few Western governments to take notice dismissed that Milošević speech as a purely rhetorical outing designed to nudge along his rise to the top of the Serb establishment. Thaçi, though, had understood the message: 'It was a declaration of war. He was saying there could be no independent existence for Kosovo Albanians since that would pose an existential challenge for Serbia and Yugoslavia.'

It took Milošević another year of outflanking his political rivals in Belgrade and in swelling rallies across Serbia – dubbed 'Meetings of Truth' – to turn himself into the premier champion of the Kosovan Serb minority and the standard-bearer of a nationalist revival. 'Every nation has a love that warms its heart. For Serbia, it is Kosovo,' he told a gathering of one million Serbs in Belgrade. 'We are not afraid.'[1]

---

1 Milošević quotes are taken from an author interview with Adam LeBor, biographer of the Serb leader.

And on the Kosovo fields, in his elaborately staged commemoration of the 1389 battle, he strongly hinted that he was about to unleash an extraordinary wave of violence.

Posters of Milošević – still some way from seizing the Serbian presidency – were pinned up in barber shops and cafés. For many of his fans he was simply 'Slobo'; Serbia was readying itself for radical change but not the kind that would, as in the rest of Eastern Europe, encourage crowds to sing along to Beethoven's 'Ode to Joy'. This was to be a rebirth that reached back into a long resentful history of blood and retribution.

The Belgrade choreography began to unfold rapidly. The head of the Kosovo Albanian communist party Azem Vllasi opposed any attempt to further sap the province's fragile autonomy. So Milošević had him arrested, accused of 'counter-revolutionary activities', and replaced by a more loyal placeman. Miners from Trepča – pit workers had played an important role in both the Polish and Romanian revolutions – barricaded themselves underground and threatened to blow themselves up unless Vllasi was reinstated and discrimination was ended against Kosovo Albanians. Some 300,000 Albanians took to the streets of Pristina in sympathy. Kosovo was the poorest region in Yugoslavia, hopelessly underfunded, with a young population faced with a choice between unemployment or emigration.

Milošević demanded that the Yugoslav army be deployed to restore order and choke off the 'separatists'. Croatia and Slovenia opposed any slide towards martial law, fearing (not unreasonably) that once Kosovo was crushed, they would be next. Both republics felt trapped in the decrepit, inefficient and Serb-dominated Yugoslavia. Milošević, meanwhile, accused them of financing the Kosovo miners because they wanted to foment the destruction of Yugoslavia. And he swiftly played his next card – he had hundreds of thousands of Serb workers bussed into Belgrade to protest outside the federal Yugoslav Parliament, threatening to ransack the capital unless action was taken immediately against the Kosovars in Pristina.

Milošević got his way. In March 1989, the tanks of the Yugoslav army rolled into Pristina. The miners' strike was ended. The Serbian Parliament abolished even the limited autonomy that had been granted to Kosovo by the late dictator Tito; it was now little better than an occupied colony. And Milošević sensed that one man with strong will and a simple vision, at the head of an unbeatably strong army, could remake the husk of Yugoslavia into a Greater Serbia, the dominant power of south-east Europe.

Thaçi, watching the Serb's manoeuvring, understood, with a young man's intuition, that Kosovo was the starting pistol for a round of Balkan wars – and that they would only end after Kosovo had secured a just peace and independence from Belgrade. The young men from the Drenica Valley had always assumed that their region would be the crucible of opposition to Serbian rule. The mountains and dense woodland had provided cover to earlier rebellions, notably the Kaçak uprising against the Serb occupation of Kosovo after the First World War. The rebels demanded Albanian-language schools and self-administration, but were beaten down. Now it seemed that Pristina too was going to be in the front line. And since 1981 – when a student fished a cockroach out of his meal in the refectory – the university had been in political ferment. Already, at the age of fifteen, as news of the cockroach uprising reached his parents' smallholding, it was clear what he wanted to do: study history at that hotbed.

A simple protest by a few hundred students fed up with living conditions had rolled into a month of stone-throwing and open confrontation with the authorities. Their slogans mutated from 'Better food!' to 'We are Albanians – not Yugoslavs' and 'Kosovo Republic!' There was, so it seemed from the vantage point of the valley, revolutionary potential in the capital too. Stiff jail sentences were handed down to more than 1,200 people; many were just leaving prison when Thaçi arrived at the university, determined to stir things up.

Why history? One of his associates – who would later emerge as the country's very active foreign minister – remembers that it was the most free-thinking of faculties. 'Promoting Albanian history, that was a way of framing our thoughts about national identity,' he says.[2] In the cafés of Pristina, as the Milošević crackdown got more and more oppressive, Hoxhaj, Thaçi and others thrashed out what could and what should be done against the overpowering existential threat posed by Milošević.

It seemed as if a Greater Serbia entailed the wiping out of all Albanian cultural memory. Place names were changed to Serbian. The shutters were pulled down on the Kosovo ballet, the Kosovo theatre, the Kosovo Academy of Sciences. More than a dozen Albanian journalists were jailed. All state-employed Albanians – and the state was by far the largest employer – were forced to swear an oath of loyalty to Serbia or face instant dismissal. Serb authorities began to pulp Albanian language books in the Pristina National Library. Over the coming years, two-thirds of Kosovo's 180 libraries were shut down; 900,000 books destroyed.

But, just as Thaçi had seen Pristina University as a magnet for resistance, so Milošević saw it as a prime target. If he was to eliminate the very idea of Kosovan independence then he had to start by killing its brain. Quotas were imposed on university enrolment by Kosovo Albanians; the ceiling was set at 18,000 rather than the 40,000 that usually attended lectures. Separate entrances were installed for ethnic Albanians and for Kosovo Serbs. 'It was tantamount to apartheid,'

---

2 Author interview with Hoxhaj

says Thaçi.[3] When lecturers protested, 863 were sacked. Many were accused of 'separatism', although the actual physical separation was being commanded by the Serbian authorities. Public gatherings were outlawed.

The crackdown reached all levels of the educational system. Serb and Albanian children had to study in separate classrooms and on different shifts. Dozens of Albanian-language primary schools were closed. The number of ethnic Albanians allowed to continue schooling after the age of sixteen was drastically thinned. As a result, the Kosovars devised their own shadow system of education, similar to the 'Flying University' set up by Polish and Czech dissidents in the 1970s. A typical lecture or classroom might be set up in an old shop, hidden from view by lace curtains, planks on bricks substituting for desks. Albanian-language textbooks were smuggled into Kosovo by pack donkeys. Serb police would stop buses coming into Pristina and check the documents of those of university age. '"Why do you study when you have no university?" That's what the cops would yell,' said one former underground student, now a businessman in Germany. Typically, another student recalls fleeing across the mountains to Macedonia after particularly brutal police treatment. He would return to sit clandestine exams, the results of which would be duly entered into his Index, a record of university achievement.

Hashim Thaçi was elected pro-rector by the student body, essentially their spokesman and organiser. He had stood out as someone with absolute clarity of purpose and the attributes of Lech Wałęsa or Václav Havel. 'I was always convinced,' he says, 'that our right would triumph over Milošević's might.' Above all he grasped, and was willing to fight

---

3   Author interview with Hashim Thaçi. Unless otherwise stated, all Thaçi quotes are taken from twenty hours of interviews with Thaçi conducted between 2015 and 2017.

against, Belgrade's plan to decapitate the up-and-coming generation of leaders in Kosovo. 'By 1991, our educational system had largely shifted underground, so I would move between sacked lecturers and secret students, from one private apartment to another,' he said. Thaçi was under observation by the Serbian security police. 'I had to be extremely careful. I never used a phone or a fax if I could avoid it,' he said. Despite having become an object of interest for Belgrade, he enjoyed a special freedom, helped by the fact that he was paid 80 German Marks a month from funds raised by Kosovo émigrés. 'It was a time when I began to understand what Kosovo's political aims should be, not just those of the students. I tried to lead a normal life as a student but then at night get back to Drenica where we would discuss how to organise resistance with the likes of Adem Jashari, one of the most vocal leaders of resistance in the region.'

Thaçi capitalised on the anger of the Kosovo Albanians as they strained under the yoke of Milošević:

> Back in 1989, there was nothing they could do about football matches between Pristina and Belgrade. They were real grudge games. The whole of the capital filled the stadium, there was a lot of fighting on the pitch; nationalist slogans off it. So of course everything we couldn't say on the street we shouted out in the stadium. Every match became a political demonstration not just by fans but everyone who felt the deep disappointment of occupation.

'Of course he got roughed up sometimes by the police,' says his friend Enver Hoxhaj. 'But it wasn't all about brutal confrontation.'[4] They met

---

4 Author interview with Hoxhaj

in cafés and apartments, drank beer together and debated the issue that gripped the whole of their generation: what next?

'It was a heavy burden to be so young and to be so public,' reflects Thaçi. 'I could have continued with a good life as a young man. I had siblings living in the diaspora – so it wasn't easy at the age of twenty-two or twenty-three to go off and start a war. It could have been different – but I never regretted it.'

CHAPTER 2

LEARNING FROM THE NEIGHBOURS

wo days before Romania's ruling couple Nicolae and Elena Ceauşescu were gunned down by a firing squad, Kosovo Albanian dissidents formally set up the LDK, the Democratic League of Kosovo. In the same month, December 1989, dissidents across the province were gathering together to give a formal face to the civil resistance to Milošević and the brutality of martial law: Adem Demaçi established a human rights council, while Veton Surroi founded the Pristina branch of the Yugoslav Democratic Initiative and immediately spoke out in favour of striking building workers. Suddenly there were free trade unionists, a liberal party, a national party: all talking shops designed to vent the Kosovar frustration with Serbian rule, all inspired by the splintering of communist authority in Eastern Europe. But the most enduring group was the LDK, which would define Kosovan politics for almost the whole of the following decade.

The outside world barely noticed. Blood was flowing in Romania and there was a real risk that a year of peaceful change in central Europe was about to give way to broader chaos. Milošević, despite his incendiary speech-making, was not seen as a problem by Western analysts. As long as he presented himself as a non-ideological reformer (he had, after all, been a banker in New York, at a time when that was still a mark of acumen) and as someone who would not allow regional upheavals to change borders, then he was viewed by foreign diplomats as a stabilising factor. Kosovo, instead of being seen as the potential trigger for new devastating Balkan wars, became the stuff of unread memos in the chancelleries of Europe. Vital was the future of Germany, the explosive potential for full-scale confrontation with the Soviet Union and the dangerously orphaned Red Army tank regiments stranded on the frontline of a crumbling Warsaw Pact.

The Kosovo Albanians were in an unfortunate situation, but they were out of step, it seemed, with the great march of history. The West, and the United States in particular, wanted to be reassured that Yugoslavia was not going to fall apart. The great minds of NATO could only deal with one crisis at a time. When James Baker, the US Secretary of State, turned up in Belgrade in June 1991, he spoke as a southerner, an American whose ancestors had experienced the devastation of a long civil war: 'We don't have a dog in this fight,' he announced, telling pro-independence republics that they could not expect recognition from Washington.

That was a depressing signal for the Kosovars.

Abandon your dreams, the US administration of George H. W. Bush seemed to be saying, don't rock the boat. In this cautious and naive worldview, the literary critic Ibrahim Rugova appeared to be the right man in the right place: someone in tune with the more peaceful rhythms of 1989, an intellectual who behind his smudged glasses seemed to be a Balkan equivalent of Václav Havel, Europe's favourite chain-smoking revolutionary. Rugova's father and paternal grandfather had been killed by Tito's partisans, he spoke foreign languages, wrote poetry and preached a non-violent resistance against the troops of Milošević. That was an attractive pose not just for Washington but also for some Kosovan Albanians, who were all too aware they were overwhelmingly outgunned and outmanned by the Serbs. And Western diplomats were willing to overlook Rugova's chronic alcohol problem and his manifest weakness as a leader in return for policies that avoided confrontation. In the summer of 1990, Kosovo Albanian representatives went to Parliament to declare limited independence from Serbia, found their way blocked by police and so made their statement on the steps instead. When the LDK eventually met to draw up their new constitution for a Republic of Kosovo it had to do so in secret and Rugova's ambition was clear: Kosovo was not striving for statehood but to be a republic with equal status with other constituent parts of a Yugoslav confederation.

For Thaçi, this kind of self-limiting revolution could lead nowhere except the further draining of Kosovo, its continued subservience to Serbia. Thaçi's yardstick, as he transformed himself from student protest leader into the leader of a national insurgency, was not the appeasement of Rugova but rather the dignified defiance of Adem Jashari, a rugged smallholder from the Drenica Valley, a man with a clear understanding of the sacrifices needed to move forward. For Jashari, fifteen years his senior, the balance of forces between the Kosovo Albanians and Belgrade had to be changed. That could not be achieved by essentially abandoning armed struggle and allowing the Serbs to treat the Kosovo Albanians as colonial serfs.

'I had admired him since I was in high school. He was a special man for me,' says Thaçi.

Jashari had taken part in the 1989 demonstrations. I became engaged with the illegal political organisation the People's

13

Movement for Kosovo through Kadri Veseli. Adem Jashari and two activists, Zahir Pajaziti and Sali Çekaj, led groups that travelled to Albania for military training. At the end of December 1991, the Serb police tried to raid his home and, together with his brothers, his father and the whole village, he fought back.

After that we met only secretly during my tenure as pro-rector, to discuss seriously about how to organise resistance in the towns. During the 1989 protests, I saw Adem Jashari for the first time fully armed and together we threw Molotov cocktails at the Serbian armoured vehicles.

And that was to be one of Thaçi's great early contributions to the uprising: to bring disciplined thought, structure and system to the uprising, to identify its leading lights.

He was a real military leader, the symbol of the still-undeclared Kosovo Liberation Army, the UÇK. In May 1992, a student was killed by the Serb police in Skenderaj. Ten thousand turned up for his funeral and I spoke in my capacity as student rector. 'If repression continues, it will lead to open, armed resistance,' I told the mourners.

After the funeral, Thaçi drove to Jashari's house, a large compound that had been fortified following the Serb attack five months before.

"'Hashim, you did the right thing,' he told me. "We have to tell the truth openly about war – but be careful.'"

Thaçi was indeed careful. Kosovo was in no sense prepared to wage a war against the heavy weaponry of Milošević. Although most farms had a few rudimentary weapons, there was no great hidden arsenal. Despite Jashari's mission to Albania, there was precious little training.

And the people of Kosovo had yet to be convinced that rising up against the Serbs was not, as Rugova portrayed it, a suicide mission, an invitation to be steamrollered out of existence. Thaçi, moving secretly, taking long walks in the open, embarked on an elaborate act of national persuasion.

'This was going to be an authentic movement,' he recalls,

> not something grafted onto society. It was clear what the uprising shouldn't be. I had watched a lot of movies about partisans fighting Germans – films from the era of Tito or the Albanian Enver Hoxha – you know, with brave heroes singlehandedly killing ten Germans at a go. I never believed that stuff.
>
> And of course I watched John Wayne too, but real life was different from the heroism I saw in socialist or Hollywood cinema, though I obviously preferred the Hollywood movies.

Real-life examples were even less useful. 'I read a lot about the IRA, the Kurdish PKK and the ETA group in the Basque land. But I didn't want a terror group that would harm civilians, not the IRA and not the Palestine Liberation Organization. The KLA would never plant bombs in Serbian cities to hit soft targets or civilians.' Thaçi was chiefly concerned that the frustration of Kosovo Albanians would turn into a doomed intifada, squashing the hopes of a generation.

'That was dangerous,' he says. 'When I talked to the Marxists in the resistance, they said: "We have to prepare the people for the uprising." But from my reading, that wouldn't work either.'

The Kosovan cause could not flourish as an ideologically driven movement, least of all a Marxist one at a time when communist rule was being discredited and toppled throughout Europe. Strategic patience wasn't the answer either; it smacked too much of Rugova's all-too-passive resistance. Rugova's approach wasn't even Gandhian; Gandhi, after all, had called for constant demonstrations against the colonial ruler. Rugova judged even this to be too risky. Instead, Thaçi calculated, a war had to be organised and orchestrated. It had to be seen as just by the outside world, it had to be adequately financed and it had to have the central aim not of the glorious battlefield victories that fuelled Serbian dreams but of outwitting and exposing the cruelty of an oppressive dictator.

The beefing up of the LDK and other groups was thus important to Thaçi even though he was sure that only a combination of political and military means could bring about a desirable political outcome. The executive of the LDK included not only home-based Kosovars but representatives from the diaspora in Europe and the United States; it was less of a party than an NGO, one with over 500 branches. That was a source of strength for the resistance but also a cause of friction – notably between the government-in-exile of Bujar Bukoshi (Cabinet sessions were held in Zürich's Mövenpick Hotel) and Rugova in Pristina.

The power of the diaspora was in the first place financial. Kosovo Albanians inside and outside the country were contributing financially to the establishment of a 'parallel state'. Voluntary contributions from the many Albanians and Kosovo Albanians working abroad in Germany and Switzerland raised at least 120 million Deutschmarks between 1990 and 1999. This money was transferred to the Dardania Bank in Tirana and then physically carried across the border into Kosovo to fund the some half a million students in the underground education system and the 166 impromptu clinics. Thaçi as pro-rector knew exactly how these sums were distributed and their value to the running of the shadow society. Kosovo was a remittance society surviving on the cash sent home by the hundreds of thousands of Kosovars working as *Gastarbeiter*, 'guest-workers', in the foundries and factories of German-speaking Europe and Scandinavia. The government-in-exile asked that they sacrifice 3 per cent of their wage packets – or 10 per cent of business profits from the wealthier emigrants – to keep the homeland alive.

They gave above all because of the sense of menace in the Balkans. What would happen to their family smallholdings, their kinfolk, the graves of their ancestors, if Kosovo was to be swallowed up by war? Their fears were reinforced by events in Slovenia and Croatia. On 25 June 1991, Slovenia defied James Baker's warnings, raised its flag, tugged down the Yugoslav one, declared independence and took control of its borders. The Yugoslav general staff had drawn up two plans. The first entailed the deployment of 2,000 troops to take back border crossings and Ljubljana airport. The second was a proper invasion and occupation of Slovenia by the Yugoslav army's Fifth Military District.

The first, more modest, plan was implemented – and Slovenia plunged headfirst into war. It was a short, limited conflict: Slovenian militia besieged Yugoslav army bases, cutting off their water, telephones and electricity. A Yugoslav helicopter was shot down and in ten days of fighting, forty-four Yugoslav soldiers were killed against only a handful of Slovenian fatalities. And, despite the anger of some Yugoslav generals, Slobodan Milošević let it happen. His scheme was to pretend to fight for the integrity of Yugoslavia while in fact laying the groundwork for a new Serbian order, a kind of Serboslavia. While paying lip service to the independence of republics within a Yugoslav federation, he was in fact paving the way for a nation that would unite all Serb minorities. Tiny Alpine Slovenia was 90 per cent inhabited by Slovenians. There were, however, 600,000 Serbs in Croatia; in Bosnia 31 per cent of the population was made up of Serbs. Slovenia could go free – it sounded the death knell for a Yugoslavia in which Milošević was no longer interested and ushered in the beginnings of a new Greater Serbia baptised by blood.

For Thaçi, the Slovenian war and the rapid unfolding of violence in Croatia and Bosnia carried important lessons. One was that the US administration really did not see Milošević in the same way as the toppled tyrants of Eastern Europe. 'Americans will not support those who seek independence in order to replace a far-off tyranny with a local despotism,' said George H. W. Bush in August 1991. That line – in favour of Yugoslavia sticking together with Milošević as its natural leader – had to be changed. But how? Second, Slovenia had shown how to get ready for an intelligent war: its 35,000 men were well trained and highly motivated. The Slovenian defence minister Janez Janša had been buying arms, including anti-tank weapons. True, Slovenia enjoyed certain advantages – it was rich, Kosovo poor. It was a republic, not a subjugated province. It had no emotional significance, unlike Kosovo, for Serbian identity. Yet Kosovo too, with careful planning, with the funds from its countrymen abroad, with the help of neighbouring Albania, could become a fighting nation in its own right. All it needed was leadership – and guile.

Croatia was the real target of Milošević. In Slovenia, the Serbian leader had essentially struck a deal with Milan Kuçan: get out of Yugoslavia and leave me free to create a Serboslavia, a Greater Serbia that would link up the Serb communities in Croatia and, even more explosively, Bosnia and Herzegovina. The troops that were being taken by train in the direction of Slovenia were in fact intended to fight for the Serb minority in Croatia. The outline of a Greater Serbia had been drawn up by the Serbian Academy of Arts and Sciences on the basis of the works of the nineteenth-century nationalist Ilija Garašanin. His idea had been to dispatch spies into targeted territories, to set up parallel military and security forces and prepare them for annexation. That was exactly the plan followed in 1990 as Milošević's men started to arm up Serb militants in Krajina; control Krajina and you can separate the Croatian capital Zagreb from the Croatian coastline. The Milošević response to the collapse of European communism was thus to return to the nineteenth century with twentieth-century armaments.

The war unfurled quickly. Around Knin, the main city in Krajina, the local Serbs blocked access roads with timber, creating checkpoints for the new border. They were under the command of a fanatical ultranationalist dentist, Milan Babić, who in turn took orders from Belgrade. Elsewhere, in western Slavonia – inhabited for centuries by Croats and Serbs – talks on a shared school curriculum, a joint police force, bilingual street names, came to nothing. On 22 December 1990, the Croatian Parliament adopted a Croatian constitution. And after a referendum in May 1991, Croatia declared independence. The Yugoslav navy proceeded to shell the ancient UNESCO-protected city of Dubrovnik. It was a popular tourist destination – and Europe woke up. The cobblestoned city of Vukovar was besieged and ruthlessly shelled. Serb nationalist militiamen, toting the long, bushy beards of the wartime Chetnik partisans, moved in and executed Croatian residents, dumping them in mass graves. It introduced shocked but largely powerless Western Europeans to the idea of ethnic cleansing and the possibility that the new post-communist world would be one where states could be dismembered by force.

By the time a kind of peace was struck at the end of 1991, it was plain that the next step would entail Serbs and Croats working together to smash Bosnia. And it was clear to Kosovars that war would roll on and destroy any hopes of claiming independence for their province. The Croatian war had really struck home for Kosovars. The country had been a natural haven for Albanians as they sought to escape from the waves of persecution in the 1980s; along the Adriatic they had set up restaurants and shops. Dissident intellectuals had set up a Pan-Albanian group in the Croatian township of Stubičke Toplice in early 1991 and had discussed the possibility of setting up an army that could defend the ethnic Albanians of Kosovo, Macedonia, Preševo and Montenegro. That was a purely theoretical discussion. More important for the long-term outcome of the Kosovo battle for independence was the fighting experience gained by Albanian conscripts who had deserted from the Serb-dominated Yugoslav army to join the Croatian forces. Crucial figures in the future Kosovo Liberation Army, generals like Agim Çeku, had fought in the Croatian ranks and had been schooled in tactical warfare at the Zagreb military academy.

The tension of wars spreading through the neighbourhood, the naked aggression of Serb military and paramilitary units, prompted the Kosovo 'government in exile'– set up by Rugova – to appoint a 'minister of defence'. Rugova's titular Prime Minister Bujar Bukoshi (a German-trained doctor) argued that there should be more – that funds should be raised from the many Kosovars abroad to establish a military force. Rugova was opposed and stuck to his leitmotif of passive resistance although much of the Balkans was already in flames. There were arguments about money and a general lack of leadership, ideas and direction.

For Hashim Thaçi, this was an irrelevance to the people on the ground in Kosovo. The way forward was to create sleeper cells, sometimes made up of no more than three people, and start a flow of guns: prepare an army of resistance. No amount of posturing abroad, he believed, would change the balance of forces. The Serbs had begun what they saw as the accelerated colonisation of Kosovo, requisitioning apartments abandoned by or seized from ethnic Albanians. The well-informed hierarchy of the Serbian Orthodox Church was so sure that war was coming to Kosovo that it ordered the urgent removal to Belgrade of the valuable icons from the church of Gračanica for 'restoration'. And across the border in Albania, the Tirana government criticised the Serbian leadership and prepared for the spillover of war. With barely 35,000 troops and an arsenal of vintage Chinese weapons, it did not stand a chance in a future war.

Thaçi understood: time was running out. Nobody seemed to have the strength or the will to stop Milošević in his tracks.

CHAPTER 3

THE SCREWDRIVER KILLING

War begets war. As the arson and pillage spread from Croatia into Bosnia and Herzegovina, it became all too clear to Thaçi that his fellow Kosovars were facing full-scale catastrophe. The idea of a Greater Serbia was not just about redrawing the map but also creating an ethnic Serbian hegemony and destroying the multiculturalism that had allowed Christians and Muslims to live cheek by jowl in the Balkans. It was a kind of madness. A joke from Belgrade in the 1990s mocks Milošević's claim that Serbia exists wherever a Serb has lived and died. According to the gag, told across the Balkans, a crew of astronauts is sent to the moon to see whether Yugoslavia can be re-created if not in Europe, then at least in outer space. Between the Croat, the Bosnian and two Serb spacemen an argument breaks out immediately on landing as to which flag should be planted. The Croat claims the moon, with its mountains and craters, as it most resembles his country. The Bosnian points out that the space team, comprising a Muslim, a Croat and a Serb, most resembles Yugoslavia and the appropriate flag should be unfurled. Then one of the Serbs takes out a gun, shoots the other and announces: 'A Serb has died here. This is Serbia.'

Serbia believed it had been held back by stagnant population growth for decades. The population of Muslim Bosnia, by contrast, had risen by 15 per cent in the 1980s and in Kosovo it had soared by 20 per cent. Milošević wanted to expand Serbian terrain – but saw the demographic decline of Serbs as part of a clash of civilisations. Between 1961 and 1981, the Muslim proportion of the Bosnian population jumped from 26 to 40 per cent, while the Albanian share of the Kosovan population rose from 67 to 77 per cent. Milošević thus waged war claiming to defend embattled Serbian values. But the deployment of vicious cutthroat militias, from the 'White Eagles' of Mirko Jović to the 'Tigers of Arkan' (Željko Ražnatović), showed that the Serbian leadership was driven by an exterminationist ideology: ethnic cleansing, the mass murder of men, the mass rape of women. It could be a short step from the subjugation of Muslims to their elimination.

These horrors lurked for Kosovo, too. Arkan, rewarded for his slaughtering crusade in Bosnia, was put up as a candidate for Kosovo in the Serbian parliamentary elections. Surrounded by his thugs, he took up residence in Pristina's Grand Hotel. Milošević, brushing off Arkan's crimes to a Croatian envoy in November 1993, declared: 'I too must have people to do certain kinds of dirty work for me.' Then he laughed out loud. They weren't laughing in Pristina. The candidacy of Arkan, says the Harvard-educated Minister of Dialogue Edita Tahiri, a formidable negotiator, 'held up a mirror to the future of Serbian democracy'.

For Thaçi, the massacre of Bosnian Muslims at Srebrenica in July 1995 changed the terms of his campaign to organise armed resistance to Serbia. He had left Kosovo in 1993 to study together with his friend Enver Hoxhaj in Vienna. The move was partly prompted by fears for his safety – his family house had been searched, his father questioned by the Serbian security police – and his stay abroad was in part financially supported by his businessmen brothers. Things were getting hotter for Thaçi at home and were obviously about to get hotter. The first Serbian arrest warrant against him was in 1993, for membership of an illegal organisation – a broad charge that could be taken out against any activist in Kosovo since such a large chunk of society was functioning underground. A second warrant was issued in 1994 for subversive activity, which carried a possible fifteen years. During the 1990s, Thaçi dodged the Serb authorities with a full deck of fake cards – five forged Serbian IDs, a Macedonian, Albanian and – thanks to a successful asylum claim – Swiss passport. Both he and Enver enrolled at Vienna University to study south-east European history but Thaçi concentrated on learning German. 'After about six months, Hashim moved to Switzerland while I stayed in Austria,' remembers Enver Hoxhaj. 'He had made his choice – there was no better place than Switzerland to get the diaspora involved in building up the KLA.' Thaçi led a parallel life there – studying, taking jobs, but also putting together a network of sympathisers for the fightback, and on short missions diving back into Kosovo.

Srebrenica was important. For some Kosovars, it still signalled the need to keep their heads down. 'They would say: "Hold off on that army,"' recalls Thaçi.

> And of course I disagreed with them. We were losing time and Milošević was getting stronger. They would say: 'Just look at Srebrenica – he can do what he wants.' The Yugoslav army was too powerful and the situation was hopeless. So we had to be really patient. To communicate. And, despite their doubts, start the clandestine organisation.

The killings in Srebrenica had done more than expose a Serb agenda, although that was alarming enough. The Bosnian Serb commander

Ratko Mladić had told his men before the onslaught: 'Finally after the rebellion of the Dahijas [the Serb rebellion against Ottoman rule in 1804], the time has come to take revenge on the Turks in this region.' The slaughter went accordingly: the younger women set aside for rape, the men and boys, some 7,000 of them, for execution. But the event had demonstrated, even more than the long siege of Sarajevo, the limitations of the West and what it takes to tip the balance in favour of military intervention.

Srebrenica had been declared a 'United Nations Safe Area', which stopped some way short of a UN commitment to defend the town. What it meant was: none of the warring parties should operate militarily within the enclaves. 'There was neither the international will, nor the necessary UN mandate to ensure that the enclaves were secure from attack,' says Adam LeBor, the biographer of Milošević. And the Serb leader understood throughout his many wars how he could hold the West – nervous not only about military intervention but about how NATO should evolve in the post-Cold War era – in check by cultivating the ancient ties between Belgrade and Moscow. The 110 lightly armed Dutch peacekeepers in the town were neutralised by the guile of Milošević. UN 'Safe Areas' were in fact among the most dangerous places in the world.

The fall of the town was a Western humiliation and the Bosnian Serbs revelled in it, bombarding the market place of Sarajevo despite a pledge to withdraw all of its heavy artillery. For years the West had agonised over the fate of Sarajevo, played with alternatives to military intervention such as the creation of a humanitarian corridor or the airlifting of arms to Bosnian forces. Now NATO decided to act, throwing Tomahawk cruise missiles and waves of bombers against the Bosnian Serb guns. 'Finally the decks were cleared for a real military response, not some piece of garbage,' said Richard Holbrooke, an American diplomat who had kick-started his career in Vietnam. As Milošević was pushed into peace talks with the Bosnians and Croats at the Dayton air base in Ohio, it quickly became apparent why Holbrooke was nicknamed The Bulldozer. He too had been galvanised by Srebrenica – 'the biggest single mass murder in Europe since World War II and the outside world did nothing'– and wanted to change the way that the US, Europe and NATO interacted with the Balkans. That won over Thaçi, who later became a great admirer of his. But Holbrooke's immediate task was to find a way to stop more blood being spilled between Serbia, Croatia and Bosnia. That would mean leaving Milošević in power. And it would mean allowing Milošević to keep Kosovo. That Thaçi did not like at all.

Holbrooke recalled walking around the air base with Milošević. 'About 100 local Albanian–Americans came to the outer fence of Wright-Patterson with megaphones to plead the case for Kosovo. I suggested we walk over to chat with them, but he refused, saying testily that they were obviously being paid by a foreign power.'

Kosovo barely gets a mention in Holbrooke's book about Dayton, entitled *To End a War*, which could equally have been called *To Keep a Dictator in Power and Begin a New War*. Dayton was flawed and Holbrooke's main defence of the deal was that he had succeeded in preventing Kosovo and Bosnia becoming what he called 'a single theatre of war'. He had, one could say charitably, bought Kosovo some time to get ready for the break. To Thaçi, Kosovo's exclusion from the talks was reminiscent of the 1992 London conference chaired by Lord Carrington, where Ibrahim Rugova was invited to watch proceedings on a screen from a nearby room – a brutal downgrading of the importance of Kosovo. Holbrooke conceded later that '[we] had always viewed Kosovo as the most explosive tinderbox in the region … an explosion in Kosovo, which the rest of the world recognised as a part of Yugoslavia, could trigger a wider war involving the Albanians, the Macedonians and perhaps even Greece.'

'The stark truth for us was that in order to be taken seriously we had to have a fighting force,' says Thaçi. 'In many ways, Bosnia and Croatia had it easier than us, because they had state structures in place. We had to organise a different kind of army from scratch.'

Even so, Holbrooke – who would go on to become a champion of Kosovan independence – had an enlightening, even inspiring, influence on Thaçi. Western reluctance to intervene in the Balkans had been based largely on a poor reading of history: namely that nothing could be done there because the whole region was bound up in ancient blood feuds. Rather, argued Holbrooke, the crises were erupting because the old enmities had been exploited by criminal leaders. Thaçi, who has never been the subject of a blood feud himself, found himself in agreement. Any attempt to break free of Kosovo had to be bound up not only with the smart use of force but with a clear sense of independent statehood and modern governance. A second, vital lesson from Holbrooke was that Kosovo should not become, as Bosnia and Croatia had, a political football continually passed between Europe and America. James Baker, Secretary of State under George H. W. Bush, had campaigned first for Yugoslavia to stay intact and then, when its dissolution became inevitable, to define it as a purely European problem. But Holbrooke, and eventually his President Bill Clinton, understood that if the US was striving for a peaceful new world order, it had to take the military lead on the Balkans. NATO, guided by the US, had been an important instrument in ending the conflict in Bosnia; it should also be ready to act if Milošević sought to destroy the Kosovars.

Yet the Kosovars lacked the confidence to play in the league of the big powers, to actively seek allies and protectors outside the region.

This confidence came not with Rugova, whose credibility as a decision-maker or even as a political analyst had been damaged by the neighbourhood wars – but rather with impatient young men like Thaçi. And he had understood that no army of resistance stood a chance of survival without a fallback country – a safe place to regroup, to plan attacks and seek treatment for the wounded. The natural refuge was Albania.

'Serb intelligence knew exactly when I travelled from Switzerland to Albania,' says Thaçi.

> They kept an eye on me the whole time I was in Switzerland, where I had successfully claimed asylum. My advantage in those days was that I was young, and looked young – they couldn't imagine that a student could be so deeply involved in a resistance movement. They saw me as a dangerous person, skilled with weapons. Well, they were wrong about the weapons bit, but it was good that they thought that, it made them both underestimate me – see me as a gunman – and overestimate me.

Thaçi has been shown (by a friendly Western intelligence service) the Serb observation reports: 'They had a drawing of my place, recorded the exact times that I would head out to Zürich Hauptbahnhof to catch the train to work. They didn't interfere, just railed me.' Serb intelligence had worked for years on the assumption that a secret underground army was being formed in Albania to invade Kosovo and incorporate it into a Greater Albania. That was their logical reading of history: from 1949, the communist dictator of Albania, Enver Hoxha, had indeed tried to set up fighting units in Kosovo. Mostly, though, these were crude attempts, easily broken up by Yugoslavia's Tito regime. The fear nonetheless informed the Serb security police.

'They weren't very bright,' says Thaçi. If they had been paying attention they would have realised that the trouble was brewing among Kosovo Albanians in Kosovo, funded by an increasingly sophisticated diaspora, rather than some plotting by the Albanian state across the mountains. The Kosovo Albanians abroad were no longer just downtrodden *Gastarbeiter* slogging away to earn the cash for remittances to be sent home. There were political organisations like the LPRK, which transformed itself in 1993 into Lëvizja Popullore e Kosovës (LPK – the People's Movement of Kosovo): small, secretive but increasingly influential and quite at odds with Rugova's placidly led LDK. There was serious fundraising in the form of the 'Homeland Calling' organisation, run out of Switzerland and other countries with an Albanian diaspora by an LPK stalwart, Jashar Salihu, a man who had seen the inside of Tito's prisons. Xhavit Haliti and Azem Syla, two more co-founders of the KLA, were also engaged in logistical support for the fledgling guerrilla army. Ali Ahmeti, the current political leader of Macedonian Albanians, was also a part of this initial cluster of KLA co-founders. In Kosovo itself, many community leaders became pillars of support for the KLA, while keeping their day jobs. It was a small and diverse cast of 'true believers', from Fatmir Xhelili, a psychiatrist who used his training to obtain intelligence in the field, to Memli Krasniqi, a teenage rapper who engaged youth through political songs. During a screening of the 1995 film *Braveheart* in a Pristina cinema, the excitement of youth for the new generation of resistance heroes was so palpable that the Serbian police had to intervene to stop them chanting 'Kosovo Republic' in the cinema.

Most of all, though, there was a head of steam gathering behind a more gutsy struggle against Milošević. There was the anger at the dictator's suppression of the province but also a sense – having seen regimes fall across Europe – that he could be outwitted. If there was to be a future war, it would have to be fought in a more modern way than the conflict in Bosnia and Croatia. Many exiled Kosovars now had Swisscom mobiles that could cheat any interception attempts by Serb intelligence. This was of course an optimistic assessment: any war against the Serbs would have bloody echoes of ancient clashes.

But Thaçi needed to be physically closer to the action. Albania was not a straightforward place to operate as a Kosovar insurgent. The West looked to the post-communist Albanian government of the cardiologist Sali Berisha to keep the Kosovars in check: the last thing it wanted, after the bruising experience of Srebrenica, was another Balkan conflagration. So the presence of Kosovan dissidents in Tirana was regarded by the government as hospitality towards their bullied cousins, and by the West as a useful way of keeping tabs on the situation. Naturally Tirana was also full of Serb agents of influence who made sure that diplomats there swallowed the legend that Kosovars were all involved in organised crime syndicates.

It was not an easy environment for Thaçi to manage an extended covert operation. He would cross into Kosovo, recruit his sleepers and return. Slowly an arsenal of small arms was being built up too, with guns bought off sympathisers in the Albanian army or from middlemen who demanded extortionate prices. Even guns bought from Montenegrin dealers had to pass through Albania with mark-ups along the way. The Kosovars in Tirana kept themselves to themselves. Albania was hurtling towards chaos. 'I had expected a different place,' remembers Thaçi. 'It was in a state of chaotic transition, [with] a dysfunctional administration, [and] deep animosities. Opposition leaders were being jailed all the time. Even Adem Jashari was detained at this time in Albania.' By 1995, the consumer bubble in Tirana that had followed the end of communist rule had popped. In the north, people were shifting from the country-side into towns; in the south, the young were moving to Greece to work.

The chromium mines were grinding to a halt; across the country families were feuding – often in bloody vendettas – over disputed property. Sanitary conditions were breaking down. Cholera was rife.

The exiled Kosovo Albanians, though, stayed out of Albanian politics. They did not want to attract the attention of agents of SHIK, the Albanian secret police. Instead, like Bekim Çollaku, their future Minister for Europe, they studied and kept their heads down, or, like Thaçi, plotted and kept their heads down. Çollaku, who was later to become Thaçi's chief of staff, remembers being awestruck when he first met Thaçi in Albanian exile.

> He came with friends to my rented flat and brought a cake. The KLA, just a couple of years before it went to war, was pretty much a secret even from its natural sympathisers. Rugova, worried that KLA fundraising would siphon off donations from his LDK, described them as isolated Marxist cells. It seemed that everyone in the game had an interest in playing down the force.[5]

Yet, when the Berisha administration was dragged under by the collapse of a pyramid banking scheme in March 1997, Thaçi with Kadri Veseli and other fellow KLA founders suddenly found that their military future had been transformed. Furious Albanians demanding the return of their savings stormed the banks. Nervous soldiers and policemen stopped guarding barracks and armouries and headed to their home villages. 'The Albanian collapse was unexpected,' says Thaçi,

> but it was a real opportunity. Villagers ransacked army warehouses and all of a sudden we had our guns too. I couldn't believe

---

5 Author interview with Bekim Çollaku

what I was seeing – there would be people in Tirana drinking coffee with their Kalashnikovs, old ladies with Kalashnikovs, children with Kalashnikovs. We had this extraordinary chance to expand our weapons base.

In northern Albania, Shkodër, close to the Kosovo border, became a staging post for smuggled petrol, cigarettes – and guns.

Although there are photographs showing Thaçi holding an automatic rifle, he is adamant that he is not a gunman. 'I knew how to handle a weapon, of course, but I never served as a regular army soldier,' he says. In 1996, though, diplomatic sources say he did leave Albania for a short spell of training with foreign military advisors.

Perhaps that was enough to attract the attention of a hostile faction in the Albanian secret service. It was July 1997, in the anarchic days before President Berisha, having rigged an election, was forced to resign. Thaçi had just returned to Tirana from another clandestine trip to Kosovo.

It was about six in the evening and I was having a coffee in a bar with friends who had got hold of some magazines of ammunition that they wanted to give to the KLA. So we took the bag, put them in the back of a cab so we could drop them at the apartment where I was staying.

Minutes later, the taxi was surrounded by masked men and blocked by three police vehicles – 'as if we were the most wanted people on earth'. Thaçi and his two companions were confused, since in the mayhem of Albania in 1997 the assailants could have come from any number of crime gangs, factions within the fast-splintering police or agents acting on behalf of the Serbs. Thaçi was not short of enemies. 'They yelled

"Out! Out!", shoved us around a bit, handcuffed us. What were they up to? It's not as if we had bags of cash. They quickly found the magazines in the boot though.'

The men demanded to know which of the group owned the magazines. 'I knew one of my comrades in the car would be jailed if he were identified, so I claimed them,' says Thaçi. They were taken to a police station, surrounded by ten officers shouting and cursing at them in Albanian. That at least seemed to rule out a Serbian covert operation.

Thaçi was locked up alone in a cell – 'hot, sweaty, mosquitos, *incommunicado*', he recalls – and it was only early the next morning when he grabbed a few words with some other newly arrested Albanians that he began to understand the background. 'One of them told me: "Ali has been killed" – that is, my flatmate in Tirana, a journalist from Pristina who would distribute his articles through the international media, a good friend.' That evening Thaçi was brought out of his cell for interrogation.

'The interrogator was an intelligent young man. He didn't beat me up. He just asked very knowledgeable questions about my activities and said again and again: "Go back to Switzerland! Go back to being a student!"'

Thaçi did not give ground, though he was sure the next stage would be a beating.

'I just said: "I'm a member of the Kosovo Liberation Army, I'm not answering anything."'

A senior officer, 'a big man with hands like hams', came into the room and tried a different approach: unless Thaçi cooperated, he would publicly brand Thaçi not as a soldier, not as an oppositionist, but as a common criminal, destroying his credibility. 'You will talk, you will talk,' he said, and ordered a recording team into the interrogation room. A camera was set up.

'That's when I became really angry,' says Thaçi. 'I knew that whatever they filmed would be edited in a slanted way, shown on Albanian television – and watched by everybody in Kosovo.' That would have handed a propaganda victory to the Serbs.

'I'm not an arms dealer,' Thaçi said fiercely. 'The weapons were intended for the armed resistance in Kosovo, for the KLA. Now switch off those damned cameras – you're putting our friends in danger!'

The officers stopped recording. By midnight he had been released, some say thanks to the influence of the Albanian officer Adem Copani, who was a sympathiser with the KLA. 'All I knew was: orders from high up,' says Thaçi.

He was given twenty-four hours to leave Albania for Switzerland. 'It was only when I arrived in Zürich that I found out more about the death of my flatmate. He had been stabbed in the neck again and again with a screwdriver.' The murder squads, steered perhaps from Belgrade, were targeting KLA supporters and activists everywhere. Thaçi understood: he might have been the real intended target of the screwdriver assassination.

CHAPTER 4

THE END OF EXILE

It was the season of funerals. In late 1997, the quiet, mumbling rebellion of the Kosovars erupted into ever-more frequent gunfights with Serb police patrols. Thaçi, still living abroad, did not attend many of the burials – they were very public events – but he understood that each gathering at a cemetery intensified the anger. Rugova's pacifism was looking more and more like passivity in the face of an oppressor; he was manifestly losing the confidence of students (beaten down by police in Pristina in October protests) and the people in the countryside. The funeral of Thaçi's KLA friend Adrian Krasniqi was attended by a throng of 10,000. By late November, with the winter winds already chilling the Drenica Valley, a teacher called Halit Gecaj was laid to rest. He had been a participant, perhaps only a bystander killed by a stray bullet, in an exchange of fire between KLA fighters and a Serb police unit. After the funeral, three armed KLA men addressed the some 20,000 mourners. It turned out to be a carefully choreographed outing, filmed so that it could be broadcast out of Tirana to be viewed within Kosovo. Two of the fighters stripped off their balaclavas, raised their fists and shouted:

'Serbia is slaughtering Albanians! Only the KLA can fight for Kosovo's freedom and nationhood!' The mourners immediately understood this was an important moment. An underground movement was emerging into the daylight and laying claim to be the true voice of Kosovo. It was a declaration of war. They responded with the chant: 'UÇK! UÇK! [KLA, KLA]' Many balled their raised fists: the symbol of the KLA.

Belgrade registered the incident and drew the wrong conclusion. The root of the problem, it was decided in the security apparatus, was Drenica and its dogged hatred of the Serbs. The leaders of the rebellion had to be picked off, one by one. Their plan was to hold off until a fortnight after the end of the Orthodox Christmas, when the Serbian Interior Ministry (MUP) police numbers would be back to full strength. This was partly down to the sluggish rhythm of the security establishment but also because there was still a vagueness about the KLA's command structure in the Drenica. There were almost no Serbs, and hence very few informants, in the valley.

One thing every Serb intelligence officer in Kosovo knew, however, was that some of the most determined opposition to Serb rule was led by the Jashari brothers, above all bushy-bearded Adem, who had actually taken a group of fighters for training in northern Albania. Their hostility had passed from generation to generation; they were highlanders and well armed. Serbia did not fully understand the relationship of the Jasharis to the KLA, but no matter. If you broke the power of the family, thus ran the logic of the Serb secret police, you could cow Drenica. And so, just before dawn on 22 January 1998, police units surrounded the family compound in Donji Prekaz and attempted to arrest him. It was a typical highland estate with houses for different wings of the family, fortified a little since an earlier assault at the end of 1991: a 'No Serb Police Zone'. The Serbs had not reckoned, however, on the intensity of fire coming from the main building and the outhouses. Nor, as the fight raged on, on the silent arrival of KLA men slipping down from the woods to guard the flanks of the compound. The police, chastened and smarting with humiliation, withdrew.

The thwarted assault on the Jasharis was important for Thaçi. 'Adem's resistance was an important factor that inspired many youngsters,' he says. 'We had talked for years about the need for armed resistance. I had spent time in that compound and felt myself almost to be one of the family.'

Although the Serbs had been fought off in Prekaz, there was a sense that this was only the beginning. The more that the KLA showed itself in public, the greater the pressure would be from the full spectrum of the Serb authorities – the MUP police, the army, intelligence and the propaganda machine. And it was getting personal – very personal – for Thaçi. Earlier, his relatives had been interrogated; now, they were becoming particularly vulnerable.

'My parents knew I was doing something big, something dangerous,' remembers Thaçi. 'Before it reached the critical moment, I was sitting in the yard with my father when he leant over and said: "Don't worry about Serbia. Care about your honour, yourself and your friends."'[6] By the end of 1997, there was another big decision for Thaçi. He proposed and married Lume. They had met as students in 1993 in Pristina and they dated on and off throughout the following years. She followed him to Switzerland and they tied the knot in a small ceremony without the nearest family members, who were all in Kosovo. They visited Albania after the ceremony for a modest honeymoon, but the situation in Kosovo was unravelling and Lume saw little of Thaçi in the subsequent few years. Her family did pay a heavy price for the love they shared. In May 1999, Lume's brother was murdered by Serbian police.

---

6 Author interview with Thaçi

By 1998, it was impossible for Thaçi not to be concerned about Serbia and its intensifying repression. He was hurtling towards a showdown with a dictator who had wrought terrible vengeance on Croats and Bosnians for having the temerity to seek independence.

Belgrade was on the lookout for pretexts to crack down, to turn Kosovo into a huge military garrison. In the summer of 1998, a KLA commander had briefly taken the Trepča mines – an important economic asset for Kosovo – and the Serbian police and army attacked with all guns blazing. Four days later, it was back in Serb hands, and the ethnic cleansing began. Kosovan Albanians were driven out of mixed neighbourhoods, their houses looted. By early 1998, the Serbian government was blaming all violence on Kosovan provocation. The Serb police spokesman claimed that, in January and February of 1998, the KLA had mounted sixty-six attacks and that Belgrade was merely trying to defend the rights of threatened Serbs. The International Crisis Group, taking a longer perspective, came out with a more modern assessment of Kosovan military strength in March 1998: 'Kosovar observers calculate that since 1996, the organisation (the KLA) has claimed responsibility for the killing of twenty-one citizens in the province including five policemen, five Serb civilians and eleven Kosovars accused of collaborating with the Serbian regime.' Not exactly indicative of a full-blown war on the part of the Kosovars; rather a low-intensity insurgency, fuelled by the Serb offensive against Albanian villagers, that was only just beginning to gather pace.

Thanks to the breaking open of arsenals across the border in Albania, weapons were flowing into the province at a much faster rate. But there was still nothing like the kind of force that could repel the might of the rump Yugoslav army with its military academies, tanks, air power and artillery. A former doctor with the KLA at that time recalls the precarious process of smuggling guns across the border:

The grenades were loaded into panniers on the mules and we walked behind them, prodding the animals a little. All the time I thought – those grenades, they were Chinese, made for the Albanian army, pretty old and unstable. One slip by the mule on a loose rock and we would have been blown to Kingdom come.

Once in Kosovo, those same unstable grenades would have to be stored, then taken on bumpy roads to Thaçi's KLA sleeper cells and put in storage again for the next raid on a police station.

In truth, the KLA wasn't quite ready. It was to some extent a self-recruiting army, with local groups declaring themselves to be KLA without any real sense of a central command. Pleurat Sejdiu told the journalist-historian Tim Judah that 'the plan was for 1999, to start a war then, bombing depots and so on. We considered that by that time we could have the structures and the people ready.'[7] The pace of conflict, however, was moving faster than anyone had calculated. Serb forces were using armed helicopters to outwit KLA units. In late February 1998, police tried to stop what they believed to be a rendezvous of KLA chieftains in a village outside Cirez. A gunfight ensued and four policemen were killed. The KLA members in the incident included Adem Jashari and Sylejman Selimi, who would go on to become the KLA commander in the Drenica. The police called up an attack helicopter and a rocket was fired at one of the getaway cars. Furious, the Serb police set out on the path of revenge. Armoured personnel carriers were used to ram private compounds; at least twenty-five Kosovo Albanians, many of them civilians, were killed in the coming days.

More funerals, attended again by thousands. Every incident, it seemed, was a further step towards the radicalisation of the entire province,

---

7   Tim Judah, *Kosovo: War and Revenge* (2002), p. 141

not just the Drenica and Dukagjini, two strongholds of the KLA. But the anger also sat deep in the Serbian police command. They were now more determined than ever to eliminate the Jasharis and in so doing break the spine of resistance. This could not have been a local decision. Milošević had passed down the word: Kosovo was to be brought to heel once and for all. He could not tolerate the idea that his country had no-go areas for Serbs.

A day after the Cirez funerals, Serb troops took over an old munitions factory on a hill overlooking the Jashari clan's homestead. The lesson had been learned from the unsuccessful January assault on the Jasharis: if the Serbs could shell from higher ground they could turn the family's walled defences into a mantrap. Before dawn, an armoured column moved into the village while from above, from the gun emplacements set up in the disused plant, shells rained down. When the Serbs sent in helicopter gunships, it was plain that the Jasharis would not be able to escape with their lives. To ensure that KLA fighters would not this time be able to come to Jashari's assistance, the Serbian military had cordoned off fifteen surrounding villages. It was a ruthless battle. By the end of the Serbian operation, fifty-eight people in the compound had been slaughtered, twenty of them members of the Jashari family, including women and children. Adem Jashari was dead – and the KLA had its martyr.

Thaçi was deeply moved and knew that his time in Swiss exile was over. He had been given political asylum there, his wife had joined him from Pristina, there was a baby son on the way – but he could see that Jashari's death was critically important.

'He was a legendary commander, the still-undeclared leader of the KLA, charismatic, a symbol,' says Thaçi. Jashari's death was a bugle call to battle. Politically, the assault on the Jasharis was a clinching argument against the do-nothing-to-cause-trouble pacifism of Rugova. Morally, it demonstrated to any undecided Kosovars that there was a unifying national cause worth fighting for. And militarily, it showed that the KLA had to be ready for all-out war.

The Drenica was thirsting for revenge and the Serb police braced itself for a counter-attack; hunkered down behind sandbags. The massacre had turned the whole province against them; there was no longer any sensible distinction between the mountain fighters and the student revolutionaries. Abroad, in the wide-ranging Albanian diaspora, there was also a shift of support in favour of the KLA. Two days after the Jashari clan was killed, a rally was held in New York and an astonishing $270,000 was raised, much of it from small contributions.

One of the great hubs of fundraising was Bruno's, an ethnic Albanian restaurant set up in 1979 on East 58th Street by Bruno Selimaj. He was an Albanian from Montenegro who had worked his way up from dish-washing. After the Jashari massacre, Bruno closed for an evening and some forty potential donors met in the upstairs private dining room to work out the implications for exiled Kosovars who had always been solidly behind Ibrahim Rugova and the concept of a peaceful parallel state. Other Albanian Americans, such as Dino Hasanaj, Nazar Mehmeti, Shaqir Gashi and Salo Rusi, were the driving force behind much of the early fundraising. 'Bruno, Dino and Nazar were true patriots, extraordinary people serving their homeland in extraordinary times,' says Thaçi. Similar discussions were being held across the diaspora, in Germany and Switzerland. 'Our fellow countrymen, our cousins, were quite clearly up against a madman willing to flatten our homeland,' says one of the Bruno regulars from 1998. 'It would have been irresponsible to continue in the old way – the guys needed to be able to defend themselves.'[8] Some asked why the US wasn't supplying arms to the

---

8 David L. Phillips, *Liberating Kosovo: Coercive Diplomacy and US Intervention* (2012), p. 85

Kosovars; soon the exiles upstairs in Bruno's would get the chance to ask the State Department themselves as the architect of the Dayton deal, Richard Holbrooke, was brought back to troubleshoot on Kosovo.

In the Balkans, there were plenty of sceptics about Dayton, which had not only ignored – some would say sold out – Kosovo but enhanced and protected the standing of Milošević. In Western capitals, though, Dayton still ranked as a masterpiece of diplomacy, supposedly a sign that the savagery of war could be tamed and brought to order inside a rules-based international system. No one's reputation hinged so hugely on the Dayton outcomes as Dick Holbrooke's. He was all too aware that a Kosovo war, the return of violence to the Balkans, would have reopened the wounds of the early 1990s.

On 16 March, Rugova – imagining that he could head off a war with Belgrade – wrote to Madeleine Albright, asking her to bring Holbrooke back on board: 'I am writing to inform you that I am ready to meet President Slobodan Milošević without any preconditions, under the mediation of the US. I urge you to appoint Richard Holbrooke as a mediator.' He sent a copy of the letter to Holbrooke and added: 'I look forward to working closely with you for the benefit of peace and stability in the region.'

For Thaçi, Rugova's proposal to meet Milošević without conditions was dangerously naive. And if Holbrooke's mission was to produce another Dayton, papering over the cracks, giving Kosovo a little more autonomy in return for perpetuating Milošević's rule, then it could only end badly. 'Milošević was always the problem, never the means to a solution,' says Thaçi.

These doubts were shared by those around the table at Bruno's when Holbrooke started to visit. He suddenly started turning up every six weeks or so in the spring and summer of 1998, trying to understand the gossamer threads that link Kosovars abroad with the homeland. 'We were simple people and he would sit with us, expressed himself well and never lost his cool,' Sami Repishti told David Phillips, a diplomat who worked closely with Richard Holbrooke on the Balkans. Another participant from the diaspora in America, expecting 'Bulldozer' Holbrooke, was pleasantly surprised too and noted that the Kosovo Albanians didn't lay into him for neglecting Kosovo over the years. 'It was amazing to me how carefully the Albanians chose their words. Nobody was harsh.'

Plainly, Holbrooke had got the tone right. He was asking for understanding for a public diplomacy which needed to talk Milošević down from further escalation. But at the same time he was letting the Kosovars know through nudges and winks that the US was not out to betray them. Holbrooke was of course not freestyling; he had the imprimatur of Madeleine Albright herself. 'We are not going to stand by and watch the Serbian authorities do in Kosovo what they can no longer get away with doing in Bosnia,' she said.

The Kosovars, at least those trying to win him over round the dinner table, gave Holbrooke the benefit of the doubt. If only because the existing US emissary – Bob Gelbard, Albright's special representative for the implementation of Dayton – had done so much damage. Holbrooke had to be better. After a meeting with Milošević on 23 February, Gelbard had summoned a press conference in Belgrade and described the KLA as terrorists. It was no excuse, but one of his previous jobs had been to head the Bureau of International Narcotics and Law Enforcement – 'the department of thugs and drugs' in the Washington slang. He seemed to think Kosovo was Bolivia and it was through this prism that he saw the KLA. For sure, some Kosovan exiles in Germany were involved in organised crime, in protection rackets, car theft and the narcotics trade. The collapse of communist rule across Europe had seen a surge in cross-frontier crime. And the KLA was buying guns on a large scale. Enough, it seems, for Gelbard to add apples to pears and come up with bananas. Milošević, though annoyed at Gelbard's confrontational manner, was delighted with his characterisation of the KLA: the US had publicly bought into the Serbian narrative. And Gelbard did not just stick to his press conference utterances, he went further. 'I know a terrorist when I see one, and these men are terrorists.' Most damaging of all, he branded the KLA as an Islamic terrorist group. The evidence for this was non-existent. Thaçi, aware that some jihadists had fought with Muslim forces in Bosnia, had been careful to ensure there was no radical infiltration of his guerrilla army. 'I made certain that we had a strict policy against religious symbolisms,' he said. Gelbard's comments, Thaçi said at the time, had been 'coordinated with Rugova and Milošević to discredit the KLA'. Though one has to acknowledge that Gelbard later realised his mistake and became a staunch supporter of bombing Serbia and of Kosovan independence.

It would take more than the appointment of Holbrooke, working alongside an increasingly irritated Gelbard, to undo the damage. Milošević could now present himself as a US ally in an early version of the war against terror. Some Kosovars still see a connection between Gelbard's comments and Milošević giving the green light to wipe out the Jashari household. And, to some in the international community, the Gelbard intervention seemed to boost the credibility of Rugova.

Although the State Department distanced itself from the terror branding of the KLA, the US seemed to be occupying a position of calculated ambiguity. A declassified phone conversation between Bill Clinton and Tony Blair ends, after much discussion about the fine detail of a Northern Ireland settlement, with a presidential outburst on Kosovo: 'We're not going to let ourselves become the air force of the KLA.' This became a mantra across the US political elite. Madeleine Albright, despite the massive displacement of ethnic Albanians, was still sceptical in mid-1998 about the KLA.

There does not seem to be much Jeffersonian thinking within the KLA. Often indiscriminate in their attacks, they seemed intent on provoking a massive Serb response so that international intervention would be unavoidable. I wanted to stop Milošević marauding through Kosovo, but I didn't want that determination exploited by the KLA for purposes we opposed. We therefore took pains to insist that we would not operate as the KLA's air force or rescue the KLA if it got into trouble as a result of its own actions.

Yet, within a year, that is exactly what the US became. It was Thaçi who convinced Albright that the KLA leadership could indeed be Jeffersonian, that wars with US help could be short and effective, and that the post-war outcome would not end up a gangster-state. Could the KLA have succeeded without American assistance? Almost certainly not. There was no European alternative. It was US military might that had brought a belated resolution to Bosnia. By hook or by crook, the leaders of the KLA had to persuade Washington that it was in America's self-interest to re-engage in the Balkans, secure a better-than-Dayton deal and permanently neuter or even topple Milošević. The US, in short, needed the KLA almost as much as the KLA needed American muscle. Simply sticking with Rugova would have been an abdication of policy; it would have turned Kosovo into a Serbian slave colony and exposed the ineffectiveness of the West and its institutions. Holbrooke, though, did not even know the names of the leaders of the KLA. The Albanian-Americans at Bruno's consulted with the KLA and decided to hand him a scrap of paper. On it were three names, three mobile phone numbers: Hashim Thaçi, Xhavit Haliti and Azem Syla. It was a beginning.

Milošević pushed ahead with his war on 'separatists and terrorists'. In Belgrade, the governing coalition now included, as well as his SPS party and 'Yugoslav United Left', the Serbian Radical Party led by the ultra-nationalist Vojislav Šešelj. Milošević had in other words ended his charade of presenting himself as a post-communist liberal and made common cause with a man who had put together one of the most savage paramilitary units to shed blood in Bosnia and Croatia. Šešelj's party programme made plain the government's intentions. It demanded the permanent expulsion of 360,000 Kosovars to Albania, and the creation of a security cordon of 20–50 kilometres along the Albania–Serbia border since Albania was a 'hostile state'. That was a political blueprint for the ethnic cleansing of Kosovo. According to Šešelj's plan, the Kosovo Parliament would be closed down until such a time as the Serb minority in the population became a clear majority.

The KLA leaders, above all Thaçi, grasped that Milošević was preparing a war of ethnic elimination. High time, then, to be less clandestine – to stir Western media interest in the insurgency and to issue a clear statement about the KLA's aims. On 27 April 1998, the KLA general staff issued a nine-point programme. The aims of the army, it said, were both defensive and liberating. It would respect the international conventions of the United Nations and the conventions of war; it denounced terrorism and violence against civilians. There could be no peace struck with Milošević without the say-so of the KLA: 'We reject any agreement reached with the enemy without the approval of the KLA.' And the charter set out the cornerstone of its policy – to internationalise the conflict as soon as possible. 'For the sake of peace in the region, we appeal to international decision-makers and in particular to the US and the EU to exert pressure upon the occupiers and to give their support to the just war of the Albanian people in Yugoslavia.'

That was a rather desperate call. The Yugoslav/Serb army – many of them battle-hardened from the Bosnian and Croatian wars – were now shelling indiscriminately the villages of Drenica. Some 30,000 locals had fled for their lives. Šešelj's plan had not quite been realised but Serb forces had set up an 8-kilometre-wide buffer zone along the border with Albania, planting a dense network of anti-personnel mines. That was supposed to stop the flow of weapons from Albania and to bottle up the Kosovo Albanian population.

Thaçi understood that international engagement in Kosovo would follow logically from recent experience; political responses to atrocity in a media age were informed by images of how events had unfolded over the previous decade. The fall of the Berlin Wall and the lifting of the Iron Curtain was a defining moment less than a decade earlier – yet now Serbia was laying minefields to blow up people. There was no major state in Europe that had been unaffected by the Bosnian refugee crisis – yet now Kosovars were scrambling for the borders. Germany in particular knew what that meant – the social strain of the Bosnian influx had spawned a neo-Nazi movement and a surge in xenophobia. The Balkan atrocities of the early 1990s had exposed the fragility of the UN and international institutions; an already confused NATO had become even more uncertain about its role. It had taken the international community three years to respond effectively to the Bosnian crisis. The KLA didn't have that long. Thaçi and Veseli as two of the co-founders of the KLA had to find a platform from which to persuade the West that delay or inaction could only harm Western interests.

For the time being, though, he was dependent on Holbrooke. A head of steam was gathering behind the US mediator. Washington's goal was straightforward: to bring Rugova and Milošević together, to kick off a 'process' that would see the Serbs withdraw from the province and the KLA hold back from its guerrilla hit-and-run attacks. Leading, ultimately, to a semi-detached relationship between Belgrade and Pristina that would respect the human rights of Kosovo.

The project was doomed. Milošević had no real incentive to abandon the Serbian interest. Rugova was nervous, aware that he had no bargaining muscle to use against one of the most unscrupulous of European autocrats. Thaçi knew that any deal worked out between Rugova and Milošević would work against the KLA and the long-term interests of Kosovo. And he was furious that Rugova could have placed Kosovo in this supplicant position. Irritated, too, that the US was applying so much pressure on the Kosovars, simply in the name of establishing a false sense of security. What was the point of 'averting' war if the price was bitterness and betrayal and the certainty of an even bigger and more explosive confrontation?

The Belgrade meeting between Rugova and Milošević went ahead. The Serbian leader had agreed because he knew the alternative was heavier sanctions; if he pretended to make a success of it, he had been promised that an investment ban on Yugoslavia would be lifted. Serbian television filmed the occasion and the footage showed Rugova laughing nervously. Tim Judah quotes a Kosovan politician who watched the spectacle on TV: 'While Rugova laughs, half of Kosovo is bleeding.' The two men agreed to regular meetings to ease the plight of Kosovo. Predictably, nothing came of that.

Rugova reaped one reward though: a meeting with Bill Clinton in the White House. In Kosovo, calls were increasing for NATO intervention. The number of displaced people was growing by the day – by September, 300,000 Kosovo Albanians would have been forced to leave their homes. The Rugova talks were sandwiched between National Security Council meetings on a flare-up between two nuclear powers, India and Pakistan. Kosovo was suddenly very low on the White House agenda. As they were rushed into the talks, news came through from Kosovo: a massacre of civilians had taken place in Peja, in the Kosovo–Albania border region. The Serb army had been stepping up its operations in the area but KLA tactics had become increasingly effective, using roadblocks to control the Pristina–Peja road, encircling police and civilians in Kijevo. Thaçi recalls that Holbrooke called the KLA leadership and gave a clear warning: "'If you attack Kijevo, forget about American support. You will pay a price.' We kept our word and refrained from an all-out assault on Kijevo.' They were fighting now in the daytime, making open contact with the locals. The Serbs had decided on a punitive response.

The information seemed to bewilder Rugova. He was incapable of improvising or using the new twist on the battlefield to dramatise his demands from the US. Two national security advisors present, Sandy Berger and Leon Fuerth, noted that after a few introductory sentences, Rugova seemed to slump, paralysed by anxiety. Veton Surroi, one of the delegation, took up the slack, arguing that before serious negotiations could start, Milošević's troops had to leave Kosovo and be replaced by an international force.

That, the US decided, was a reasonable place to begin. Holbrooke started to commute frenetically between Belgrade and Pristina – and trying to make contact with the KLA. In June, he passed the last Serb checkpoint in the Dukagjini region, drove a bit faster, and suddenly found himself surrounded by men in KLA uniforms. He got out and walked to a farmhouse with a machine gun mounted on a pick-up truck trained on him. Holbrooke's aim was to hard-talk the KLA general staff into dismantling road blocks. But the commanders decided it was too risky to meet him (and pointless to give up the tactical advantage of blocking roads). So the US envoy took off his shoes, entered the farmhouse and supped tea with two local KLA men.

Suddenly a photographer appeared and snapped him, apparently socialising with armed insurgents. 'It was a good public relations moment for us,' says Thaçi, smiling. 'And in general it was really valuable that he took the trouble to travel down muddy dirt tracks to see us. You have to understand that until then, we were being portrayed as outlaws.' Even if it was unintentional, Holbrooke had helped to patch up the damage done by Gelbard's labelling of the KLA as terrorists. Informally, but very publicly, the KLA was becoming part of the political equation.

Step by step, Holbrooke piled on the threats to Milošević. At the UN General Assembly session that September, Tony Blair warned of an imminent humanitarian disaster. Two days later, Britain launched UN Security Council Resolution 1199, which demanded a ceasefire. It was increasingly obvious, though, that the West would have to roll out the guns if it was going to secure a Serb withdrawal. NATO defence ministers agreed to issue an Activation Warning Order, the first step towards a mobilisation. Holbrooke decided to take General Wes Clark, Supreme Allied Commander of forces in Europe, to his next meeting with Milošević. Any NATO bombing raid on Serbia would be far, far worse than the damage inflicted by the Nazis on Belgrade in 1941, Clark told the Serbian leader.

The critical juncture came in the transit lounge of Heathrow airport on 8 October. Holbrooke briefed the international contact group that Milošević was not giving ground. On the contrary, Serb behaviour in Kosovo was getting ever more brutal. Milošević was using the diplomatic process to buy himself time to consolidate his power in the province. Crucially, Holbrooke won Russian approval to push the threat level against Milošević even higher. Holbrooke returned to Belgrade. Another NATO mobilisation order was issued. It was a gun at Milošević's head: he had ninety-six hours to comply otherwise he would face the firepower of the NATO alliance. Until now, Milošević had been counting on the West backing down. In 1995, when Banja Luka was about to crumple – a move that would surely have brought down Milošević – Washington ordered a halt to the ground offensive of the Croats and Bosnians. That saved Milošević's skin and had reinforced in him the idea that he was considered an indispensable player in global diplomacy.

Now, though, he was forced to blink. He agreed to a ceasefire. Serbian forces would be partially withdrawn. Aid agencies would be given access to the needy. Displaced people would be helped to return to their homes. More autonomy could be granted to the Kosovars. And, for the first time since expelling the Organisation for Security and Cooperation in Europe (OSCE) mission in 1992,[9] he said he was ready to let in foreign observers.

The deal was never going to stick. Every item on the agenda was open to manipulation. The observers – the Kosovo Verification Mission – were supposed to be 2,000 unarmed policemen or ex-military people ready to interpose themselves between opposing sides. Thaçi saw that the deal would lead nowhere. It let Milošević keep a significant force in the province. And the KVM observers were supposed to report on KLA activities and movements – information that would surely get back to the Serbs and give them a tactical advantage. Unarmed referees in a shifting battle zone? It was a policy made up on the hoof.

David Phillips recalls a lunch at Bruno's in which the NYPD commissioner Howard Safir – whose son was married to the daughter of the Kosovan émigré Sami Repishti – called together about fifty Albanian-origin New York cops to persuade them to join the monitors. They were offered a fully paid six-month leave of absence to go to their ancestral home and keep the peace.

'Some were administrative types,' says Phillips. 'Others worked on homicide and narcotics. There were several women officers who had been working undercover. It was a rough bunch. Not only were they New York cops; they were also Albanians.'

---

9   The OSCE was given the thankless task of promoting dialogue between the Yugoslav authorities and communities in Kosovo. The mission collapsed within months when the Yugoslav leadership was accused of breaching OSCE principles.

They were told that NATO would set up a rapid-reaction force – an 'extraction force' – in Macedonia to drag them out of danger. But they were not convinced. 'Go to Kosovo without a sidearm?' said one of the officers present. 'You must be crazy.' Nobody volunteered.

General Clark shared their fears. If Srebrenica was anything to go by, Serb forces could easily seize them and use them as hostages in case of a NATO attack. The simple reality, Thaçi understood, was that only direct NATO military action would be able to check Milošević. The ceasefire deal had only one merit: it internationalised the Kosovo conflict, it showed that all peaceful options were being tried and it bought the KLA time to regroup and organise for the battle ahead. The breathing space would not last long.

CHAPTER 5

THE HIKE TO RAMBOUILLET

The first time that Thaçi heard the name 'Rambouillet' was when he entered a private room in Heathrow airport crowded with worried foreign ministers and diplomats. They were panicking about the latest massacre in Kosovo, a massacre that, this time, would prove to be a tipping point against Milošević. And for the first time it became clear to Thaçi that he was being eyed as someone who could be used to broker some kind of peace deal.

It was January 1999. A few days earlier, on the 15th, Serb Ministry of Interior units had gone into the central Kosovan village of Račak at dawn and started shooting, demanding people come out of their snow-covered homes. The buildings in the hamlet, sheltered from bleak winter winds only by a craggy hill, had already been pounded since dawn by Yugoslav army artillery. Old men and boys were ordered up a hill and shot. Witnesses said that some of the bodies were mutilated – either beheaded or with limbs removed. The final death toll was forty-five.

Račak was regarded as a KLA neighbourhood, close to the market place in Shtime, where fighters could get food supplies to their forest hideouts. It was strategically important, too, because it allowed the rebels to descend to the Pristina–Prizren road and mount ambushes.

But the Serb assault was not about gaining the military upper hand; it was about revenge. And it was a revenge attack that, unknown to Milošević, would mark a tipping point for him and prod the West, once and for all, to bomb Serbia out of Kosovo. The bullets fired at old men in Račak – no different from any other atrocity in the Kosovar war – would start the clock ticking for independence.

Belgrade had become increasingly angry about the KLA hit-and-run tactics. Serb policemen had been killed in a firefight in the area. Earlier, some Serb teenagers had been killed by masked men in a shoot-out at a billiards café. Thousands of local Serbs had turned out at the funerals and demanded that Belgrade step up their protection. A decade later, Serbian Prime Minister Vučić would state that the brutal murders of Serbian teenagers in Peja had not actually been committed by 'Albanian extremists', leading some observers to conclude that the crimes were the work of the notorious Serbian intelligence agency itself, in order to blame the KLA and incite a greater wave of violence.[10]

The Serb response was an atrocity. The troopers encircled Račak and then moved in street by street, shooting any villagers who took flight. A group of forty-five men, teenagers and old men included, hid in a basement but were smoked out, beaten up and then taken up the hillside. A Human Rights Watch team later concluded that the men had been killed at close range.

> Their clothes were bloody, with slashes and holes at the same
> spots as their bullet entry and exit wounds which argues against

---

10 https://www.tagesanzeiger.ch/ausland/europa/Einst-Kriegshetzer-heute-schaemt-er-sich-dafuer/story/14696826, accessed 5 September 2017

government claims that the victims were KLA soldiers who were dressed in civilian clothes only after they had been killed. All of them were wearing rubber boots typical of Kosovo farmers rather than military footwear.

Nine KLA men had indeed been killed but the final death toll included elderly men, three women and a twelve-year-old boy. William Walker, head of the Kosovo Verification Mission, rushed to Račak and, knowing that Belgrade would try to muddy the waters, declared: 'As a layman it looks to me like executions.' It was, he said, 'an unspeakable atrocity and a crime very much against humanity'. The Serb propaganda machine, helped, perhaps unwittingly, by Walker's French deputy head of mission – Gabriel Keller – who tried to cast doubt on the 'massacre', suggesting that the KLA had staged an event designed to pull the West into a bombing campaign against Milošević.

Yet all the signs suggested it was a vicious attack on civilians by a force that was acting like an unrestrained occupation army. Walker was declared *persona non grata* and ordered to go back over the border. Louise Arbour, head of the International Criminal Tribunal in The Hague, was refused entry to Yugoslavia to investigate the crime. When an EU forensics team was eventually allowed into Račak, it declared: 'There were no indications of the people being other than unarmed civilians.'

The international community, having learned how swiftly Milošević had covered up and deflected from atrocities in Bosnia, moved faster. James Pardew of the State Department – regarded as a Milošević expert ever since the Dayton peace talks – was sent to confront the Serb leader in his presidential villa. 'Walker is a horse's ass,' Milošević blustered to Pardew. Milošević was urged to pull back his forces, to start talking seriously about autonomy for Kosovo, but gave no ground. 'Milošević had built up a command around Kosovo and it looked like he was going to launch a full-scale invasion, Pardew told State Department Balkan expert David Phillips.

Two days later, Madeleine Albright, deeply upset, immediately called a meeting of the Contact Group – the US, Britain, France, Italy, Germany and Russia – in London. And it was here that the next chapter of Thaçi's career would be born.

Pressure had to be piled on Milošević, she believed, in order to head off a Serbian spring offensive against Kosovo – one which would make no distinction between those who were wearing KLA uniforms and those who were not. That meant coercive diplomacy: building up a credible threat of bombing Belgrade to push the Serb leader into making a deal. The alternative was an unfolding chain of Račak-style killings – another Bosnia. Both sides had to be persuaded to sit in a room together, or at least agree on common concerns. Yet, unlike Bosnia, the two sides were not suffering from war fatigue; the war could theoretically linger on for years, with KLA hit-and-run raids prompting disproportionate responses from Belgrade until finally the whole province became a killing field.

This time, peace negotiations had to be different.

In the brown-windowed, soundproofed Heathrow meeting room, the Contact Group agreed a date for new peace talks – it was to be 6 February, and they would take place in the beautiful fourteenth-century Château de Rambouillet, around 50km from central Paris. With a massive lake, gardens and forest, the official summer residence of the French President had hosted Napoleon on his way to St Helena and Charles de Gaulle from where he plotted the liberation of Paris. The talks were to be chaired by the French foreign minister Hubert Védrine, the NATO ally most sympathetic to Serbia, and the British Foreign Secretary Robin Cook. This time, however, unlike other Balkan peace talks, Thaçi would finally be allowed to sit at the top table.

The likes of Noam Chomsky claimed that Rambouillet was part of a charade, a token attempt at diplomacy designed to persuade a sceptical Western public of the need to deploy force. Milošević showed every sign of not wanting to cooperate, but most Western governments still believed that he would rather strike a deal (that averted Kosovan independence) rather than risk the destruction of his country. Certainly, there was no enthusiasm for deeper involvement.

Alastair Campbell, Tony Blair's press secretary and strategist, recorded a meeting at 10 Downing Street on 16 January to assess the Račak massacre. George Robertson, the defence secretary, was there, so was Chief of Defence Staff Charles Guthrie, along with Robin Cook. 'They agreed we could not bomb at the moment because there was no political process and the KLA were not much better than the Serbs and just looking to NATO to be their defence arm and bomb Milošević for them.'

Robertson whinged that 27 per cent of the British army was already involved in other conflicts. Guthrie said it would be difficult to sustain a long-term UK ground troop commitment 'if we ever got to that'.

'TB [Tony Blair] said everyone accepts Milošević is a dreadful man, but if we bomb as things stand, what is the process we are trying to bring about?'[11]

That, then, was the scale of the challenge to Thaçi. He did not have to convince the West or even Russia that Milošević was a war criminal. He did, however, have to persuade the West that the KLA were civilised amateurs and a potential ruling class, not a bunch of gangsters. He had to make plain that the Kosovan goal was full-blown independence rather than some form of self-government within Serbia. Kosovo had enjoyed those rights before under the Tito-era 1974 constitution – and Milošević had trampled on them, unchecked. And he had to make sure

---

11 Alastair Campbell, *The Blair Years* (2007), p. 362

that all members of the Contact Group understood that the KLA had to be the dominant part of any negotiating team since it would have to sell the outcome to its fighters. And the clearest voice coming out of the KLA was that of Thaçi.

First, though, Thaçi had to find out where the conference was actually happening. 'I had visited Versailles – I knew where that was, but I had never heard of Rambouillet.'

But he knew, sure enough, that whatever drama unfolded in the château could transform not only the future of Kosovo, but also his own fortunes.

As it turned out, Rambouillet would transform him from a guerrilla leader to a statesman on the world stage, capable of playing hardball with international leaders, and getting his own way.

As soon as the invitation was extended to the KLA, Thaçi and other leaders met to agree that they should attend but, critically, to decide who would be the group's main spokesman.

'I was keen to make it happen. The summit was to be of utmost importance for Kosovo,' Thaçi recalled in an interview in Switzerland in December 2015.

> Non-participation would have had very bad repercussions for both the KLA and for Kosovo. We would have been playing into Russia's hands. We would have been blamed for the failure of a political solution – we would have been the pariah. Publicly, we would have been lynched in the media. Albania would have stopped us from moving freely in and out of their country and the pressure on Milošević would have subsided. Our own society would have split as well.
>
> In truth, while I had the absolute conviction that we had to attend Rambouillet, I also knew that we [the KLA] were

suffering rapidly depleting resources. Our forces were tired. It would have been stupid to turn down the promise of finding a political solution because we had always said that such a solution was the only solution for us. We knew of the political risks, but I knew that to turn it down would be seen historically as the wrong thing to do. I knew that this could be the beginning of the next stage.

It was Wolfgang Petritsch, erstwhile Austrian ambassador to Belgrade, and Chris Hill, America's special representative to Kosovo, who had talent-spotted Thaçi. In November 1998, a meeting had been arranged in a safe house with the man who described himself as the political director of the KLA. Weapons were stacked outside. Thaçi offered them tea; they sat on a carpet on a bare floor and discussed a working document for a possible peace deal. Thaçi dismissed it out of hand – it gave Serbia far too much – but for Petritsch, the international negotiator who had the best inside knowledge of the KLA, it was clear that Thaçi spoke with authority, and that was a starting point. There would be two problems on the Kosovo side: who was to represent the province as a whole at any talks and who would represent the KLA? Thaçi, though young, seemed to be the clear answer. Ibrahim Rugova, battling depression and a drink problem, was admired and even revered by many Kosovars, yet he was deemed likely to cave under pressure from Milošević. Veton Surroi, publisher of the newspaper *Koha Ditore*, was liked by Western diplomats and journalists but had little sway within the KLA. Rexhep Qosja was another intellectual close to the KLA, but was aggressively antagonistic to Rugova and was considered to be too aloof. Adem Demaçi, the old dissident who had won the prestigious Sakharov Prize in the European Parliament and subsequently became the KLA's political spokesman, saw dialogue with the Serbs as a kind of surrender. His lesson from Račak had been to carry on fighting and demand more weapons from Western governments.

Thaçi recalled that around 70 per cent of KLA top brass were in favour of attending the conference, and realised that it was his job to convince the final 30 per cent. The most demanding would certainly be Demaçi and it would fall to Thaçi to convince him that a compromise which traded the prospect of independence for the disarming of the KLA would not end up as a sell-out. Petritsch – who was to join Hill and the Russian Boris Mayorski as Rambouillet mediators – had chosen wisely. Out of the sixteen-strong Albanian delegation – Rugova, Bujar Bukoshi and Fehmi Agani, the KLA men Xhavit Haliti and Rame Buja, as well as civil society leaders such as Shala, Surroi and others – Thaçi stood out as the most soldierly of the politicians and the most political of the soldiers. They voted among themselves and chose Thaçi, providing that he secured consensus on all decisions. Recalling his appointment as head of the delegation, US diplomat Jamie Rubin says: 'People thought so at the time, but Thaçi wasn't chosen by the Americans. Albanians chose Thaçi but we worked closely with him once he got elected.'

It was not just a third of the KLA who needed persuading. The French did not want the KLA there and whispered their reservations about Marxist hardliners to the French press. Serbia tried to block them from attending, denouncing them as terrorists. Petritsch tartly asked how Serbia imagined that it would solve the problem, talking to no one but themselves. Chris Hill was equally disdainful: there would be no meaning to Rambouillet without the KLA. And the message from Madeleine Albright was loud and clear: 'Don't just show up, get serious.' But, in a clever strategy, the Kosovars attending the talks stood firm – there would be no Rambouillet without the KLA. 'It was smart,'

Thaçi said, 'because it showed unity between us and meant that we could speak on behalf of each other.'

On 4 February, two days before the Rambouillet talks were due to begin, Thaçi and his small KLA team left the forests of Kosovo to head for France. But the Serbs intended to block even this step: a Kosovan no-show could be hailed as an easy victory. A French plane was allowed to land in Pristina airport to wait for the delegates. The KLA delegates, however, were travelling without valid passports. So it was uncertain whether they would even manage to pass the Serb police control points on the airport road. In the end, the French and Americans secured them safe passage.

Thaçi, though, had an arrest warrant outstanding against him and he knew that the Serbs were ready to try every trick in the book to stop him going. If Belgrade could stop him turning up, then internal divisions on the Kosovo team would allow Serbia to box through its points.

And so Thaçi put on his hiking boots and walked to the talks.

Fit and fast, he was long-accustomed to walking over the Albanian border to smuggle arms, meet other KLA operatives and to hide there. But this was different. In 1997, his regular walks over the border took seventy-two hours. This time, he did not have three days. Instead, he resolved to take the shortest and most treacherous route straight through the mountains, densely patrolled by armed border police along tracks littered with land mines, in freezing February weather. This route – if he were to survive it – would take just six hours, but it would require the discreet help of loyalist villagers who knew the shortest way through the mines. 'The villagers took me along a river route, walking by night. They knew the best routes.'

Over the border, Thaçi and Veseli took a village taxi to Tirana, the Albanian capital, reaching the airport just in time to catch a flight to Zürich, a city he knew well from his exiled student days. On the long walk across the mountains, Thaçi had only carried a modest rucksack with basic provisions, and was clothed for a below-zero hike. He was not dressed to appear before world statesmen.

'Close to Zürich airport was a gentleman's outfitters called Gladbrook. English tailors. I think they are still there and I kitted myself out for diplomacy. I think it was a grey suit,' Thaçi recalled. From there they flew to Paris Charles de Gaulle airport.

'We arranged for a taxi to pick us up and said: "Rambouillet! As fast as you can!"'

In the one-hour cab ride to the château through the end of the Paris evening rush hour, Thaçi was deep in thought. He had just metamorphised from khaki-clad rebel leader into a diplomatic negotiator. Slobodan Milošević would not be there, but his arch-enemy would be transmitting orders to the Serb delegation through the embassy in Paris (which had set up a special communications link with Belgrade). Thaçi was just two months shy of his thirty-first birthday and somehow he had to find a way of wrong-footing a powerful and slippery dictator without losing the support of his soldiers and citizens.

The cab ride took him through Versailles, where the peace treaty that ended the First World War had split the rubble of empires and had imposed such punitive reparations on Germany it had helped spawn a new world war. The Rambouillet stakes were just as high for Thaçi. How to wrestle a deal from the Serbs that could set Kosovo on a path to independence knowing that Belgrade would block such ambitions all the way? And how, when forced to publicly compromise, could he sell it back home to KLA shivering in trenches, running out of men and arms, and, more critically, sell such a compromise to the wealthy Kosovar diaspora who had funded him and the KLA for a decade? Despite Thaçi's quiet, stubborn confidence, he could not have predicted that within two months of arriving at Rambouillet, he would walk away with a straight flush: the right for Kosovars to self-determination, albeit three years hence, and the might of NATO to bomb Serbia out of the war.

'We arrived at Rambouillet about 9 p.m. It was already dark when the cab pulled up. Three diplomats were waiting for me. Young Austrian diplomat Jan Kickert, who would later become an ambassador to the UN, the British liaison officer David Slinn, and Axel Dittmann, the German diplomat – they all came to meet me at the main gate. They were pretty surprised,' Thaçi said.

> But we got there hours after everyone else. They had already started the proceedings – breaking into separate working groups. I was the only person who missed the beginning of all the meetings.
>
> While I was walking over the Albanian border, Chirac had opened the conference – talking about the importance of reaching a solution for peace. He stressed that it was France and Germany who had to broker a peace deal. Robin Cook spoke as well. He said the decisions taken now will affect all of our futures. 'This castle', he said, 'is not as peaceful as you might think. The British bombed it three times.' I regret missing his joke.
>
> That night I met the Kosovan delegation and I proposed that we start to organise ourselves into working groups, carving out one group that represented our Presidency, if you like. The delegation nominated me to lead the talks. It was a huge relief that they chose me and not [President] Rugova.

Rugova had had his chance and had blown it four years before. While lauded in the West for his insistence on a Gandhi-style passive resistance, keen to avoid the violence unleashed on Bosnia and Croatia,

Kosovo had been so marginalised that it was not even written as a foot-note into the Dayton Agreement of 1995. Now, on the first floor of the château, 2,500km from Pristina, Rugova's eclipse first by the KLA and now by Thaçi himself was complete. It was obvious to all in the Kosovan delegation – and to those back in Pristina – that the passive 55-year-old expert on sixteenth-century Albanian literary criticism was not the man to represent the country at the peace talks. And for the conference to succeed, it would have to be better than Dayton.

> When I arrived at Rambouillet that night, it was clear that Rugova had been living in a cocoon. He was isolated from everyone else within the Kosovan delegation. He was making odd statements. What I knew we needed was an agreement – signed – one that would provide us with long-term durability. That was all that was on my mind. But Rugova spoke only three times publicly during the whole of Rambouillet – he was very passive and withdrawn.
>
> This was the first ever international conference where Kosovo was the subject of it. Kosovo was represented by sixteen legitimate leaders' representatives. In the past, it was always others who spoke on our behalf. We were traded. We never represented ourselves. In Dayton we weren't even at the table.
>
> We sent the best of us to represent Kosovo. The highest quality of political leadership we had. Milošević sent a team who had no shred of credibility and, critically, no ability to make any decisions on behalf of Serbia. I saw some Albanians that were part of the Serbian delegation. That was the first and last I ever saw of them.

The summit was structured so that the Serbian delegation and the Kosovars were kept physically separate from each other except for scheduled meetings and dinner. The Kosovan living quarters were on the top floor of the château, which, while grand on the outside, was pokey inside. Thaçi's own room was modern and small, 'overlooking the pond, a sort of small lake. We were all sleeping in tiny rooms. My legs always stuck out of the end of the bed' – Thaçi is over 6ft tall. The shared bathroom was at the end of the corridor. The Serbs were given the floor underneath.

But most of them were never there. They seemed to spend their time playing the piano. I'm not sure where the piano came from, maybe Milošević sent it with them to give them something to do. I remember hearing them singing Serbian nationalist songs, and they certainly arrived with a lot of raki.

Rattling along the corridors and staircases of the castle, American, Russian and EU envoys broke into separate working groups, each shuffling working documents between them. The idea of the draft papers was to try to establish basic principles of the future deal between Serbia and Kosovo, which, line by line, detail by detail, would be put to Thaçi and the Serbs to see if they would agree.

The very first political documents produced in Rambouillet were far from favourable for Kosovo. The very first principle they addressed was the territorial integrity of Yugoslavia – i.e. that Kosovo would stay in, that at best we would be gifted a kind of second-rate autonomy.

We rejected that out of hand. Then we were given another first draft. This one projected some sort of autonomy but even less than what we already had. Theoretically, we already had our own government and our own constitution. Even then, the focus was not on strengthening Pristina but on giving us expanded, decentralised rights within the Serbian state.

They wanted us to specify the number of Kosovan military personnel that we would agree to reduce by, but there was no inclusion of any clause that monitored how many Serbs were left in Kosovo.

Even some of the earliest – and what the Americans and EU had hoped would be the easiest – principles to agree on became immediate sticking points, including the right of refugees to return home and reclaim their property and belongings unhindered.

Each of the three chief international power-brokers in the talks – Chris Hill, US special envoy to Kosovo; Wolfgang Petritsch, the Austrian EU chief negotiator for Rambouillet; and Boris Mayorsky, Russia's mediator for Kosovo – was supposed to be neutral.

'Hill was pretty even-handed,' Thaçi said, 'but the Russians were forever leaking drafts to the Serbs – I suppose as you would expect.'

With turrets, grand ballrooms and five floors, the château was gated – not just to keep the media out, but to keep the delegates in. Once in the grounds of Rambouillet, 'no one could come in to visit, and not a soul could go out', Thaçi remembers.

But in the hundreds of acres of medieval forest, lakes and tree-lined avenues, Thaçi jogged every day. Later in the conference he would embark on long walks with various envoys, most notably Jamie Rubin, the chief spokesman to the US State Department and Madeleine Albright's right-hand man. Just beyond the grounds, scores of satellite television vans were camped outside and Balkans journalists occupied the bars and cafés near the château, one of the few places that the small town of Rambouillet could offer an internet connection. Mobile phone usage within the château was supposed to be strictly limited, and calls to the media forbidden. At one point, there were so many broadcast crews based in the town hall that Rambouillet deployed riot police to control the traffic.

> Outside the formal talks we were allowed to be in the same room as the Serbs over dinner. On the second floor there was a kitchen – the Serbs had one table, we had another. The French laid on pretty rich food and mountains of cheese. We had wine in the evenings. Rugova, however, drank cognac pretty heavily. The Serbs were often drunk.
>
> In the first days of the summit, everybody just wanted an agreement. By now, there was a natural sympathy for the Kosovars from both the Europeans and the Americans. It was a sympathy connected to the fact that everyone loathed Milošević, which in the early days translated into everyone having very little sympathy for the Serbian cause.

The French had banked on the Rambouillet summit lasting seven days, 'but it took ten days just to get a first draft agreed. Tiny changes to sentences in new drafts were taken up and down between the two floors.'

Within the first week of the summit, it became clear that the talks were stalling, fatally.

Thaçi was overwhelmed by bullying down his satellite phone from some KLA commanders, who would threaten to kill him on return to Kosovo if he compromised with Serbia, and from rich members of the Kosovar diaspora who had funded his years in exile. He admits that he began to regularly ignore new written amendments on drafts and the Serbs tried to avoid delivering any written remarks on the Kosovo documents.

Worse, while Thaçi had, in principle, the credibility to agree to new parts of a peace deal, but did not want to do so, Hill and Petritsch realised that the Serb delegation had no authority to approve any principles of an agreement. Any member of the Serb delegation had to phone Milošević in Belgrade and neither the Serbs nor Milošević had any interest in doing so.

'The internationals [*sic*] realised that the Serb delegation had no political gravity. They were just hanging out. Drinking, eating, sleeping. The only legitimate comments from the Serb side were coming out of Belgrade – often through the media – not out of Rambouillet.'

After the first ten days of the summit, on 16 February, a new draft was delivered to Thaçi, a document that would mark a breakthrough in the talks. Entitled an 'Interim Agreement', NATO added one new annex.

> It was called the 'B' Annex and added a military mechanism to the agreement. We fully agreed with this annex, NATO troops to be given the ability to move across the entire territory of Yugoslavia, unhindered – from Belgrade to Pristina, so they could move freely in and out of Kosovo. However, Annex B made the Serbs look even more distant in the negotiations.

His plan was to make an international peacekeeping force police any deal that Belgrade signed up to. But it would have marked a humiliation for Milošević.

The psychological pressure on the thirty-year-old was immense. 'The international envoys just assumed we would accept anything that was offered. They believed that they had us – and me – cornered.'

As if the stakes were not high enough, the Serbs ramped up attacks on Kosovan soil while Thaçi and the cream of the political wing of the KLA were distracted in France.

Throughout the entire conference, the Serbs were killing

Kosovars. Every morning the Americans and the rest of the international team would give us briefings on the daily military operations that were happening in Kosovo. It was all orchestrated out of Belgrade to add to the psychological pressure and make us agree to their terms.

As the summit threatened to drag into its third week, it became clear that the prospect of an agreement was rapidly diminishing.

CHAPTER 6

POWER PLAY IN THE CHÂTEAU

It had become clear to everyone in Rambouillet that the peace talks were beginning to fall apart. With the Serb delegation made up of non-entities with no authority to agree to anything without a phone call back to Belgrade, any serious movement would have to come from Milošević himself. But the Serb leader seemed convinced that Western unity would dissolve as soon as the delegations moved from Jaw-Jaw to War-War. Bill Clinton gave an ultimatum to Belgrade: sign up for a peace accord in a week or we start bombing Serbian targets. But Milošević sat tight. He remembered how long it had taken the US to get involved in Bosnia; this was a crisis that he could survive. Above all, after decades – indeed centuries – of Serbs treating the Albanians as an *Unter-Volk*, it was impossible for him to believe that he could be outwitted by them. He knew Rugova, knew that he would bend. Of Thaçi, Milošević knew little, only the scribblings of his secret policemen. In a matter of weeks, he would understand his cardinal error: his underestimation of Thaçi. Milošević had been a banker in New York, Thaçi was a boy from hilly Drenica. How could Thaçi possibly have a better sense of US intentions than himself?

On the eve of the new deadline, Madeleine Albright, whose reputation was riding on a peace deal, flew into Paris to try to salvage an agreement.

Arriving in Paris on 14 February – day eight of what was originally scheduled to be a seven-day summit – Albright, donning a brown trilby, told reporters: 'I am ready to work.' Decoded: it was now up to the US to lead. The implication was clear: the Europeans who felt sidelined at Dayton thought that they could corral the two sides into a subtle understanding. The Dayton military base did not even have a cappuccino machine. Rambouillet had tapestries, fine wine and diplomats schooled in the legal niceties of European collaboration. It was a natural habit of European diplomacy. But they had not produced a result: if the ultimate argument was to be the likely use of NATO firepower, then the US had to be there, banging the château's fine walnut tables.

On her journey from the Paris Hotel InterContinental to Rambouillet, Albright must have known that the Serbs would never sign any deal that brought NATO troops onto its soil. Kosovo was the site of a historic Serb defeat. Milošević would have to fight for his throne if he allowed a foreign enemy army to take the province away from him. 'Albright hoped that Rambouillet would end the brutality against the Kosovars, but she was also prepared for the meeting to fail, and thereby all options for avoiding military conflict would be exhausted,' says Marc Grossman, who was US Assistant Secretary of State for Europe at the time. 'Her idea was that we had to be seen to be doing everything we could diplomatically, including her continued presence, so that if Rambouillet was a failure there could be no further excuses against taking action.'[12]

---

12 David L. Phillips, *Liberating Kosovo*, p. 103

The mission was clear: the restoration and enhancement of Kosovo's autonomy for an interim period until its final status could be determined by a referendum. The tactical objectives?

To give energy to the flagging European efforts, and to avoid a situation where both Milošević and Thaçi said no to what was on the table. A Milošević 'no' would bring the bombing war that she privately thought was becoming inevitable. A Thaçi 'no' would be worse – it would wreck the credibility of NATO, leave the West without any kind of Balkan strategy and keep Milošević in power, cocking a snook at America. And what if both sides said 'yes'? That, Albright confided to an aide, would be a miracle.

Western embassies were already bracing for imminent NATO air-strikes and had begun withdrawing their staff. Instructions had been issued to Richard Miles, the US ambassador to Belgrade, to shred all documents and to weld shut the doors to the embassy's communications and encryption room as soon as it looked as if NATO strikes were about to start. Plans were put in place to evacuate the 1,300 international monitors in Kosovo lest they be held as hostages or used as human shields.

Albright arrived at the château with what Thaçi described as 'a brilliant team of advisors'. The Kosovo negotiating team – not having the kind of constitutional legal advice available to the Serbs – had been allowed counsellors, including US diplomat and Dayton veteran Morton Abramowitz and the German-born, Cambridge-based constitutional lawyer Marc Weller. Yet Thaçi felt that the Kosovo team, though it was thoroughly commenting on every aspect of the Rambouillet draft presented to them – usually along the lines of: 'Yes, agreed, but…' – was not being taken seriously. He hoped that the new influx of people with Albright would tip the scales.

'She brought military and legal advisors, and they really were impeccable, especially Jamie Rubin and Jim O'Brien and John Levicki, while the advisors for the Kosovo delegation were the likes of Morton Abramowitz, a former Assistant Secretary of State in the Department for Intelligence, as well as Paul Williams, a constitutional lawyer and a veteran of the Dayton Agreement,' Thaçi said.

Even the new arrivals from Washington, though, failed to understand the group dynamics at first. Marc Weller recalls how the supposed peace process proceeded in the first weeks. Kosovo would go through the Contact Group draft paragraph by paragraph, in scholarly detail. 'Rather than appreciate the miracle of having obtained comments which sought to improve on that initial draft, and instead of fundamentally questioning the draft, the negotiators continued to ignore the comments until the Yugoslav/Serb delegation had submitted its own text a week or more later.' And the upshot was: reduce your demands to make them acceptable to Belgrade.

Thaçi was livid. The day before Albright's arrival, Chris Hill had flown to Belgrade to meet Milošević. 'I was furious. Apart from anything else, they [the Contact Group] had set up rules that prevented any of us from leaving Rambouillet. Now Chris was going to Belgrade to meet Milošević. Why didn't Milošević just come to Rambouillet himself?' The truth was that Milošević did not want to place himself on an equal footing with the Kosovo Albanians. Nor did he want to expose himself to additional pressure from the international community. It suited him just fine to have diplomats seek an audience with him in his palace.

When Hill returned to Rambouillet, it was plain that nothing Milošević had to offer worked for the Kosovars. Any change in the future constitutional status of Kosovo would have to be firmly within the context of a sovereign and intact Serbia. He wanted strict curbs set on the authority of Kosovo institutions. And all national communities within Kosovo – notably, of course, the Serbs – should have the right to veto legislation passed by a Kosovo assembly. It was a blueprint for a paralysed Kosovo, and it would remain essentially a colony dependent on the goodwill of Belgrade. 'He was telling the Kosovars to piss off,' said a diplomat familiar with the talks.

'I met Chris as he walked up the steps to the château, when he returned,' Thaçi recalls. 'He told me that Milošević had said no to everything in the draft agreement and said that he was really disappointed with the visit to Belgrade. I told Chris how happy I was that he was disappointed.'

Thaçi was convinced that Milošević would eventually walk into a trap of his own making. The problem was finding a way of justifying the continuation of the talks to the increasingly sceptical KLA commanders at home. How, cooped up in the château, could he argue the case with his soldiers? On the phone to Kosovo he picked up rumours that plans were afoot to oust him. And Adem Demaçi, a spokesman for the KLA and one of the key supporters, was threatening to leave the movement altogether, complaining that Thaçi was preparing to sign away Kosovo's right to a referendum on independence. Demaçi, a hero among Albanian Kosovars after serving more than two decades in Serbian prisons, was also fearful that Thaçi would buckle over insisting on the deployment of NATO troops to enforce any peace agreement. What credibility would Thaçi have if he asked the KLA to surrender their weapons? This was a painful struggle for Thaçi, who shared Demaçi's views on many things, above all a contempt for the pacifism of Rugova. Now it seemed that Demaçi, the voice of conscience of the Kosovo resistance, was lumping Thaçi together with Rugova as appeasers.

Fearing that the KLA was fragmenting back home and that he was about to be unseated, Thaçi decided to leave the château. If Hill could travel to Milošević, he argued, then it was only right that he should be able to consult someone who would be vital to the success or failure of whatever emerged from Rambouillet.

I requested the next day to leave the conference to meet Adem.

A sudden coup was happening. I travelled from Paris to Ljubljana to meet Adem. He came from Pristina. The Slovenians hosted a meeting for the two of us at the Presidential residence. There were sub-zero temperatures, the wrought-iron tables and chairs blanketed in ice. The atmosphere with Demaçi was chilly too. There was one metre of snow on the ground but we still sat in the garden.

The Prime Minister of Slovenia [Janez Drnovšek] was really helpful. He was very pro-Kosovo and pro-NATO and had experience of dealing with Serbia. He still supported us. I had a very heavy-hearted talk with Adem.

Adem said that even if we didn't sign the agreement, we could still have another [peace] conference in America. I pleaded with him to go to Rambouillet but he just refused to join the delegation. In the end, we hosted a press conference at the gates of Ljubljana airport. We agreed to spare each other fighting in front of the press. We tried to present a unified front, but we departed from each other with opposite opinions. He was staunchly opposed to signing the accords at all.

Just two weeks later, Demaçi would publicly resign as political leader of the KLA. At a press conference, he would further challenge Thaçi, saying that the deal the Kosovars were on the brink of signing 'will not liberate Kosovo from Serbian slavery' and that it was 'not even close to what we have fought for and we are fighting for'.

Thaçi said that he returned to Rambouillet with 'greater clarity of mind'. It was the kind of clarity that comes briefly after emerging from the wreckage of a car. Under pressure from the KLA hardliners, under pressure from Albright, who was the key to any future NATO intervention, surrounded by backstabbing European diplomats claiming to have Kosovo's best interests at heart, his delegation divided, Thaçi was close to breakdown. 'These were among the heaviest days of my life,' he confesses.

In truth, everybody was under pressure. Albright had been due to fly to China but found herself instead commuting between Paris and Rambouillet, between the delegations in the château and between the Europeans. Not everyone in the State Department was convinced that she was heading in the right direction. To her critics, she seemed to be steering towards a US-led war on behalf of the KLA, who on closer inspection in the château seemed to be out of their league. And the White House was wondering why Albright was not, as advertised, banging heads together. The French were grumbling about Albright and had dubbed her Madame Bomber. A British official complained to the *New York Times* that 'she was speaking loudly and carrying a toothpick, not a big stick in her handbag'. Her whole strategy was misguided; a 'European policymaker' told the newspaper: 'If NATO failed to act against Serbian troop build-ups or even the massacre of civilians in December why would anyone think that the alliance will steel itself to launch air strikes now that there is at least a semblance of talking going on?'

Reasonable questions which could play into Milošević's hands. Yet Albright had intuitively understood what had been going wrong with the negotiations so far. The Kosovars had felt that they were being taken for granted. The Contact Group had assumed that Kosovo would fall into line – that it would put on hold its push for independence and that it would shut down its army in return for keeping Milošević at bay. The effect was that all the pressure fell on the shoulders of Thaçi rather than Milošević. She needed to construct a narrative for Thaçi that would allow him to convince or at least marginalise Demaçi. It was simply this:

the US was ready to make war if Thaçi signed but Milošević did not. The Albanians had to be unmistakably on the right side. But it wasn't just Milošević who opposed a rush to independence; many in the US establishment were anxious about the further splintering of the region.

Thaçi noted the change of tone. Albright bullied but also listened. And her particularly able spokesman Jamie Rubin became his boss's explainer, an introduction for Thaçi to a different world. So he set out Kosovo's objections, more confident that they would not be lost in the diplomatic blancmange favoured by the Contact Group.

'I started by stating to her that I agreed with the accords but I needed any reference to the "demilitarisation" of the KLA to be removed. Instead the document should refer to the "transformation" of the KLA.'

That was one of the fundamental criticisms levelled against him by the hardliners at home. Second, he was worried that Kosovo was being 'parked': that is, put on hold in the hope that problems would find their own solution.

> I made it pretty plain [that] any agreement I signed would only be applicable for the next three to five years. It had to be clear that it was an 'interim' agreement. After that interim period, there must be written into the deal that the people of Kosovo had the right to vote for their future. I was categorical: the people of Kosovo must have written into the agreement that they had the right to a referendum for independence.
>
> Albright walked into our delegation room and said: 'Be real guys, you have to be realistic. We're not asking you to give up on your dreams but you need to sign this agreement.'

Albright then pointed at Thaçi and, referring to the leader of Sinn Féin who was instrumental in the Irish peace deal, said: 'I can see Gerry Adams here.' Thaçi stresses that he certainly does not see himself in the Adams mould. 'The KLA was never like the IRA,' he says, with feeling. 'That was obvious the moment that the Republicans started a bombing campaign in England. We would never have acted as terrorists in Serbia – we acted within Kosovo against an occupying army.' Even so, Enver Hoxhaj, an old friend and one of Thaçi's foreign policy advisors, remembers watching the film *Michael Collins* together with Thaçi and being struck by the parallels. Collins (played by Liam Neeson in the movie) is the Irish revolutionary leader who ended up making enemies within his own ranks by striking a deal with the hated British to win statehood. But what Albright really meant was that two peace processes were under way in 1999 – Ireland and Kosovo – and decision-makers like Albright and especially Tony Blair were constantly switching from one negotiating crisis to another.

The Gerry Adams comparison was supposed to flatter Thaçi. That, too, was part of the Albright strategy. She had described him as a 'wonderful' person; it was important the Americans decided to publicly acknowledge that Thaçi, not the elected President Rugova, was the pivotal person in the delegation. And to reassure him that the US understood the personal and political risks he was taking. Although Thaçi acknowledges that Albright singled him out for special treatment, he flatly denies that he had become the favourite of the US Secretary of State.

'I had some very rough talks with Albright. They could be really hard going. She refused to back down. But we were both right. I couldn't say no to any of her arguments and she couldn't say no to any of my demands. She wanted a longer "interim" period.' That is, the US wanted to stretch out Kosovo's period of limbo as a largely autonomous but still non-independent part of Serbia.

But Thaçi stuck to his guns:

I was adamant about the referendum issue, we had to have a solid pledge to a vote on our future. And we had to have some certainty of what would happen after the so-called interim period. More: the wording had to be right on the KLA – we couldn't say 'disbanded'. It was all about phrasing. I knew how much that mattered in nailing down the Serbs in the future. So instead of the word 'referendum', we would accept the words 'will of the people'.

Rambouillet had become a game of what has been described as 'creative ambiguities'. How to covertly promise a referendum to the Kosovars – the very least that would satisfy hardliners in Pristina – without giving the Serbs the impression that the West was actively planning the dismantling of their country? And how to get Serbia to accept an armed international force to implement any deal without making it look as if NATO was about to march in?

At this point in the talks, the Serbs did not yet realise what Albright was about to throw their way. Accounts vary between members of the Serb delegation and the Russians, but both accuse Albright's team of sneaking a new clause into the draft peace accord – known as military Annex B. The new annex demanded that Belgrade agree NATO troops should effectively be able to occupy the whole of Yugoslavia as guardians of any peace deal, and to do so with immunity. Annex B stated that 'NATO personnel shall enjoy, together with their vehicles, vessels, aircraft and equipment, free and unrestricted passage and unimpeded access throughout the FRY (Federal Republic of Yugoslavia) including associated air space and territorial waters.'

According to the annexes, NATO would establish a force known as Kfor (Kosovo Force), operating under the NATO chain of command. Other states – a reference to Russia – could take part in the military implementation. Kfor would have a broader mandate than the international armed presence in Bosnia – it could support civilian aspects of Rambouillet as well as military. Those were extensive powers that could be expanded even further.

Goran Matić, a minister in Milošević's government, claimed that the annex was shown to the Serbs in the second week of March. Others claim they discovered it 'in the minute before midnight' of the final March deadline. Western negotiators say the broad outlines of the military implementation were communicated well ahead of the deadline and that its details were only ever going to be tackled when the rest of the agreement was ready. It was not an attempt to bamboozle the Serbs but rather, as one diplomat said, 'an attempt not to put the cart before the horse'. And, they say, the rights demanded by NATO were akin to those required in the Dayton Agreement.

Nonetheless, Annex B has become part of the Serb version of Western perfidy; an attempt to present Belgrade as the obstacle to peace and therefore the legitimate target of a bombing campaign. Whenever the NATO occupation clause was written in, it is clear that the Americans knew Belgrade would reject it, and that they could use Serbia's refusal to sign a peace deal as the excuse they needed to bomb them and finish the war.

The Serb view – that Rambouillet was specifically designed to pave the way for a military attack on Milošević – was shared by many in Western establishments, not just conspiracy theorists. Lord Gilbert, junior foreign minister in the UK, admitted to the House of Commons Select Committee on Defence that:

> I think certain people were spoiling for a fight in NATO at that time. If you ask my personal view, I think the terms put to Milošević at Rambouillet were absolutely intolerable; how could he possibly accept them? It was quite deliberate. That does

not excuse an awful lot of other things, but we were at a point when some people felt that something had to be done, so you just provoked a fight.

In the days that followed, rumours buzzed in the château about Annex B and that Chris Hill had gone to Belgrade for a second time to meet Milošević and present Annex B to him in return for Kosovo agreeing to disband the KLA and drop the word referendum. To Thaçi's great pleasure, Milošević simply refused to meet Hill. The trip had been even more of a waste of time than the first.

'Hill returned [from Belgrade] even more disappointed,' Thaçi said. At that point the mood really soured against Serbia. 'Milošević needs to wake up and smell the coffee,' Albright told the press.

'Albright and I were meeting very frequently,' recalls Thaçi:

On one occasion, we had a very long lunch and a very frank, direct discussion. It was very heavy for me – she had the best of intentions but they were unacceptable. I could not sign anything that did not give us clarity about our future.

What I was being pressured to do at that lunch – it was a dilemma I had never faced in my life before. She said: 'I need your signature if we are to use NATO against the Serbs. If you do not sign, then Belgrade and Pristina will be jointly responsible for everything that happened in Kosovo.

The Secretary of State went public with her frustrations: 'The Kosovan Albanians must do their part by giving a clear and unequivocal yes. It is up to them to create a black and white situation,' she told reporters.

For the thirty-year-old exile, the burden on his shoulders to secure the future of Kosovo was becoming almost unbearable. The stakes were enormous. Any deal he signed he had to be able to sell to KLA commanders, and to the powerful and wealthy Kosovan diaspora. A fudged, meaningless compromise would not only rob his country of a future free of Milošević, it could cost him his life – Thaçi had received death threats from Kosovars who threatened to wreak revenge on the 'betrayal' of signing. Any deal had to justify more than a decade for him living on the run, and for an eighteen-month insurgency that had killed more than 2,000 Kosovars, civilians and fighters.

> What was being presented to me at that lunch – it was enormous.
> I remember my breathing became very slow and very heavy.
> The last two years flashed in front of me. I said: 'OK. I will
> sign but only if the word transformation [of the KLA] replaces
> disbanding [of the KLA] and there had to be a mention of "the
> will of the people".'

Wolfgang Petritsch, the wily EU negotiator, understood better than most what Thaçi was going through. How was this inexperienced political operator going to be able to make the bridge between great power diplomacy and the muscular politics of the Balkans? On the night of 19 February, he agreed with Thaçi he would help persuade KLA commanders – some of whom he knew personally – that it was worth laying down their arms. 'We would have to make it clear that, by signing up to Rambouillet, their organisation, their military organisation, [would] have to be disbanded.' That tense meeting happened on 5 March, in the pause in the Rambouillet talks, and it provided important flanking support for Thaçi. 'These were active rebels, or military or paramilitary, whatever you want to call them, and for them it was clear that they would hand over their weapons and uniforms.'

That was a welcome intervention for Thaçi, but his choices remained crushingly complex. By the evening of 20 February – more than two weeks into the summit – the Contact Group met with a take-it-or-leave-it ultimatum. Thaçi dug in his heels and stuck to his two demands. According to Thaçi, the Serbs made no new demands, and Russia 'had nothing to say any more'.

'Milošević was being informed all the time by phone. He was gambling that we would not sign, and that the whole peace conference would fail, no resolution,' Thaçi said. Milošević was almost certainly being informed by the Russians about the internal splits in the Contact Group. Italy could not see how the question of self-determination versus territorial integrity could be resolved without Thaçi in effect surrendering everything the KLA had been fighting for. It stressed there should be no attempt to smuggle even the most disguised reference to independence in the documents.

The Italian Foreign Affairs Under Secretary – Umberto Ranieri – collared Thaçi. 'Are you accepting or refusing? Don't give me answers with footnotes!'

Thaçi pleaded with Ranieri: 'This is very difficult for me. My fate and Kosovo's fate depends on this,' and then he reiterated his two demands:

'I was afraid that the extra words I wanted – that as a result I would be blamed for the whole failure of the conference,' he recalled. This was a dilemma not just for Thaçi but for Albright. As Michael Ignatieff makes clear in his post-Rambouillet book:

> The real point of Rambouillet was to persuade the Europeans, especially the Italians who tended to think of the Albanians as terrorists and drug traffickers, that they were actually 'the good guys'. Rambouillet was necessary in other words to get the Europeans to stop blaming the victims and to build the resolve at NATO to use force.

With a show of reluctance – 'as a professor, I don't like to give extensions'– Albright gave Thaçi breathing space by allocating another three days of negotiation. 'I became the happiest of men,' he said.

Now they had until 23 February to get a deal. For Thaçi, that meant working only with Albright and Rubin on finding the sufficiently open-ended wording for a referendum that the Serbs might agree to. 'It was clear the word referendum would not have the backing of the international community, including the Russians,' admitted Thaçi.

During the next three days, Thaçi stuck close to Albright and Rubin. Meetings with the Secretary of State were often followed by long walks with Rubin through the grounds of the château, round a vast lake, Marie Antoinette's dairy and a cottage, despite the freezing February weather.

It was clear Rubin had managed to calm Thaçi. 'I spent a lot of time with Jamie. The green space. The long walks. We talked about everything.' Albright had been firm that the three-year interim status for Kosovo could be presented by Thaçi to his people as a strategic victory. It was, she said, about giving Kosovo the time to elect their own officials, have their local police, their own schools and relate differently to Belgrade. That was not very convincing to Thaçi; he understood all too well how quickly Milošević could extinguish those rights.

It was up to Rubin to fill in the gaps. How would Serbia look in three years' time? Perhaps, with the help of the US, Milošević would be toppled by a growing opposition of young people. And without Milošević, the whole relationship between Serbia and Kosovo would change. Force an early referendum on Serbia and the result could be counter-productive.

One thing Thaçi and Rubin had in common was their youth, unlike many of the other ageing delegates. Rubin, thirty-eight, was just eight years older than Thaçi. Already chief spokesman for the US State Department, Rubin was the closest Rambouillet got to glamour. Less than a year before, society columns and celebrity magazines had drooled over the wedding guest list for Rubin and his wife-to-be Christiane Amanpour, the highly renowned CNN war reporter. They had met in Bosnia. John Kennedy and his wife Carolyn Bessette were guests, and their wedding pictures were taken by Annie Leibovitz, the world-famous photographer. Somewhat less glamorous, but nonetheless telling: Richard Holbrooke also attended the wedding.

'We didn't just talk about Kosovo. We discussed the Balkans as a whole. We even talked about what a great Hollywood film this would make and the clothes that the delegates were wearing,' Thaçi recalls. These were eye-opening moments for Thaçi. He began to understand that Kosovo needed not just US firepower to beat back the Serbs but long-term political support too. If a Kosovo nation was going to be built, then it would have to be with massive US-led investment. And so far, at least, he was the closest the US had to a personal ally in this venture. He no longer doubted that Albright was ready to wage a war but he needed to figure out a relationship with the US that would endure into the post-war period. And if he said 'no' to Rambouillet, if he failed to deliver the KLA, then he would lose all influence – and the new world that was being so eloquently conjured up by Rubin.

During the next few days, Thaçi barely slept. Talks with the Albanian delegation in their conference room dragged into the early hours of the mornings. The other Albanians all agreed to sign, without any clause in the peace accord to a referendum. Thaçi held out.

> I was aware that I was the only one blocking the deal. I was very upset and exhausted – both the hours that we were keeping but also dreadful insomnia from the stress of it all. But I was determined to stand firm. All the time I had in the back of my mind that I was not just representing Kosovo. I was representing

the Kosovan armed resistance, the so-called famous freedom fighters. I was representing the toughest of men. I was a man of independence, not autonomy.

Thaçi explained:

> I was only twenty-three when we started to establish the armed resistance. I think the Rambouillet diplomats saw my youth as an advantage. None of us in the KLA had any experience of international summits. But at least I had read about them. I'd been to other capital cities – some members of the Albanian delegation had never been further than Belgrade in their lives.

While the sixteen-man Albanian delegation had experienced members such as the 54-year-old Rugova and Bujar Bukoshi, the President was remote and disengaged. Much of the delegation were, like Thaçi, relatively young. They included Xhavit Haliti, a co-founder of the KLA and ten years older than Thaçi, and the journalist Blerim Shala, still in his late twenties. Shala would years later become a crucial coordinator of dialogue with Serbia in all stages of the process.

Thaçi recalls how many in the delegation simply could not envisage an independent Kosovo, and as such were prepared to give up any pledge for a referendum. They were ready to give in.

'It was a very lonely time for me,' Thaçi said.

> Some of them [the Albanian delegation] just did not believe that the Serbian army would ever leave Kosovo. One member of the Kosovan team basically thought that as long as we are at peace and we could bring the fighting to an end, he didn't really mind Serbia being in Kosovo. I said to him: 'You might be able to live

in peace in Kosovo but most Kosovo Albanians – me included – will never be able to live in peace in Kosovo under Serbia.'

According to Thaçi, the prevailing view among the Albanian delegation was that the real problem for Kosovo lay on the shoulders of one man – Milošević – and that after his downfall everything would be fine.

> I had a problem with Milošević. But unlike them, I had a problem with Serbia being in Kosovo at all.
>
> I was stubborn – yes. But what upset me was that, at the end of the day, these diplomats just want such summits to look like they have ended with something resembling a success. It's good for their careers. But without a referendum, without Kosovo being able to choose whether it wanted to be independent from Serbia, it was clear to me that the diplomats were not solving a crisis, they were postponing one.

Thaçi admits that the psychological pressure was wearing him down.

Exhausted and anxious that, even if he could get a deal in Rambouillet, he might not be able to sell it back home, Thaçi became agitated and depressed. In the view of some participants, he was also taking on paranoid characteristics.

Some of the fears were probably justified. The whole Albanian delegation was convinced they were being bugged by the Americans. The French had a van with blacked-out windows parked outside the château and their intelligence service was collating a daily report on the activities at the conference. Mayorsky was in regular contact with the Russian embassy, which almost certainly passed information on to Belgrade. Dukagjin Gorani, Thaçi's personal translator, revealed in a Channel 4 documentary broadcast in the UK that 'we were [often] in the toilet because we realised that was the safest place to discuss [matters]'. The meeting rooms also had CCTV cameras.

Thaçi's dark state of mind did not go unnoticed by the Americans, some of whom he would share a drink with every evening:

> One American diplomat opened a bottle of cognac one night and handed me a glass. When instead I asked if I could have a glass of wine, he presumed that I believed the cognac to be poisoned. They just thought I was paranoid. In truth, I'm just not a heavy drinker, I never have been. I don't drink incessantly and, more to the point, I don't like cognac.

In an attempt to manage his anxiety, Thaçi began running for an hour every day around Rambouillet's grounds. In the ten years before, it had been long hikes across the Albanian mountains which had helped him formulate plans for the KLA and to arm the movement. Now, it was to be running that would help him clear his mind and pursue his dream of Kosovan nationhood.

A new draft was written up throughout the night of 21 February, with US lawyers and the Albanian delegation.

By dawn of 22 February, the Albanian delegation delivered an amended draft to Albright. They beefed up the phrase 'will of the people' to 'expressed will of the people'. The KLA members including Thaçi still refused to sign it on the grounds that the word 'referendum' was absent.

Buckling under pressure from incessant satellite phone calls between Pristina, Rambouillet and the Kosovan diaspora around the world, all except Thaçi agreed to sign.

'I threatened to resign as head of the delegation if they signed without "referendum"', Thaçi said. 'But they wouldn't accept it. It was a very lonely time.'

The Russians were furious at the phrase 'expressed will of the people', the Albanians were in a state of anguished stalemate, bullied on all sides, and Albright was facing the very real prospect that she would not get her deal.

Then both Albright and Thaçi began to budge. 'She decided to provide personal guarantees that some sort of referendum would be granted. The phrase they provided was "aspirations of the Kosovar people would be expressed after three years". Those words were good enough for me. It was code for the future of Kosovo.'

But Thaçi now faced a new, even bigger obstacle: he had to sell the deal to the KLA.

> I talked at length to Rubin about how to convince KLA commanders. I told him that I would sign the peace deal a few days later but that I first needed to consult KLA leaders back in Kosovo. Jamie and I left it that I would initial the document, effectively agreeing to its content, but that I could only sign once I had returned from talking to the KLA.

In a bid to appease the Americans and buy time, the Albanian delegation promised to form an interim Kosovar government that would include representatives of the main factions of Pristina, including the KLA. 'It was a voluntary act. A side agreement that we signed as a gesture of unity and our endorsement of Rambouillet. They liked it,' Thaçi said.

Sensing that they could secure a deal, the Contact Group gave Thaçi two weeks to go home and win over the KLA. The prospect overwhelmed him.

What lay behind him was the international community, the might of the Americans, and the risk that, without a deal, not just Kosovo, but Thaçi himself would be blamed for wrecking their best chance of peace.

In front of him lay the wrath of the KLA, who believed Thaçi was about to sell them a weak offer of autonomy for Kosovo. Their bubbling anger was already evident. After all, Thaçi, supposedly their man, had been closeted together not only with the Serbs, but allies of the Serbs, and with Rugova, a man who had not concealed his contempt for the KLA. How could any agreement signed on those terms be worth the sacrifice? Many were waiting for their moment to brand Thaçi a traitor to his face.

More trouble loomed. As Thaçi prepared to leave Rambouillet for Pristina, the Serbs issued a second international arrest warrant for him.

'The French flew me back in a military plane to Tirana – I dared not fly direct to Pristina because of the arrest warrant. Albania was providing support and cover for us, but all the decisions I always took independently from Tirana. The issue I had with Albanian politicians is that they didn't believe that Kosovo could become fully independent.'

Yet again, Thaçi walked from Albania through the mountain pass into Kosovo to evade arrest. This time, however, he was not a gun-runner, arming a rebel movement; this time, he was a man with a peace deal, an interim government to form and the future of Kosovo on his shoulders.

––––––––––

Back in Kosovo, he convened a meeting of all the KLA commanders from every region. All of them remained loyal to Thaçi and backed him as their leader in a new government. But Demaçi and his close associates within the KLA began to accuse Thaçi of betrayal at Rambouillet, alleging that the Kosovan delegation was preparing to just accept autonomy. 'They made stupid [death] threats against me. But I knew that the threats were empty – because I knew they had no weapons left for me,' Thaçi said.

Even so, he had to persuade them that he was not, as Demaçi had claimed, a traitor.

> The tables had turned. In Rambouillet everyone was trying to convince me to sign. Now, I was trying to convince them [the commanders]. I went to Drenica – my home region – and the meeting was very emotional. The whole brigade there wanted to see me – to hear what I had to say. I knew every one of them.
>
> I had grown up with these men. I loved and respected them dearly and they respected me. Going back to Drenica, trying to sell this deal, it was like going back to where it had all started. These men were the bread and butter of the KLA. I had been in a château in France for weeks but they had been in the trenches.

Under the terms of the Rambouillet proposed deal, the KLA would agree to 'transform' itself. While Thaçi had refused the word 'disbandment' of the KLA, it effectively meant the same thing. If they went ahead with the deal, the KLA would agree to a ceasefire and a handover of weapons.

'In my experience', Thaçi said, 'it is easier to convince people to pick up weapons than to put them down.'

The Drenica commanders were not sold on the deal. In family homes, round breakfast tables, they drank black tea in Ottoman glasses, chain-smoking cigarettes as Thaçi tried to persuade them throughout one long night to endorse the deal.

'Some of them were saying that they didn't want to sign. "Why did our friends die, our neighbours?" they asked me.'

The diaspora – many of whom lived in exile in Germany and Switzer-land – piled on the pressure, phoning Thaçi on his satellite phone, pleading with the KLA, whom they had largely funded, not to sign.

'But they were warm in their living rooms in Zürich and Munich. We were in the Drenica Valley, with no electricity, drinking tea.'

Thaçi played hardball.

> I told them, speaking from my mind and heart: 'Our soldiers have no more than thirty bullets each. We have been a resistance movement for seven years. Will we be able to keep up militarily if we do not sign this agreement?' I thought I was bringing a dose of realism, but they reacted angrily. 'Hashim – why are you saying this? We started this war with broken handguns.'

Thaçi replied: 'This is not seven years ago. If you want Kalashnikovs to become F-16 bombers, then we have to sign or we will be finished in Kosovo and forgotten by the world.'

All but two agreed to sign the Rambouillet deal, and the two who refused said they would effectively abstain. It had taken almost two weeks to convince KLA commanders, knowing he could not return to Rambouillet without their endorsement. Now, he had a deal.

The first thing Thaçi did was to phone Rubin at the State Department in Washington. Through a translator and down Thaçi's satellite phone, he told Rubin: 'I've kept my word. I have kept my word to the USA.' Rubin was elated.

The second thing Thaçi did was to get a haircut.

In the village of Malisheve in the Drenica Valley, he convened a press conference. 'My shirt looked like a pyjama top – I had been up all night.' At the press conference, Thaçi confirmed that a Kosovan delegation would go to Paris to sign the Rambouillet deal and that he had secured the full backing of the KLA.

Thaçi was on his way to making history.

It was a feat that Milošević and the Serb delegation had clearly not banked on happening. Throughout Rambouillet, Milošević bet that the Kosovars would never sign and Belgrade would never accept NATO troops on the ground in Yugoslavia.

The Americans went ahead regardless. As the Conference Centre on the Avenue Kléber in Paris was booked for the signing ceremony, a draft copy of the peace treaty was filed in the House of Commons library. Critically, however, the draft did not contain the all-important Annex B – that which allowed the deployment of 30,000 NATO troops across Yugoslavia, with full freedom of movement and immunity from prosecution.

According to the Serbs, the Belgrade delegation did not know about Annex B until they arrived in Paris for the peace deal.

Thaçi, meanwhile, was on his way to Paris. Nervous that the Serbs would try to block his passage to Pristina airport, Shaun Byrnes, a US diplomat working with the OSCE mission, promised to transport him in an American convoy to get his flight. Thaçi recalls:

> I was imagining the situation with me trying to get to France only weeks before. I had no faith that the Serbs would allow me to travel to the airport. They had assassinated others ... and I had several arrest warrants out for me. But the Americans said they would deliver me safely. They transported me in a convoy of bright orange vehicles along with American diplomats. I was in an orange Humvee. It was like the parting of the Red Sea. I was in this US convoy travelling through Serb-controlled territory. This would be my first ever flight from the Pristina airport and I had no passport, just two hand grenades in my pockets,

for my own safety. At the airport, it was full of Serbian police and a number of Serbian intelligence officials, some taking photos of me. I was transported onto a French military plane and on board was the entire Kosovan delegation waiting for me. It was the first time I had seen them since Rambouillet.

CHAPTER 7

NATO AT WAR

'It seemed like a dream to us all,' says Thaçi, reconstructing the moments before the start of the NATO bombing campaign against the troops of Milošević. When it became clear that Serbia was not going to sign up for Rambouillet, the machinery of war cranked into action. 'To start as we did, without guns, without resources, no people, no international support – and then suddenly to have the world's most powerful military alliance on our side, that was a real political success,' he recalls. 'It meant that we had changed, that we were being accepted as part of the Euro-Atlantic family of nations. And it meant that Serbia was being seen as in opposition to Western values. We were for Western values, they were against them.'

The victory of the KLA was always going to be more political than military. At Rambouillet, Thaçi had repositioned the KLA to such an extent that whatever Milošević did next would throw the Serb leader onto the back foot. In chess – Thaçi's game – that is known as zugzwang. 'It was probably the weakest insurgent force ever to achieve the key items on its political agenda,' says strategic analyst

James Gow. 'It had done so because of the peculiar circumstances of NATO involvement.'[13]

Thaçi's silent ally in this manoeuvring was Wes Clark, Supreme Allied Commander Europe, a bright, awkward American general whose sharp political analysis and understanding of Milošević (gleaned at Holbrooke's side during the Dayton process) had convinced him that negotiations with tyrants had to be backed by the credible threat of force. How best to convey that threat, project that power? NATO was struggling to find a new mission after the breakdown of communist rule in Eastern Europe; it needed to try out different forms of deployment, be more flexible. The whole idea of military command had changed, had become more politically proactive. Since Milošević's men had moved from village to village in the spring and summer of 1998, torching houses and driving people out of the province, it had become obvious to Clark that commanders had the right to argue for military options. The beginnings of the Bosnian conflagration were fresh in everyone's memory yet the implications of that war for the relationship between military commanders and the political elite had not been understood. Now, in Kosovo, a leader – the same leader that inflicted atrocities on Bosnia – was grossly violating humanitarian norms. And it was right, Clark believed, that US and European decision-makers be made aware of how armed force could be used to stave off another disaster.

At the peak of the bombing campaign, Thaçi travelled to Brussels, shook hands with Clark, talked to him in German. Thaçi grasped what was at stake. For over a year he had been wrestling with the question of how the international community could come to the aid of Kosovo and the KLA. And at the nub of the issue was the one bothering Clark: how could one threaten Milošević with different gradations of force

---

13 James Gow, *The Serbian Project and Its Adversaries: A Strategy of War Crimes* (2003)

to change his behaviour – and yet rule out the deployment of ground forces, the one sure measure that would bring a result? Politicians across the alliance were, however, queasy at the very idea.

Wes Clark had to use smoke and mirrors, building up an army presence in Albania and Macedonia, gambling that this would be enough to rattle Milošević into cutting a deal. As his memoir *Waging Modern Warfare* makes plain, the KLA was never considered a substitute for an allied ground force. By Clark's calculations, at least 175,000 men would be needed to seize control of Kosovo; the KLA, though its numbers were growing, had barely a few thousand under-equipped fighters. At the outset of the war, Clark was convinced that the KLA would have its uses; its knowledge of the terrain could not be bettered by any number of drones or manned reconnaissance flights, but it would be no more than a supernumerary force, not a war-winning factor.

Thaçi's task was to change that perception over the coming months. If the KLA was to emerge from a victorious war as the natural backbone of a new nation, part of its founding myth, then its contribution would have to be presented as a heroic partnership with NATO. Not just a modest, locally based self-defence force, but as an army that sent Milošević scurrying for cover. Already, on the first day of war, Thaçi was pondering the possible post-war outcomes.

Much, though, was out of his hands, and there were plenty of risks – and misery – ahead. Some fears were not realised. There was always a chance, for example, that the Kosovo Verification Mission, the 2,000 or so unarmed observers, could be seized by Serb troops and held hostage. Imprisoned perhaps in the vicinity of likely NATO bombing targets as human shields to deter the attacks. To Clark's relief, however, the observers were allowed to leave Kosovo and entered Macedonia unimpeded by 20 March.

That same afternoon, Milošević decided to demonstrate that allowing the departure of the KVM observers was not an act of weakness. His troops – military and police units – resumed their ethnic cleansing, this time in the village of Skenderaj. The *Times* war correspondent Anthony Loyd was there and tells how the Serb police units, dressed in black balaclavas and strange white overalls, had forced civilians out of their homes at gunpoint, ordering several groups of young men to make a run for it. 'As they did so, they were fired upon,' says Loyd. 'It seemed that the murders were part of an opportunistic entertainment designed with no more aim than to get the men of Kosovo to move at speed.' He reported one horrific detail: 'a truck-mounted anti-aircraft gun was used to strafe some of the runners, tearing them apart as they tried to make it to the cover of woodland at the town's periphery.' Later the killings would be notched up as a successful Serbian battle against the KLA rather than for what it was – one of many atrocities.

Years after the 78-day bombing campaign, critics such as the American activist and philosopher Noam Chomsky would argue that the Western offensive accelerated or even caused ethnic cleansing. Yet the Serbs had never made a secret of their intention to drive Kosovo Albanians out of the province and replace them with Serb settlers. The critics did have a partial point. There were no real calculations as to how air power was supposed to stop ethnic cleansing. Nor, despite the recent experience of Bosnia, was any serious consideration given to the flow of refugees to the borders. How was the new variant of air warfare going to solve these problems?

Clark was running the first NATO war of its kind. NATO had been conceived as a defensive alliance. Now it was going on the offensive without a real sense of how the political restraints of collective decision-making would impact the war. The alliance's proximate goal was to persuade Milošević to change his mind, sign Rambouillet, stop the killing and displacement of Kosovars and ensure that he didn't cheat his way to some kind of victory for Serbia. This translated into two strategic aims: to hit the heartland of Serbia, including Belgrade, to destroy the military chain of command and to encourage the Yugoslav/Serb order to break Milošević. And secondly – once Serbian air defences had been smashed – to stop the massacre of civilians.

But these military missions were heavily influenced by politics. In his address to the nation, Bill Clinton had rules about the use of US ground troops – a statement that both Holbrooke and Clark considered to be a mistake since it sent out the wrong signals not only to Milošević but to NATO allies who now had an excuse for holding back. 'Saying in his initial speech that ground troops would not be needed', said Holbrooke, 'was one of Clinton's biggest foreign policy errors.'

It was going to be a war by committee. If only one of NATO's nineteen national governments decided that its electorate couldn't stomach the sight of bombs dropping on Belgrade institutions, then those buildings were taken off the target list. And there were plenty of reservations from the very outset. Wrecking a power station could blindside a Serbian army base but also switch off the electricity of a hospital. If children were shown freezing on television screens as a result of NATO raids, then public opinion could curdle in several member states. Apparently wracked by conscience, a French agent had betrayed many of the planned targets to Belgrade. New targets had to be found and, to stop planes being shot down, pilots had to fly at 15,000 feet. The result: a heightened risk of missing targets and hitting civilians.

This was a war everyone felt would be fought in the full glare of television. It had to be legally foolproof. Some states were insisting that military force should only be used with the support of a United Nations Security Council resolution, yet Russia would almost certainly veto such a move if it felt that its traditional ally Serbia was being disadvantaged. The US (which faces a similar dilemma when acting today in the Middle East and other trouble spots) chafed under this restraint to its foreign policy. Months before the start of the war, in the autumn of 1998, these issues had been played out. They were fundamental to the question of how power should be projected in the post-communist world. Holbrooke, the tough pragmatist, summed up how Russian resistance to NATO action was splitting the West: 'On the one hand you have us, and on the other you have the French. Then you have the Germans who usually go to us, reluctantly. Thus Britain is often the key to NATO decision-making.'

In this scenario it was always clear that Tony Blair and his Foreign Secretary Robin Cook were going to emerge as the best European allies of Kosovo. But the atrocities of late summer 1998, the ethnic cleansing, did help change minds. By 6 October 1998, President Jacques Chirac showed that he was ready to make a U-turn: 'If it appeared that the situation required it, then France would not hesitate to join those who would like to intervene in order to help those who are in danger.' Paris, in other words, was ready after all to go ahead without a UN resolution. Defence minister Alain Richard played a crucial role to ensure France's inclusion in the possible military strikes. The Germans, too – the newly elected Red-Green government led by Social Democrat Gerhard Schröder and his Green foreign minister Joschka Fischer – were prepared to find ways of joining a military operation. Across the West, the consensus had been shifting in favour of Kosovo. But it came at a price: in Germany, finance minister Oskar Lafontaine walked out of the government and a pacifist Green activist flung a can of blood-coloured paint into Fischer's face. There was consensus, but it was fickle.

What then if, mid-war, these allies wavered? What if they lost their nerve and handed a victory, another political victory, to Milošević?

It would spell the end of Kosovo's dream of independence for generations to come. Was it conceivable that what Thaçi called the 'world's
most powerful alliance' could be outwitted by Milošević, defeated by
their own lack of resolve?

Wes Clark had to factor this into his calculations – and the possibility
that Milošević would try to regionalise the war:

> I was worried about some Serb artillery that was stationed
> in southern Serbia but was aimed at Macedonia. It wasn't
> participating in the ethnic cleansing but it was aiming south.
> Some of our troops were within its range. If we could attack
> and destroy it all at once, all well and good. If we attacked and
> they responded, then we would have brought a shooting war to
> Macedonia.

That is, to a country – with a large Albanian population – that was one
of the two key destinations for Kosovars being hounded out of their
homes. Was it possible to justify shifting planes away from preventing
ethnic cleansing in Kosovo, the prime motivation for what NATO was
now labelling Operation Allied Force?

The answer to these and other pressing conundrums was to make it
a short war, to secure Milošević's compliance before the ground forces
decision pushed itself to the top of the agenda, before the conflict could
spread and Western public opinion turn sour. Wes Clark was sure the
war could be wrapped up quickly. 'Wes's strongly held view was: "If we
just threaten to bomb, he'll fold. I know this guy, this won't last"', says
one Clinton-era Defense Department official. This conviction was
based on a special kind of hubris that was guaranteed to make Clark
enemies in the Pentagon. Because Clark had sat alongside Holbrooke
at Dayton, he was convinced that he had unparalleled knowledge of

Milošević's poker tactics. 'I'm the only commander in the twentieth century, I think, that really knew his adversary.'

The war was not short. It lasted eleven weeks, not forty-eight hours. NATO aircraft from thirteen countries flew 38,400 sorties, including 10,484 strike missions, in which 26,614 air munitions were dropped. It wasn't short, and it wasn't simple. And historians have been arguing for fifteen years as to why Milošević folded when he did.

Clark believed in what he called 'compellent diplomacy' because he thought he had seen it at work in Dayton. Bosnia, though, was a different kind of war: it had been a republic within federal Yugoslavia, unlike Kosovo's shrivelled autonomy. In Bosnia, NATO bombs had nudged the battle against Milošević after Croatian ground troops had already notched up successes against the Serbs. In Kosovo, by contrast, Milošević was assuming that he could wipe the floor with the KLA within ten days. Thaçi's men were growing in confidence with better arms and training but they remained, in Milošević's assessment, hit-and-run insurgents. And the emotional power of Kosovo, talked up by Milošević since 1987, was such that there was little room for diplomatic finesse. The Serbs would never forgive Milošević if he lost Kosovo.

All of Thaçi's instincts told him that Milošević would not cave in in a matter of days. Air was unpredictable, dependent on the weather. Bombs on Belgrade would almost certainly stiffen the Serb resolve to fight to the finish. Since the KVM were out of the country, the US did not have many eyes on the ground. The Serbs could create decoys, fake military installations, to draw down bombs on civilians rather than soldiers. From their high cruising height it would be difficult for pilots to make a clear distinction between columns of refugees on tractors and columns of armoured vehicles.

When the bombardment began, the problems and the possibilities of the forthcoming campaign were thrown into sudden, startling focus. Three of Milošević's MiG-29s were shot down on the first night, one by a Dutch F-16. That was good for NATO and for Washington, which wanted to demonstrate that this was not just a duel between America and Serbia. But the Dutch pleaded with Clark not to publicise their success – it could have caused domestic political strife. The Greeks were nervous from the very first shootings and wanted the bombing to stop to give Milošević another chance to 'reconsider'. Italy asked if the bombing could be suspended until the government had won parliamentary approval. Across the alliance, member states quickly sensed that this war was going to drag on for much longer than Clark had promised.

Milošević had not activated his full air defences. That meant two things: that Belgrade was going to make a fight out of it, and that it was going to be cautious about activating air defences lest they draw down US firepower. The longer the war, the more likely it would be that Milošević would drive a wedge between NATO members. As a result, political considerations intruded on every level of NATO's military calculations. Could Milošević be brought to his knees by Easter, Javier Solana, the NATO Secretary-General asked Clark? Easter fell on 4 April that year, less than a fortnight into the campaign, and Solana's fear was that the Pope's Easter sermon would call for an end to the bombing and boost public opposition to the war.

From a military point of view, a bombing pause made no sense. The lesson of Vietnam, said Clark, was that air was a race between 'destruction' and 'reconstruction'. 'We had to destroy and disable our targets faster than Milošević could repair or work around them.'

The key to a successful campaign then was going to have to comprise three components: the constant persuasion by political elites that the campaign would lead to a change in Milošević's behaviour; that pinpoint targeting was relieving human suffering, not adding to it; and that if air war failed, the allies had a follow-up plan. Thaçi was to play a significant role in realising all three elements of victory.

After Rambouillet, he had become the international face of Kosovo, but he was also the symbol of a broader-based sentiment in Europe that someone had to stand up to Milošević. It was difficult for many in the West that Milošević had quite literally got away with murder in Bosnia. Thaçi, straight-talking and straight-backed, was the kind of underdog favoured by the media – and by governments anxious to justify their new war in the Balkans. Kosovo, as Thaçi presented the country, was not just a passive consumer of NATO security. Nor, as he stressed to various NATO ministers, was he trying to drag a reluctant alliance into an unnecessary war. Rather, Kosovo, brave and responsibly led, could work together with the Western alliance to steer it out of an emergency. NATO, an alliance in search of a mission, could only benefit from cooperating with the KLA.

Whether the alliance bought into the Thaçi line or not, he was soon on the ground, making himself useful. With a satellite phone supplied by NATO, Thaçi rang out of Kosovo to key leaders and allies. 'They needed to know what was happening on the ground, and they were our friends, they had a right to know,' he says. 'Foreign ministers Robin Cook, Joschka Fischer of Germany, Madeleine Albright.' The relationship between the KLA leadership and the US Secretary of State had, thanks to Thaçi, become a solid factor in the crisis. Quite an advance from Rambouillet, when, early in the talks, Albright popped spontaneously into the room being used by the Kosovar negotiators to work out the next day's tactics. 'Come back later, we're busy,' grunted one of the team, thinking that the US official – then routinely described as one of the most powerful women in the world – was the cleaning lady. With the official monitors out of the province, the KLA saw it as essential that they feed coordinates into the targeting process. Apart from anything else, they didn't want to be accidentally bombed.

Thaçi, as political director and the man best known to the international community, took on the task of channelling information out of the country. But if the KLA mission was to succeed beyond the technical level of merely spotting the enemy, coordination had to deepen; the KLA had to earn its spurs as an ally of the US and the alliance. It was the first European war to be fought with mobile phones rather than radios and though they were cumbersome Nokia bricks it was a sign that Kosovo, unlike Bosnia, was in effect a post-modern conflict. The Serb/Yugoslav forces fought the same war as they had fought in Bosnia earlier in the decade, with urban sieges, heavy armour surrounding and shelling villages. Most commanders had learned their tactics from old Soviet textbooks; the chain of command was long, slow and bureaucratic. The KLA responded with highly mobile tactics, avoiding pitched battles and wherever possible seeking control of the roads which since Ottoman days had been the key to conquest.

And so it was that the KLA – not just Thaçi – started to identify targets and phone out the information to a unit in the Albanian 2nd Army that then passed it on to US intelligence. The point was to avoid direct contact with the US army but the whole communications scheme had been devised and was supervised by the Central Intelligence Agency. The intelligence coming out of Kosovo was gauged, plotted and then passed on to the bomber and fighter squadrons. Soon enough, the KLA was working hand in glove with the Americans. Serb troops could be provoked out of their cover, tanks goaded out of their camouflaged barns and enter what US military jargon dubs 'killboxes', a defined target area for fighter jets. If the Serbs dispersed, aware that they had been lured into an ambush, the KLA would be able to pick them off.

Did all targets offered by the KLA correspond to those on the NATO list? Probably not. But the dawning realisation that this was not going to be a US blitzkrieg meant that the Pentagon was running out of targets. Too much responsibility was being laid on the shoulders of forward airborne observers and too many mistakes were being made. There were serious NATO bombing errors in Kosovo – most notoriously a refugee convoy mistaken for an army column – but the most politically sensitive blunders were occurring in or around Belgrade on the basis of out-of-date CIA intelligence. The most damaging was probably the bombing of the Chinese embassy in Belgrade.

Thaçi was not and never claimed to be a great military commander or even a particularly brilliant soldier. He admits to carrying a Makarov pistol throughout the war and is coy about being caught up in occasional firefights. But his strength lay in understanding the Clausewitzian alchemy: how even limited military power could be leveraged into political advantage.

At the nub of Thaçi's political strategy was the need to turn on its head the black propaganda coming out of Belgrade. The Milošević message had for years been that the KLA were terrorists and secessionists. Belgrade thought that gave them double legitimacy. It allowed Milošević to pose as a champion against 'Islamic' terror at a time when the US was waking up to the threat. In the summer of 1998, terrorists had struck at two US embassies in east Africa, apparently in retaliation for the arrest of members of the Egyptian Islamic Jihad who had holed up in Albania. Mixing and stirring these ingredients in an attempt to blacken the KLA was a priority task for Milošević agents. Second, Milošević could claim to be fighting for national integrity. He knew that many older US officials had regretted the disintegration of Yugoslavia in the early 1990s.

Yet neither line of propaganda argument could survive the ruthless practice of ethnic cleansing. Between 24 March and 10 June, some

863,000 refugees were displaced in Kosovo; over half of the estimated Kosovan Albanian population in 1998 were forced to leave their homes. 'Serb forces would surround a village or two and attack it with grenades or artillery shelling, forcing many people to hide in basements or flee to the surrounding hills,' says the Independent International Commission, in a compilation of witness statements.

In all, more than 10,000 were killed; 3,000 were exhumed by the International Criminal Tribunal for the former Yugoslavia (ICTY) from 348 mass graves. Enough of this was obvious even during the bombing campaign to demonstrate that the primary and legitimate objective of the war was to stop war crimes being committed.

'I was visiting different regions,' says Thaçi,

> working out ways to protect them but also trying to weigh up the enormity of what was happening. I had become a public figure by then, was appearing on CNN, BBC. It's not that I ever wore a balaclava during press conferences; I never tried to hide my identity. But this was all much more – Kosovo really had become an international event, it was in the eye of the storm. Every day I was in contact with various foreign ministers about the movements of refugees. Since Milošević had imposed a media blackout for the international media, the only direct source of information to the world came from the KLA.

Air war functions cumulatively. But as the frequency of the raids increased, as the range of targets stretched to include buildings used by civilians, so too frustration and impatience swelled in the coalition. France complained that Clark had his sights on petrol storage units in Montenegro. Since NATO had not formally declared war, since the laws of warfare were not fully applicable, it would be wrong, said the French, to stop the flow of oil into Serbia. The issue was a pretext. France, like other member states, was becoming queasy about the prospect of Serb civilian casualties. Italy raised the matter too. Had the bombing offensive not slowed down the rapacity of Milošević? asked Italy. Was it not time to take stock and see if Milošević was ready to talk? The public anger against the bombing was particularly intense in Greece, a traditional friend of Serbia.

'There was extraordinary resistance,' remembers Nicholas Burns, US ambassador to Greece at the time, 'altogether fifty-three demonstrations against our embassy over a three-month period. They threw eggs, paint and rocks while the anarchists hurled Molotov cocktails.' For Serbia and for Russia, Greece was the promisingly weak link in the alliance – if Greece broke from the NATO consensus, then the whole alliance effort would be paralysed. In the end, Greece reluctantly toed the line.

Feeding the anxiety of the critics was the idea that cumulative bombing actually caused ethnic cleansing. This was wrong. The forced displacement of people in Kosovo had begun in 1998. A study by the American Association for the Advancement of the Sciences compared in detail refugee departures with the intensity of the bombing raids and could find no correlation.[14] It was, the scientists found, an organised, planned expulsion rather than panic about NATO that drove people from their homes. So-called Operation Horseshoe had set out Serbia's plans for emptying the province of Albanians. Some doubt the credibility of that blueprint for ethnic cleansing – it appears to have been first circulated by a European intelligence service – but there is plenty of evidence of planning. Before March 1999, there were only two regular trains between Pristina and the Macedonian border. When

---

14 The Kosovo Report (2000), p. 304

the bombing began, Serbian railways suddenly found the rolling stock to lay on three or four extra trains a day, each with twenty carriages.

The deportation of ethnic Albanians has been a leitmotif of Serbian policy in Kosovo throughout its modern history, writes Dr Zamir Shtylla, formerly of Tirana University. 'The main route for the deportation of the Albanians from their territories between 1918 and 1941 was through what is now the Former Yugoslav Republic of Macedonia via the Shkup–Salonika [Skopje–Thessaloniki] railway and thence by either rail or sea to Istanbul.' Other expulsions were to Albania. The similarity to the Milošević era was striking except for the numbers. Dr Shtylla talks of the forced deportation of between 200,000 and 300,000 in a quarter of a century. Milošević's army, his police units and his paramilitaries, trumped this figure many times over.

The expulsion of Kosovar Albanians was thus expected by both Serbs and Albanians alike; it was part of the historical pattern. And, in any case, Milošević's henchmen had demonstrated in Bosnia that rape, pillage and mass executions were all legitimate means of creating ethnic purity. Thaçi's home village was not spared, swallowed by flames like so much of the Drenica Valley. 'My parents fled,' says Thaçi. 'Our home, our entire village, was set ablaze by the Serb police. Everywhere there was the stench of burning roofs.'

The KLA did what it could to protect and warn villagers of an approaching Serb attack. Each region had its own KLA hierarchy but many of the troops on the ground were local self-defence forces, an organic resistance to invaders. Yet Thaçi understood that Kosovo needed something more. The war was, he understood, a defining moment for Kosovo, its path to independence. As such it needed a figurehead. Ibrahim Rugova, the titular President of Kosovo, was stuck in a villa surrounded by Serbs; he had become a listless, confused figure and would eventually be whisked to safety out of the province by the Italians.

He was put up in a safe house where, in the words of one ex-KLA man, 'he proceeded to have a nervous breakdown'. Thaçi contacted Albright. 'She advised me that Kosovo needed a political address. This is how I became an interim Prime Minister. We needed to be a full part of what was going on and what would happen next.'

Perhaps the most important figure at this stage – as so many NATO members fretted over the length of the bombing war – was Tony Blair. As early as June 1998, Blair had stated the need for military action if diplomacy was unable to put a stop to the crisis. It had become increasingly clear to Blair that unless NATO could credibly threaten the use of ground troops, Milošević would find a way of wriggling off the hook. He had drawn very concrete lessons from the way that the international government and the Conservative government of John Major had mishandled the ethnic cleansing in Bosnia. The UN had demanded 'safe zones' but the reluctance of member states to provide muscle on the ground turned them into potential death traps. It had been a humiliating cycle which Blair was determined to avoid this time round: the inability to deter marauding Serb forces, their cynical shelling of Sarajevo, followed by NATO air strikes which were then thwarted by the use of hapless captured peacekeepers as human shields. And most bitter of all was the Bosnian Serb massacre of Muslims after over-running the supposedly protected area of Srebrenica. The whole sorry story was only brought under control by intensified air strikes and deploying heavily armed brigades from Britain, France and the Netherlands.

For Blair, a combined services action force was the only way to prevent a repeat tragedy in the Balkans and there was little time to waste. In March, shortly before the bombing began, he had clearly stated that the war would only end when 'Milošević abides by the agreement, stops repressing the people, gets his troops back into barracks, gets his heavy artillery out of there and starts to behave like a civilised person towards Kosovo.' He was aware that Milošević was going to try to split the NATO coalition by showing bombing to be inhumane and ineffective.

But to bring him back to the negotiating table, NATO needed to demonstrate the ability to escalate. Broadly speaking, there was a fusion of interest between Wes Clark, Tony Blair and Hashim Thaçi. All three understood that Milošević would find ways of dodging air strikes. The Serb/Yugoslav army, however, was no serious match for a combination of air power and ground troops. There was then an element of bluff involved on the part of Blair and Clark; it might be enough for Milošević simply to believe that he was about to be destroyed by a huge modern army without it having to be deployed. The US creation of a forward air base in Albania, Clark's leaked demands for Apache attack helicopters, the creation of a substantial base in Macedonia by General Sir Mike Jackson: all this could have been mere pantomime to break Milošević's nerve.

It was up to Blair to convince Bill Clinton and a very sceptical Pentagon that US troops should be readied for action in the killing fields of Kosovo, even if they were never actually deployed. The British understood the military problems. The approach of ground troops into Kosovo would involve heavy armour squeezing through narrow winding mountain passes. Were Albanian ports large and deep enough to take the warships delivering equipment to the invading army? According to Wes Clark, a ground invasion would have to be launched by September before the onset of winter made the mountain roads impassable. That in turn meant operational preparations beginning in June. And that meant a political decision by May.

The ideal moment would thus have been the NATO summit scheduled in Washington for 23 April to mark the fiftieth birthday of the alliance.

It was supposed to be more than just a ceremonial event and discussion was expected on the future evolution of NATO in the post-communist world – and its first big test in Kosovo. Blair was determined to seize the chance to make a case for ground troops – he was a convinced liberal interventionist and was determined to re-shape British foreign policy accordingly. Since both he and Clinton shared ideological roots – the so-called Third Way of pragmatic, market-friendly social democracy – he was sure the Anglo-American axis could change the world. Where better to test the dynamics of the relationship than fighting together on the battlefield for democratic values? The summit was due to start on Friday and Blair arrived early, on the Wednesday evening. He headed straight into a meeting with Clinton at the White House. And the American President told him, politely, to shut up.

'The American case,' remembers Christopher Meyer, British ambassador to the US, who was present at the first part of the talks, 'rested on two propositions: that it would undermine the credibility of the air war if it became known that preparations were in hand for a ground war. And that a ground war would require calling up US reservists which would not be good politically.'[15] In the private part of the Clinton–Blair talks, the President gave other arguments: that Blair would end up splitting the alliance if he insisted on pushing for an invasion of Kosovo; that it would be difficult to raise the troop numbers and NATO could be left with egg on its face; that America was in no mood to have hostages taken by what Clinton called 'the crazies' – Serb paramilitaries – or to lose large numbers of casualties.

It was an unusually long visit to the US, stretching to four days, and the US piled pressure on Blair. When British newspapers suggested Clinton was being over-cautious on Kosovo, the President made what

---

15 Christopher Meyer, *DC Confidential* (2005), p. 102

Sir Christopher calls 'an explosive phone call to Blair'. At a speech in Chicago, just before the summit, Blair made the moral case for intervention: a doctrine for humanitarian intervention if genocide was about to be carried out or was already under way. The White House was furious about that too.

Easier by far for the White House and the Pentagon to muzzle Wes Clark. He was told that he could only come to the NATO summit if he held his tongue on the use of ground troops in Kosovo. 'Yes, Sir!' said Clark over the phone. 'I'm not going to be the skunk at the picnic.' Nonetheless, after the summit, Clark was authorised to draw up contingency plans for introducing troops into Kosovo. And, by 23 May, both Blair and Clinton had given the go-ahead to Javier Solana to draw up detailed invasion plans.

Blair's response to American doubts was to put together a potential British force big enough to demonstrate that the US would not be left fighting Milošević by itself. More than 30,000 letters were drafted, typed and prepared for dispatch to Territorial Army reservists. As soon as the invasion was agreed, the letters would be sent. George Robertson, the British defence minister, told his US counterpart William Cohen that Britain could offer 50,000 troops. That was decisive. Wes Clark was estimating that a total of 175,000 would be needed to take control of Kosovo; with a big British contingent, NATO would not have to beg for soldiers from less enthusiastic allies.

Meanwhile, on a craggy, windswept mountain on the Kosovo–Albania border, the formidable KLA general Agim Çeku had launched an all-out attack on the Serbs. The KLA had transformed itself into a force that could not only stage effective ambushes but also capture and hold territory. This was vital all along arms supply routes and there was none quite as important, for the passage of men, medicine and weapons, as Mount Paštrik.

'On the morning of 26 May,' recalls Wes Clark, 'we had considerable information about the KLA plans to attack into Kosovo.' The US estimated there were four or five battalions, 1,800 to 2,000 men, ready to go over the top of the mountain and attack Serb positions. It formed the high ground north-east of Kukës in Albania and if NATO went ahead with an invasion it would need to be in control of the slopes. Clark was worried. If, as he expected, the Serb mortars and artillery made mincemeat out of the KLA, they would push over the crest of the mountain and be able to overlook the massive refugee camps around Kukës. Call in artillery fire and they could engineer one atrocity after another. And they could target the crucial US airfield. The high ground was dangerous.

'That mountain is not going to be lost!' Clark told US commanders. 'We're not going to have Serbs on top of that mountain. We'll have to pay for the top of that hill with American blood if we don't help the KLA now.' And so it was that the relationship between the KLA and the US armed forces went quickly deeper than an exchange of intelligence. As Clark had feared, the KLA troops, outnumbered and outgunned, were pinned down by Serb fire. Clark sought and gained permission to use cluster bombs against Serb positions. The decision went as far as the White House, which had been wary of using the explosives because of the danger to civilians. Two B-52s were called in and battered the Serb gunnery; according to some accounts hundreds of their soldiers were killed. They fled – and for the KLA it was a sign that their soldiers were now full US allies. A far cry from a year earlier, when senior US officials stood up and publicly declared the KLA to be terrorists.

As the battle raged on the mountain, Thaçi was on tour persuading European ministers that they should hold firm. As the first US warplanes steered towards Mount Paštrik, Thaçi was in Italy, on the NATO base in Aviano. 'I won't forget it,' says Thaçi. 'The day before I had been in

Kosovo on the war front. Now I was watching the world's most powerful air force roar out to bomb Milošević.'

The British Foreign Secretary had urged him to get out of Kosovo for a while. It was critical now, more than ever before, that the KLA present itself not just as a guerrilla army but as a responsible political actor. The west feared above all that after driving Milošević out of Kosovo, the province would go into meltdown. 'We had come to trust Thaçi,' said one senior British official. 'He could negotiate, command and deliver – everything that Rugova was incapable of doing.' Robin Cook was the pivotal foreign minister in Europe, precisely because of Britain's relationship with the US. 'He was more decisive than some other Europeans and I had a good personal relationship with him,' says Thaçi.

> So when I flew to see him in that hot phase of the war, we were both very earnest and very open. We needed his support, political as well as military, and he needed us to demonstrate that this was to be the last of the Balkan wars.
>
> After our talks we stopped at the top of the FCO staircase and Cook patted me on the back. 'From these steps,' he said, 'de Gaulle left to liberate France. You too will soon be on your way to liberate your country.'

CHAPTER 8

VICTORY AND DEFEAT

Thaçi brimmed with pride at the KLA's part in the victory over Milošević:

> Jamie Rubin and I took a stroll through the centre of Pristina and drew up chairs at the Korza café. It was a busy place on what has once been called Tito Street, then renamed after King Lazar, the Serb hero, by Milošević. Now it is named after Mother Teresa, the newly proclaimed Albanian saint of Kosovan origin. As we sipped our coffees – and my first champagne in liberated Kosovo – a smiling crowd gathered around. It was difficult not to think back to 1993 when I had just a pair of jeans to my name, when I was being hunted by Serbia. Now, six years on, here I was – and Kosovo was free, NATO was in.

Thaçi had returned to Kosovo a few days earlier. When the bombing campaign was halted, Thaçi had travelled first to neighbouring Macedonia.

I wanted to see the Kosovan refugees there. Life had been difficult for them, and now they were living in a state of anxiety about their homes and their relatives. So I wanted to tell them they would soon be on their way back. They clapped and they cried. A great wave of relief seemed to roll over them.

Thaçi had flown in under British protection. General Mike Jackson had been based in Macedonia with the mission to create a jumping-off place for a NATO army of occupation. The final capitulation of the Serbian Army was signed in a ramshackle border restaurant named Europa 92, owned by a Macedonian Albanian. It had been a frustrating task for him, unsure of how the endgame of the bombing war would pan out. For the time being it seemed that his first task would be to send in the sappers to ensure that the approach roads to Pristina were free of mines. Would the Serbs mount a rearguard action? Would the Kosovars speed back and end up slaughtered or held hostage by Milošević's disgruntled men? How fast was he supposed to move? And would Thaçi – who seemed to the general to be improbably young – ensure that Kosovars held back their anger?

No matter: Thaçi needed his support. A Chinook was put at Thaçi's disposal and, from a muddy field in Tetovo, he was flown first into the Drenica Valley and then on to the capital. Thaçi was full of apprehension. His war aims had been relatively straightforward and the outcome was a good one. Even the fact that Milošević showed no signs of stepping down or surrendering power worked in his favour: it was going to be easier both to ensure heavy international engagement and to move faster towards independence as long as Milošević, discredited and weakened, was still in charge. The plausibility of the Kosovan cause did not need to be promoted at length; it was self-evident to almost all of the Western community that it had to protect the Kosovars from a man viewed as the Devil of the Balkans.

But he shared some of Jackson's worries. The post-war period would be complicated and dangerous. He knew that the KLA was far from being a unified force. Could he guarantee that KLA fighters would not harry the withdrawing Serb units? The international community had insisted on the disarmament of the KLA as a condition of placing its NATO contingent, the so-called Kfor, in position. But what if Kfor wasn't up to the job or if it delayed? What if a security vacuum opened up?

The Serbs, cowed by seventy-eight days of bombardment, would probably keep their promise – but what of Serbia's ally, Russia? Boris Yeltsin was unpredictable and so was his army. Moscow could make life very difficult indeed. Alastair Campbell – Tony Blair's media advisor, who had steered much of the NATO information war – took a call from Wes Clark. 'Clark said Milošević was perfectly capable of playing several moves ahead of us. He was looking for a new game to play and we had to work out what it was.' Could that involve Moscow?

The situation became clearer on Friday 11 June. The war was over, and Jackson's paratroopers and Gurkhas were supposed to lead the way into Kosovo. They anticipated victory parades. Instead news came through that a convoy of Russian armoured vehicles was on its way to Kosovo from Bosnia. 'Wes Clark called me,' remembers Campbell, 'and said that the Russian troops were moving in [to secure Pristina airport] and he had learned that they had asked for air space for six planes across Hungary. Either we go for a very risky military operation, or we risk partition, with the Russians just taking over.'[16]

No one knew if the Russians had a coherent strategy. But Thaçi knew for sure that a partition of Kosovo would have been deadly for the new

---

16 Alastair Campbell, *The Blair Years* (2007)

state. 'We were being hijacked by the Russians.' If Milošević thought he could grab northern Kosovo, take the northern city of Mitrovica and five rural municipalities, grab the Trepča mines, then Kosovo would end up as little more than a rump statelet. A few Albanian nationalists may have preferred it that way, inhabiting an ethnically pure Albanian commonwealth, but Thaçi understood that such a division would make a dysfunctional state out of a future Kosovo. And it would destabilise the region – if Kosovo Serbs formally merged with Serbia, then the ethnic Albanians in Serbia's Preševo Valley would demand to be part of Kosovo. Unrest could then spread to the Albanian population in Macedonia and Montenegro. The end of the war could thus mark the beginning of a new one. If Milošević was in cahoots with Moscow to achieve that, then he had to be stopped.

'I discovered that Clark had seemingly become obsessed by the threat of Russian troops invading the Serb enclaves, particularly in the north, and establishing a de facto partition of Kosovo,' recalls Jackson, who had pushed quickly towards Pristina airport. The airport was seen as pivotal, the gateway for the airlift of perhaps thousands of Russian troops. 'To prevent this happening, Clark wanted the runway to be blocked by Kfor headquarters.'

Jackson did not see the point. NATO already controlled the air space over Kosovo. Blocking the runway, he believed, would spark a dangerous confrontation. Jackson, a fluent Russian speaker, had approached the Russian general in charge at the airport. It was pouring with rain and drops must have seeped into the engine of the Russian commander's vehicle. As Jackson clambered in, it erupted with black smoke. The two men got out, Jackson took a bottle of Scotch from the inside of his combat jacket and, over a few drinks with his Russian counterpart, it became clear that neither Moscow nor NATO really knew what they were doing. The Kremlin, it seemed, was not after a carve-up; it wanted the brief propaganda triumph of being the first to the airport. After being on the sidelines of the NATO campaign for three months, Yeltsin wanted to leave his mark. This was not Berlin 1945, with the Red Army racing to the capital in order to enforce a division of the country.

Clark disagreed. He flew in the next day and demanded that Jackson directly challenge the Russians to withdraw. The increasingly irritated British general explained that Pristina airport had no operational value.

> 'Mike, do you understand that as a NATO commander I'm giving you a legal order, and if you don't accept that order you'll have to resign?'
> 'I do.'
> 'OK, so I'm giving you an order to block the runways at Pristina airfield. I want it done. Is that clear?'

Jackson found a way to outwit Clark. He suggested that the runways be obstructed not by helicopters but by British armoured vehicles. Clark agreed. But Jackson knew that the use of British ground troops in this way would need the explicit approval of London – and he was sure that Tony Blair would back him. Clark rang Javier Solana, the Secretary-General of NATO, and Alastair Campbell in an attempt to outflank Jackson. 'I wish to God these generals would calm down a bit,' Blair complained to Campbell.

'Sir,' said Jackson to Clark, 'I'm not going to start World War Three for you.' Blair had used exactly the same phrasing; this was going to be a stand-off that he would win. Jackson did not only have Blair's backing but those of his men facing the Russian contingent. One of them was Captain James Blunt, who would later go on to become an international singing star ('You're Beautiful'). The young officer declared that he would rather face court martial than shoot on the Russians. Blair rang Clinton who, in Campbell's words, made clear that he too thought 'any notion of a battle with the Russians was wrong'.[17]

And yet Wes Clark – unloved by the Pentagon – had the right instincts. Russia under Yeltsin and, soon after, under Putin would come to exploit any division in alliance ranks to strengthen Serbia at the expense of the Kosovo Albanians. It was Russia that turned the tension between post-war Serbia and Kosovo into a zero-sum game, in which Kosovo's gain could only be interpreted as Serbia's loss.

The airport crisis was resolved nonetheless in a way that fell some way short of Armageddon. The US administration asked Hungary to stop Russian military flights over its soil. Pristina airport became irrelevant. A sour taste remained though – Russia felt it had somehow been cheated by NATO and was determined from then on to find ways of impeding or punishing the Kosovars. In subsequent confrontations, Putin was careful not to be outmanoeuvred.

The question in those tense post-war months was how Kosovo should be governed. Nothing in the Rambouillet accord, or in the rushed diplomacy that followed, really gave a clue. In early June 1999, the US, Russia and six other world powers had agreed to the text of a UN Security Council resolution that satisfied NATO's key demand: the authorisation of the alliance and other international peacekeepers to enter the province after Serb troops had withdrawn. Their mission was narrowly limited to the safeguarding of hundreds of thousands of returning Albanians but it was in fact the prelude to a remarkable exercise in nation-building, the construction of a state. 'We got what we came for,' said Madeleine Albright after the decisive G8 meeting in

---

17 Quotations drawn from the diaries of Alastair Campbell and the memoirs of Wes Clark and General Sir Mike Jackson.

Cologne on 8 June. A photograph shows Thaçi in a dark suit towering behind her and to one side the tired figure of Ibrahim Rugova, a scarf wrapped around his neck, his head bowed.

Resolution 1244, as it was designated, provided for an international civil presence alongside the armed peacekeepers. They were supposed to pave the way for domestic self-governing institutions. Some Yugoslav and Serb personnel would be allowed to return to patrol border crossings, identify minefields, to run the Serb Orthodox domain and to liaise with the new UN interim administration, known as UNMIK. That sensible arrangement had not come easily but rather as the result of some fifty hours of talks between Finnish President Martti Ahtisaari acting as the UN envoy, the Russian specialist Strobe Talbott who represented Albright and Yeltsin's man, the former Russian Prime Minister Viktor Chernomyrdin. Serbia's minimal demand had been to keep some troops in Serbia and keep NATO out – that would have been enough for Milošević to declare a tactical victory. Russia had supported this view – until, after an all-night bargaining session at the German government residence on a hilltop outside Bonn, Yeltsin called Chernomyrdin and ordered him to do everything to strike a deal. The crisis, said the bibulous Kremlin chief, had been dragging on for too long.

As demanded, Chernomyrdin performed a U-turn: Russia would agree to all Serbian units leaving Kosovo with a few specified exceptions. In return, civilian and security control of Kosovo would come under UN supervision rather than that of NATO, albeit with 'substantial NATO participation'. The generals in the Russian delegation were furious. Whichever way the resolution was read, it seemed to them that Russia would eventually be blocked out. Chernomyrdin, though, had Yeltsin's backing. It was this unresolved issue, the tension between Yeltsin and his general staff, that was at the heart of the Pristina airport showdown.

The governance of Kosovo was thus ill-starred from the very outset. It was not just the question of how and when Russia should compete or cooperate with NATO. It was also how the UN-steered administration should work with Kfor. This tangled authority made it difficult for Thaçi to chart a clear line of political leadership in the immediate post-war years. How much autonomy would there really be from Serbia? How secure would Kosovo's borders be? How limited was the role of Kosovan self-government? How long would it take before UNMIK handed over its gubernatorial powers to local politicians?

And, crucially: what kind of authority would be enjoyed by a Kosovan leader?

Kosovo had a so-called President – Rugova. They had one government in exile, run by LDK's Bujar Bukoshi. Thaçi, having declared a provisional government but still a long way from a ballot box test, decided that the best course was to consolidate his ties with Western leaders. UNMIK had to be left in no doubt as to which of the Kosovan leaders enjoyed international legitimacy. Western governments worked with Kosovo leaders as political representatives but never recognised the legality of the various Kosovo governments, as Resolution 1244 was clear in empowering UNMIK as the sole executive and judicial body in the former Serbian province: Kosovo became a de facto UN protectorate. Rugova was still sheltering in an Italian villa, withdrawn, strangely absent from the exuberance of his homeland.

It seemed natural for Thaçi to take charge. 'Rambouillet had turned me into a public figure. It was a strange but also joyous feeling to walk freely, and recognised, along the familiar streets of Pristina.' A procession of Western leaders came to Kosovo that summer eager to demonstrate to electorates back home that it has been a war well fought. FBI forensic experts were already on the ground, sifting evidence from mass graves. Joschka Fischer, the German foreign minister, was visibly shaken after visiting an opened burial site. The perpetrators, he said, would be put in the dock at The Hague. 'The work will only be done', he said, 'when we have not only a liberated Kosovo but also a democratic Kosovo.' That was an important signal: the toppling of Milošević and placing him before an international tribunal was now a clear aim. It was based on the perhaps naive hope that a post-Milošević government would feel confident enough to loosen its grip on Kosovo. But Kosovars took the statement at face value: that the West was committed to Kosovo for the long haul. And, for Fischer, the trip to Kosovo was part of an ideological passage. 'I used to be a supporter of appeasement, and for good reasons,' said Fischer, who was a leading light in the pacifist Green party. 'I changed my mind after Srebrenica. It became clear to me that appeasement towards Milošević would just lead to more and more mass graves.'

The British Foreign Secretary Robin Cook was also on the left and as passionate a convert to liberal interventionism as Fischer. That June he visited the site of a suspected massacre in Velika Kruša – and appealed to Kosovo Albanians to set aside their hatred of the Serbs and allow the United Nations 'to pursue the task of doing justice to those who died. Let us here in Kosovo break the cycle of violence and build a peaceful non-violent future for the children of all communities in Kosovo.'

Cook was to repeat those sentiments when he and Fischer saw Thaçi that summer. They made it clear they had a clear preference for Thaçi to be interim Prime Minister until democratic elections could be held; Rambouillet had built a mutual trust between them. Madeleine Albright made Western approval of Thaçi even clearer when she publicly kissed him on the cheek in Pristina. They had been through a war together, NATO's first, and it was an important bond. But for this bond to endure they needed leadership in Kosovo that would demonstrate the lasting success of the intervention. The Kosovo operation had become part of the re-branding of NATO; that strategy would be discredited if Kosovo drifted back into the world of Balkan vendetta. There had to be ambitious nation-building, a pledge from Kosovan leaders to support a multi-ethnic, multi-faith community. Liberal interventionism had to be more than the West protecting lives and ensuring that the right side won; it had to be accompanied by a deeper pledge to modernise and democratise societies. Thaçi told them he was up for the job.

'From the very first day we started to talk about the demilitarisation of the KLA,' recalls Thaçi. UNSC 1244 had stipulated that clearly: 'The KLA and the other armed Kosovo Albanian groups should end immediately all offensive actions and comply with the requirements of demilitarisation as laid down by the head of the international civil and security presence in consultation with the Special Representative of the Secretary-General.'

Thaçi knew this was going to be difficult. In the early 1990s he had called on Kosovars to arm up for an uprising against Milošević. He had smuggled weapons across the Albanian border. And he had in the middle of the Rambouillet conference gone back to sceptical commanders and told them they should be ready to give up the struggle if NATO moved in to displace Serbian troops. Now he had to go a step further and persuade the KLA to abolish itself at the moment when it was experiencing the first flush of victory.

But a deal was a deal. Hours after the Serbs agreed to withdraw its forces, Mike Jackson sent a helicopter to pick up the chief KLA commander, General Çeku, and told him in his usual gruff tone that he expected a total handover to NATO of all equipment and weapons. 'I was shocked,' Çeku told David Phillips. 'I told them I'm not representing an armed group. I'm chief of the general staff and we're partners. We have been in touch on every day of this conflict.' The KLA demob, he insisted, had to be a collective decision. Jackson agreed. KLA commanders and Thaçi – as political director the only participant apart from Jamie Rubin to be wearing civilian clothes – were flown to a barracks to negotiate with Jackson about the future of the KLA.

At Rambouillet, Thaçi had already set out the definitive phraseology: the point was not to dismember the KLA but transform it. 'We had to deliver 12,000 weapons,' says Thaçi. '5.5 million rounds of ammunition, and 27,000 handguns. And we had to stop wearing uniforms.' It was not a personal blow. 'Except for the two years of war I've never worn a gun in my belt.' For many KLA men, though, it was an extraordinary intrusion; family safety had come to mean a cache of firearms in the barn.

'These were tricky talks with Jackson and Wes Clark,' remembers Thaçi. '"Kosovo is free," I told them. "It has NATO at its side but it will not have its own defence force."' Thaçi's case had been made most eloquently by Milošević, whose 'surrender' speech had contained more than a hint of menace. 'Dear citizens,' the Serb leader had said over television, 'the aggression is over. Peace has overcome violence.' But he added: 'We won't give up Kosovo. We haven't given up Kosovo.' Milošević could return, and would as NATO left the province. If he was going to attack again, Kosovo would be left without a shield.

'So we agreed that there would be a type of national guard,' says Thaçi. 'The Trupat Mbrojtëse të Kosovës.' That was translated as the 'Kosovo Protection Corps' (KPC) but could equally well be rendered as the more muscular 'Kosovo Defence Troops'. 'It was to be 3,000 men and 2,000 reservists,' said Thaçi, and according to the terms of the deal it was supposed to 'provide disaster response services, perform search and rescue, provide capacity for humanitarian assistance in isolated areas and assist in demining and rebuilding work.'

In fact, many saw it as the kernel of a future army for an independent Kosovo. 'I didn't want them to have the Albanian eagle as its insignia, that would have sent all the wrong signals,' says Thaçi.

> So I helped design a shoulder flash that depicted the contours of Kosovo's external borders on a red background. That map has now also become the insignia used on the Kosovo flag and it is supposed to show that our territory is indivisible. The new Kosovo force had to be multi-ethnic, that is: open to Kosovan Serbs.

In fact, at a distance, the shoulder flash looks very like the old KLA badge. And the commanders of the six regional task forces of the KPC were, to no one's surprise, former KLA commanders from the same regions.

All recruits were vetted, subjected to psychological and physical tests, their attitudes to human rights and ethnic minorities scrutinised. Under OSCE supervision, a police academy was set up – based on Norwegian ideas but run by the US. As a result, some KLA men found themselves quickly in uniform. 'Most of them, though, returned to civilian life,' says Thaçi. 'Some had been students who returned to what was now a free university life.'

The Western aim was of course to ensure that the KPC, with its hardened military veterans, did not become a rival to Kfor, the NATO mission. The veterans were self-aware, blooded by combat, and sceptical about the international presence, which was swelling with military bureaucrats. The KPC was well-funded (the US forked out a third of the $40 million running costs) but resented being given what seemed to be humiliating orders from the foreign officers in Kfor. Tasks like road clearance and traffic control seemed demeaning to people who considered themselves war heroes. 'As a result, many just ended up drinking coffee all day,' says Terence Billingham, KPC coordinator in the flashpoint of Mitrovica.[18] A confidential NATO report in 2000 said some KPC officers had 'ties with criminal organisations' and profited from the seizure of vacant apartments.

Thaçi had taken over as provisional Prime Minister, having formed a new party: the Democratic Party of Kosovo (PDK). It was essentially a Victory Party. Thaçi had begun organising the team at Rambouillet, and established it in exile in the second week of the NATO bombing campaign. By June 1999, it was able to set up skeleton councils in twenty-seven out of the twenty-nine Albanian-dominated municipalities. It drew its legitimacy from the success of Thaçi at Rambouillet, the support of the West – in particular Tony Blair and Bill Clinton, who were glowing with pride at the success of their military intervention – and what Thaçi calculated to be a national disdain for Rugova's policies.

This turned out to be a fragile basis for rebuilding a country that was still in shock. Statues were put up for KLA heroes and a war pensions scheme was devised. But, rather than building statues for soldiers, Kosovo's priority was to restore bridges, repair the sewage system and create a functioning electricity grid. It wanted a UN administration that genuinely addressed their problems and an efficient Prime Minister who was able to channel international funds in an equitable way. Kosovo roadsides were strewn with plastic bags filled with uncollected rubbish. Houses were being built but in a haphazard, unregulated way.

The United Nations presence – known as UNMIK – moved only sluggishly into action. The mission was led by a progressive and well-meaning French diplomat, Bernard Kouchner, who founded Doctors Without Borders. After a short honeymoon, frictions increased. Highly paid staff and consultants (some on $1,000 a day, a mind-boggling sum

---

18 Iain King and Whit Mason, *Peace at Any Price: How the World Failed Kosovo* (2006), p. 59

for the Kosovars) poured in. They treated Kosovo as a lucrative short-term contract, typically leaving for Brussels on a Thursday night and returning on Monday. One of its first errors, in the view of Kosovars, was to adopt Yugoslav law as the interim legal system. Kosovo had just fought a war for independence but was being offered instead at best limited autonomy by a profoundly inefficient alien bureaucracy.

Bernard Kouchner, the Special Representative of the UN Secretary-General, acted as if Thaçi did not enjoy popular legitimacy and coordinated instead with a transitional council that comprised delegates from the major parties. In fact, it was Kouchner who had doubtful legitimacy. He was scrambling for funds, pleading with donors so that the UN could meet its commitments. His mission was not only to repair the province but also to build the institutions of a nation-state in a place that had no immediate prospect of becoming one. His hands were tied by all the ambiguities inherent in Resolution 1244 – as in Bosnia, the UN mission had been handed a holding operation not an architect's blueprint.

'Albright had advised Kouchner not to pick a fight with Thaçi,' says an official who worked within UNMIK. Given the right set of circumstances, it might have been possible for Thaçi to build a credible problem-solving administration and exploit to his advantage the institutional quarrels between the UNHCR (United Nations High Commissioner for Refugees), the EU and the OSCE. But although Thaçi had played a weak hand brilliantly at Rambouillet, he was still an inexperienced political operator.

Around him there was chaos. That summer tens of thousands of Kosovo Albanians who had fled or been expelled from their villages during the bombing campaign trekked back into the province. Since their houses in the countryside had been ransacked and torched, they stayed in the towns and looked for work, waiting for word from relatives. The first UN Special Representative, Sérgio Vieira de Mello

– who lasted only a few months before being replaced by Kouchner – had been sent in with a staff of eight but was faced with the need to find shelter and basic services for 900,000 displaced Kosovo Albanians. Running water was a problem in Pristina; that summer there was the pervasive stench of sewage. Dogs, abandoned by fleeing Serbs, roamed the streets, feeding on scraps.

The Yugoslav army and Serbian police units withdrew from Kosovo in long convoys, in accordance with UN resolution 1244. Thousands of Serb civilians squeezed into cars and tractor-tugged carts and made a more ragged retreat, fearing the next instalment of Balkan revenge. The International Committee of the Red Cross calculated that close to 60,000 Kosovo Serbs had joined the exodus in the fortnight before 18 June. Seen from the air it yielded an extraordinary image of the end of war. Alastair Campbell recalls a trip on a low-flying Puma helicopter. 'Through the headset, I could hear the voice of the pilot spotting potential dangers, like Serb troop movements as they withdrew. We flew over some of the ethnically cleansed villages, homes that were shells of themselves, animals scavenging, lots of rough and ready graves.' He noted there was no visible wreckage of Serb tanks. It was an astute observation.

While the NATO bombardment of central Serbia had made a significant impact on everyday lives – the winter of 1999–2000 was to be a cold one in Belgrade, with at best erratic heating – it had not devastated the Serb army in Kosovo. Serb commanders had constructed dummy tanks and evaded serious damage. Perhaps air was really the road to psychological victory – the theatre of overwhelming firepower – rather than a decisive military knockout blow. According to one estimate, only thirteen tanks in Kosovo had been destroyed by NATO bombs. The true harm inflicted by Serbs in Kosovo was down to the most banal of weapons: the cigarette lighter. That was all it took to set homes on fire and, backed up by grenades, bayonets and the selective execution of young men, was enough to destroy whole communities, sending survivors on the run. Mosques were flattened. A village cow would be shot and dumped in a well, simultaneously denying the community its livelihood and poisoning its water supply. All of NATO's high-tech warfare was not able to stop that; rather, it was the fear that NATO would cripple Serbia's main cities and then bring ground troops to within striking distance of Belgrade, the fear of worse to come, that made Milošević cave in.

The returning Kosovo Albanians smelled the fear of the Serbs and remembered all too well the cruelty and the cigarette lighters. There was a thirst for revenge, a settling of scores.

'Thousands upon thousands of Kosovo Albanians were living that summer in open fields next to their burned-out houses in burned-out villages,' says Thaçi.

> The realities of the war were suddenly clear to them. And just as in Germany after the downfall of Hitler, they realised that too many people they knew had acted as Belgrade's willing executioners. So there were brutal revenge attacks. Very often the targets were immediate neighbours and it was an Old Testament reckoning: an eye for an eye, a tooth for a tooth. For me it was genuinely unexpected, a typical Balkan episode you could say, but unexpected, a total loss of control.

NATO expected Kosovo would not enter a period of peace immediately after the war ended. In those turbulent summer days after NATO entered the province, Pentagon spokesman Ken Bacon had stated clearly: 'I don't think Kosovo will be a happy place for Serbs. When NATO comes in, I don't think they will stay there.' So it happened. Many Serbs left Kosovo for ever.

The OSCE compiled lists of horrific incidents. Chiefly the attacks were against people deemed as collaborators. Not just local Serbs but Roma who were seen as being under the special protection of Belgrade. The scorched body of a Roma leader was found inside a ransacked house on the south side of the river Ibar in Mitrovica. Other Roma were abducted and tortured because their families had supposedly cooperated with the Serb police. Partly the victims were accused of having looted Albanians' homes after they had been forced to flee; not so much collaborators as profiteers. There were attacks too on Serbs, especially those of military age. Under cover of night, they would be beaten with iron rods, their throats slit with broken glass.

Kfor claimed that in June 1999, when its troops first moved in, the murder rate was fifty a week. By October, the vendetta death toll had reached 348. 'I've been a human rights activist for thirty years,' said Kouchner when he took over, 'and here I am unable to stop people being massacred.'

Most disturbing for Thaçi was the involvement of KLA members or supporters. Although he had signed the KLA demobilisation accord, the cut-off date for the surrender of guns was September. So that summer there were plenty of frustrated young men still legally armed, pumped up with adrenaline and a sense of being victors. Many of these young men were now purchasing KLA uniforms, which were being freely sold in markets. And Kfor, though more effective than any other international organisation on the ground, was wrong-footed. By late August it had 36,500 men at its disposal, but it understood its mission to be guaranteeing the safe passage of Serb soldiers from the territory of Kosovo. The priority was to ensure that Milošević would not go back on his word and suddenly attack again.

That was a reasonable assumption. General Radovan Lazarevic, commander of the Yugoslav army's Pristina Corps, made it all too plain that his men were hungry to return to their former garrison. 'As long as we defended Kosovo, the enemy did not expel the Serbs. Until we withdrew, the enemy did not capture a single metre of our country,' he said. 'Our return is our obsession … we are prepared to take back Kosovo by force.'[19]

There was probably no serious intention in Belgrade of doing that – the re-conquest of Kosovo would continue to be little more than a rhetorical or diplomatic goal. But Milošević had reneged on promises throughout his career and it could not be ruled out. Kfor was thus turned outwards not inwards. And as long as that was the case, some KLA fighters felt they could mount revenge attacks with impunity. Who could stop them?

Thaçi says he was appalled:

> At any one time in our war, the maximum number of soldiers in the KLA was between fifteen and twenty thousand. Suddenly, though, all sorts of people started to pretend that they too had been in the KLA, any eighteen-year-old kid who had bought a second-hand KLA tunic in Albania felt he could lay claim to having fought for our victory. Maybe 40,000 of them. And tragically quite a lot of them were not out to liberate Kosovo but to liberate property for themselves. I considered these men were doing enormous damage to our newly found freedom. They wanted to hit the Serbs at their weakest moment. In all, hundreds of Serbs died, though that includes people killed in the NATO military operations.

Kfor's mission was complicated by countervailing orders and political

---

19 Tim Judah, *Kosovo: War and Revenge* (2002), p. 307

quarrels. Swedish troops were earmarked to set up a camp in Prizren in
the south but were ordered at the last minute to guard Gračanica, a Serb
enclave and religious site outside Pristina. The tense city of Mitrovica,
with Serb and Albanian communities divided by the river Ibar, was
supposed to be a British sector; the French took it instead. Each change
in mission left contingents with outdated or irrelevant intelligence,
lost in the Balkan labyrinth. 'Kfor had the troops available to restore
security,' says Thaçi, 'but were unable to do so in the immediate
aftermath of the NATO bombing.'

Thaçi seems genuinely shamed by the months of reprisals. They were
carried out during the time when a new, liberated Kosovo was being
rebuilt – and they undermined his authority. His agreement with the
international community was to turn the KLA into civilians committed
to playing an important role in a new state. But precisely sealing that
deal weakened his tenuous hold over the KLA structures; he found
himself neither a proper national leader nor someone with any real legal
authority to maintain discipline in the former KLA.

'I can say only this: there was no premeditated plan to commit
systematic violence against Serbs. It happened in other places too, in
South Africa for example, that when the tables are turned in a conflict,
people seek revenge.'

'In war not everybody is an angel,' Thaçi says,

> I can't say with a clear heart that everybody stuck to the rules we
> set out. Anyone found responsible for these crimes should be put
> in the dock. I've seen Peja burned twice. First the Serbs torched
> it, then they withdrew, NATO came in. And when I joined them
> in the town I could see Serbian houses ablaze. Because especially
> in Peja people were coming back to mass graves. It turned
> my stomach.

'The fact is we never had a grudge against the Serb people, but with the vicious regime.' Yet most Serbs left Kosovo as soon as they realised their army was withdrawing completely, just as they left Sarajevo after the Bosnian war ended, or Croatia after the Croatian war. They didn't want to be a part of this new Kosovo, where century-long dominance of a minority was a mode of governance. They joined the Serbian police and army units in long caravans of tanks, armoured vehices and tractors. When Serbs were killed in a field while picking crops, Thaçi understood that the new freedom for Kosovo couldn't begin that way. 'I condemned it immediately, called it insanity.' That did not stop the rolling wave of revenge attacks by Albanians on local Serbs. On Albania's national day, 28 November, celebrated in Pristina for the first time, some young Kosovo Albanians kidnapped a Serb and torched him inside his own car.

'I realised just how deep ran the wounds in society,' says Thaçi. 'A crime wave was unfolding in front of me, committed by some of my own compatriots. And we were completely unprepared for it. People who had been criminals before the war returned to their ways, uncontrolled because there were no identity cards, no order.'

But Thaçi had inherited from the Rambouillet times the position as head of the informal provisional government. The international community expected more from Kosovan leaders: the assertion of discipline over those claiming to have been KLA fighters who were now trampling not only on Serbs and Roma but also starting to run protection rackets in the liberated province. Veton Surroi, the liberal publisher who had sided with Thaçi in Rambouillet, used his newspaper *Koha Ditore* to denounce the KLA's post-war arrogance. It was a blistering *j'accuse* that mentioned neither the KLA nor Thaçi by name.

'I know how Kosovo's remaining Serbians and indeed Roma feel because I, along with nearly two million Albanians, was in exactly the same situation only ten weeks ago. I recognise their fear. It was shameful,' said Surroi, 'to discover that we Kosovo Albanians are also capable of such monstrous acts. To hold Serbs collectively guilty for what had happened in Kosovo was to betray the point of a decade of civil resistance, the setting up of a parallel society, and the war that had just come to an end. Such attitudes are fascist.'

Many Kosovo Albanians were wounded by the tone of the attack by Thaçi's former ally. The truth was that the revenge attacks were being carried out by a small minority; Albanians were not on the whole thirsting for blood. They were, however, largely indifferent to the Serb fate. The cities emptied of Serbs and this was accepted as the natural order of things. In some places Serbs maintained a presence, guarded, if they were lucky, by Kfor. In Mitrovica, in the north the town effectively split between Serb and Albanian communities, joined by a bridge patrolled by Kfor. It was not a happy situation but, to Thaçi, it did not signal the imminent arrival of fascism.

As far as he was concerned, his task was to demonstrate that Kosovo could be governed effectively by Kosovars. That was the first basic building block for independence. The reality, though, was that Kosovan sovereignty was distinctly limited – it had become a NATO and an EU protectorate. And his own team had no experience of running a country; it was not like running the underground state that had existed under the Serbs; it certainly wasn't anything like running a partisan army. The big moral task of creating a Kosovan national identity and finding a co-existence with the Serbs had to be subordinated to the everyday chores of ensuring electricity supply, registering cars and keeping a functioning health service.

Thaçi, say even his supporters, was overwhelmed by the detail. He concentrated instead on honouring the commitments to the international community.

'We delivered the fastest demobilisation in history,' he says. Zone by zone, established commanders emptied their arsenals and surrendered 12,000 automatic weapons and millions of rounds of ammunition. The only acceptable uniforms were those worn by the KPC, who would be entitled to 200 weapons, less than one gun for every national guardsman. This was not, however, the whole story. Some arms caches remained hidden. The definition of what constituted a hunting rifle was kept deliberately vague. Many hand guns ended up on the black market. Yet it was a genuine attempt to civilianise the province, to bring down the level of communal violence and to remove Kosovo's Wild West image.

Thaçi was working sixteen-hour days just to keep up with the pace of change. It wasn't just about the breakneck attempt to create the foundations of a modern state, but also a party of government – the PDK – that went beyond the dismembered KLA. The effort may have blinded him from a stark new reality: Kosovars, while recognising his extraordinary wartime role, did not much love him. He seemed remote. There was no one around Thaçi at that time to alert him to the realities of being a peacetime politician. His first instincts had been tactical: to lock out rivals from the provisional government, and to prove that he, not Ibrahim Rugova, was the natural source of authority.

Yet Rugova, who returned only in August from his comfortable Italian exile, still retained popularity in Kosovo. Thaçi's men underestimated not only the enduring myth of Rugova but the organisational power of the LDK. By the time of Thaçi's first democratic test, the municipal elections of October 2000, the LDK had established thirty-six regional offices involved in democracy education. It won twenty-one out of twenty-seven contested municipalities and 58 per cent of the popular vote. Thaçi's PDK managed only 27 per cent.

'I was stunned,' says Thaçi.

Why did we lose? Remember it was still very soon after the end of the war. We had no real party infrastructure in place. We were having massive power blackouts, so it was easy to blame us for this inefficiency, and to trust the LDK, which had communist roots and which seemed to many voters to be better equipped to run the country. Rather than young guys with guns. 'Don't worry,' they were saying, 'when war returns we will return Thaçi to power.'

That then became Thaçi's next giant task: to demonstrate that he had the skill to be a peacetime leader, the popular touch to win democratic legitimacy. And that he retained the talent that had served him so well since his early twenties: to turn setbacks into opportunity, to alchemise bad luck into good.

CHAPTER 9

TROUBLE IN MITROVICA

On a chilly March day in 2004, Thaçi's phone rang. He was in Washington DC but he might as well have been in a café on Rexhep Luci Street in the middle of Pristina; the news from Kosovo was passed on from hour to hour. Although his PDK party had been pushed aside in the 2000 municipal elections, and although he had been denied the premiership after the 2001 general election, Thaçi was still a pivotal player in Kosovan politics. So he travelled continually, understanding that Kosovan independence would only succeed if the would-be state remained close to the centre of international attention. Kosovo had been a model for the principle of liberal intervention, but now, following a change of US President, 9/11 and the invasion of Iraq, Kosovo was in danger of becoming a footnote. As a result, for several years, Thaçi's suitcase was rarely unpacked. He had to fight to keep Kosovo relevant. 'Hashim was a perpetual motion machine,' recalls one of his closest advisors.

The call that day jerked Thaçi back from the Potomac to the Ibar river. 'It was immediately clear to me, when I was told there was trouble in Mitrovica, I had to get the next flight back,' remembers Thaçi. It had been five years since the beginning of the NATO bombing campaign and the province, impatient to move forward, was brimming with frustration at UNMIK, the UN administrators. The Kosovo Albanians had been rescued by NATO, yet the international controllers seemed sluggish and corrupt. There was anger at perceived discrimination against KLA veterans and increasingly heated claims that UNMIK was delaying the issue of final status for Kosovo. The UN protectorate seemed to veer towards a permanent political status quo – not part of Serbia any more, but not an independent nation either.

The message to Thaçi did not surprise him; he had sensed for months that something was brewing. On 12 March, a grenade had exploded outside the house of President Rugova. No one was hurt but shortly afterwards there was another symbolic explosion: a homemade bomb planted near UNMIK headquarters. Every March, Kosovars would march to commemorate the NATO air war but this year organisers wanted to use the occasion to protest against UNMIK's arrest of KLA veterans on war crimes charges. That too went off peacefully – yet there was no mistaking the mounting anger, the feeling that the international community was ready to let Kosovo slip back into Serb control. Kosovo had been Bill Clinton's war; now George W. Bush was in charge. Bush ended up visiting Kosovo only once in his career, a fleeting trip to the US base; there was no attempt to meet the leaders of the emerging free state. In Pristina, there is a large bronze statue to Bill Clinton but there was none yet dedicated to Bush. The continuing tensions in Kosovo, five years on, merely demonstrated to some in the Bush administration that US involvement in nation-building was a lost cause.

'Trouble in Mitrovica' – what did that mean? The divided northern town was Kosovo's prime flashpoint. Historically it had a majority of Kosovo Albanians but most had been pushed southwards into the province by the war. When Kfor was put into place, it offered protection to the tens of thousands of Albanians returning to the town. They stayed south of the Ibar river, in houses battered by the war. The Serbs and Roma who had occupied their homes shifted north of the river. The bridge thus became a tense fault line, much like the Glienicke Bridge between West Berlin and communist East Germany. The French contingent of Kfor troops did not enforce the property rights of ethnic Albanians displaced from their homes in the north, nor did they control the border between Serbia and northern Kosovo. It was negligent, too, in challenging the Serbian hard men who had appointed themselves 'bridge-watchers' to stop Albanians crossing the river. Their mission was to keep things quiet and out of the headlines. Given that French officers tipped off Serbia during the bombing campaign, however, it was predictable that many Albanians believed that Paris was in cahoots with Belgrade. If Serbia succeeded in partitioning Kosovo, it could well be with the help of France.

As he sped towards Dulles airport, all these thoughts whirled through Thaçi's head. It would not take much to unravel the achievements of his war of independence. The reports trickling through to him were scanty, permeated with rumour. On the early evening of 16 March, six Kosovo Albanian boys, the youngest aged nine, had been walking along the northern bank of the Ibar river. It had been a long, hard winter and it was only the third hot day of the year. The snows had melted, the river was roaring. As they walked, some Serbs yelled insults from a nearby house. They threatened to let loose their barking dog. The young boys were terrified of the dogs and this, rather than a direct attack, may have prompted three of the boys to jump into the river. They were swept under the surface and drowned.

The Kosovan national broadcasters cranked up the incident and soon headmasters were urging their pupils to demonstrate against 'this hideous crime'. A crowd of a few hundred Albanians was stopped by police on the south side of the bridge, but a second group – up to a thousand – shoved their way through a cordon of riot police and made their way across a smaller footbridge to the Serb side of the river, determined to seek vengeance. There was a bloody confrontation; the two sides shot guns and hurled petrol bombs.

The French Kfor units stood aside. One of the Serbs killed in the showdown was the father of Dragan Spasovic, leader of the 'bridge-watchers'. The fatal shot was allegedly fired by an Albanian sniper. Hour by hour, the whole architecture of international control, Kfor and UNMIK, was falling apart at the first open resurgence of Balkan fury. Half a decade after the NATO war, the supposedly civilising mission of the peacekeepers appeared to be based on little more than empty phrases.

It was this, then, that Thaçi had to fight against. He understood better than most that KLA veterans felt marginalised and that young people, seeing nothing but a dead end, were leaving the country in droves. But if the war, his war, was to make sense, it had to lead to the de-balkanisation of the Balkans; he had to ease the Kosovo Albanians out of their resentment and towards an acceptance of a multi-ethnic democracy. The Ibar river was more than an unfortunate flare-up – it could start the rapid unravelling of a dream.

'The Mitrovica riots were doomed to spread,' says Thaçi. 'It was a Serb provocation to discredit the international order and force the partitioning of Kosovo.' When he arrived on the scene, he discovered that the crisis had developed its own dynamic. It was starting to look like a civil war. 'It was never organised ethnic violence,' he stresses. 'For the most part it was kids who had slipped out of school ready to attack anybody and anything, Roma too.'

Perhaps the most critical moment came when mobs turned on Serb Orthodox churches and shrines. 'During the whole war not a single church was burned,' says Thaçi, 'and yet five years on we had churches being torched. It was devastating and unacceptable – the victims of violence were becoming the perpetrators of violence. So I said to the crowds: "If you attack churches, you attack Kosovo itself."'

But attack they did. Sometimes Kfor fought them back. NATO intelligence warned that a crowd of angry Albanians was intent on sacking the symbolically important Serb Orthodox church compound at Gračanica – a move that would surely have prompted Serb troops to roll back into the province. Kfor had withdrawn its heavy weaponry from the area years before and could not possibly have defended the monastery and its fourteenth-century frescos. Instead, under a doughty Norwegian commander, Kfor held an approach road near Čaglavica to block the march. An Italian contingent, meanwhile, fought off protestors who were hurling Molotov cocktails over the ancient walls of Visoki Dečani monastery. In a church near Peć, fifteen members of the Kosovo Police Service and six US policemen tried to save thirty Serbs from thousands of demonstrators who were determined to set it ablaze. An American policewoman warned a bellowing stick-waving Kosovar to put down his weapon – and then shot him in the chest.

More typical was the experience of a German Kfor unit in Prizren, who were supposed to be guarding the Monastery of the Holy Archangels. Outnumbered, the soldiers packed their bags and negotiated their own free passage.

In all, thirty-six Orthodox religious sites were destroyed. The paralysis of the German and other Kfor contingents was down to chaotic organisation. Twelve NATO members sent troops but attached caveats to their deployment. Each followed orders from their national capitals and down the national chain of command. The result: Kfor acted chiefly out of self-defence, cowed and suppressed. Towards the end of the riots, NATO had to send in an American admiral from his Naples base to take command.

Across the province, the depth of the opposition to the UN presence had become clear. In Pristina, their vehicles had been stoned. UN buildings were attacked, sometimes because Serbs had sought protection there. 'I was in UNMIK headquarters,' remembers the former UN advisor Carne Ross. 'We were told there was an angry crowd approaching. There was a panicky evacuation ... the UN and NATO lost control.' The fact was that UNMIK felt it had to act through the Kosovo Prime Minister Bajram Rexhepi, and called on him to dismiss any minister or mayor who had condoned the violence. That would, however, have undermined Rexhepi's power base and in the overwrought mood of the moment would have made him a target. In theory, UNMIK's head, the so-called Special Representative of the UN Secretary-General, had the authority to fire people himself, but never did so.

It was not just Thaçi who came back to fill the vacuum. Rexhepi had personally gone to the Čaglavica road to calm the protestors. Ramush Haradinaj, a former KLA commander, had urged the crowd not to attack the Dečani monastery. Even so, thirty-one people, mostly Kosovo Albanians, had been killed in the rioting, 950 – including 184 security personnel – had been injured, and almost 4,000 buildings had been destroyed. And President Rugova – who according to some reports had warned UNMIK of a possible attack two weeks in advance – remained silent.

'He just stayed at home,' says Thaçi. The riots were thus not just a collapse in international governance but also of presidential leadership. Rugova had only won the support of Thaçi's PDK in the February 2002 coalition talks in return for bartering away many of his most important presidential duties. His role had shrunk and he was sending out distorted messages, at odds with his image as a figure of Gandhian tolerance. Asked by a UNMIK official if he considered it safe for Serbs to come to Pristina, he clumsily replied that he saw no reason for them to come since 'they have everything they need in Gračanica'. The reference was to the Orthodox Church and his point was that only Serb priests could count on protection.

Thaçi for his part denies that the riots were staged or that they served some sinister purpose. Yet the political outcome of the bloody clashes worked to Thaçi's advantage; they had brought Kosovo a step closer to independence. When Chris Patten, the EU Commissioner for External Relations, came, he warned the leadership that Kosovo ran the risk of becoming a 'gangster pariah state' unless it got control over its extremists. But that was not a typical public statement. Rather, the Bush administration, previously cool to the Kosovo 'project', expressed support for the PDK leadership rather than criticising it. And the sheer force of the violence made inevitable a reappraisal of the international community's over-cautious strategy of edging towards some form of autonomy. The frustration was obvious: only full-blown independence would bring calm.

Back in December 2001, an abrasive German diplomat called Michael Steiner had been appointed Special Representative to the Secretary-General (SRSG). He had in effect been exiled to Pristina because he had politically disgraced himself as Chancellor Gerhard Schröder's high-flying foreign policy advisor. Feared for his explosive temperament, he had launched into a foul-mouthed tirade against a Russian security guard at Moscow airport. But he still enjoyed the Chancellor's confidence – and he acted accordingly in Kosovo, as if he had full authority not only to administer the UN protectorate but determine its future. His guiding principle was 'Standards before Status', whereby Kosovo's leaders had to tick eight boxes, all major reforms, before negotiations could even begin. These measures included introducing and implementing the rule of law, setting up functioning democratic institutions, dialogue with Belgrade, the safe return of displaced people and guaranteed rights for all non-Albanian minorities.

While Steiner made these legitimate demands with his customary *brio*, he failed to hand over serious responsibility to Kosovo that allowed its leaders to implement the measures. His modus operandi was to infantilise Kosovo, to put it in a position where it was constantly being judged while being left in the dark as to what was supposed to happen next. As Carne Ross puts it: 'Standards before Status was a constant state of coitus interruptus.' That may have been fine with the otherwise-engaged Bush team, but it was always going to stoke up dangerous levels of impatience. Inevitably, the UN was seen by the Kosovars less as a protector and more and more as a restrainer.

Steiner, described by a former UNMIK official as possessing the manner of a 'choleric schoolmaster', symbolised the Kosovan dilemma: it had exchanged brutal Serb domination for a kind of heavy-handed colonial administration.

It took an outbreak of sustained violence to get world attention again and restore the momentum towards independence. Thaçi, who had so artfully nudged NATO into a war against Serbia in 1999, understood better than anyone else in the game how to exploit anger for political gain.

The UN's answer to the spring riots of 2004 was Søren Jessen-Petersen, a shrewd Dane and former professional footballer who had worked with the UNHCR in Bosnia and Croatia. Kofi Annan had selected him as special representative because he was unlikely to be hoodwinked by Belgrade and because, unlike Steiner, he understood the need for strategic patience in the Balkans. He was ready to put independence at the top of the agenda rather than make the province jump through a seemingly endless series of hoops. He told Annan: 'Mitrovica has made it very clear that we have to move at an accelerated pace. I needed to hold out the prospect of further hope. That would be my goal – to prepare the Kosovars for the inevitable outcome, which was independence.'

When his appointment was announced, publisher Veton Surroi – writing in his paper *Koha Ditore* – warned the Dane about the limitations of his post. 'You'll have god-like status in Kosovo, but no real power: no army, no central bank, no prosecutor, no constitution and no friends … the fact that you are omnipotent with a UN mandate does not add up to much.' Jessen-Petersen had come up with a formula which he thought he could implement even within the constraints set out with such acid accuracy by Surroi.

The Dane would persuade the international community to lower its expectations for Kosovo, persuade the mediocre political class to show willing, and declare the project to be a victory. That in turn would allow a quick forward shift towards some kind of independence and a scaling down of the international presence. Rather than a rigid 'Standards before Status' regimen, he would usher in Standards-Lite and a faster pace of change.

The approach was guided in part by Kai Eide, an experienced Norwegian diplomat who had been coaxed by Kofi Annan into writing a report about what was going wrong in Kosovo. It was frank about the failings of the international community. Kfor in particular was seen as being a serial bungler. 'It failed to read the mood of the majority population,' wrote Eide, 'its frustration and impatience. It also failed to understand the potential for extremists to mobilise support for ethnic violence and the vulnerability of minorities, in particular the Serb population.' Kosovo, he concluded, was 'characterised by growing dissatisfaction and frustration. Our current policies are seen as static and unable to face up to the real problems facing it.' Thus, Eide's report enabled the opening of the issue of the status of Kosovo.

Jessen-Petersen's first task, having arrived three months after the riots, was to bring to justice the ringleaders. By the end of October 2004, more than 100 cases had been completed; eighty-five led to conviction. Many more should have been imprisoned but all too often witnesses were intimidated and courts were instructed not to convict on hearsay. Some culprits picked up medical exemption chits after developing improbable diseases. Others feigned mental disorders. Jessen-Petersen was convinced: Kosovo's limbo status did not encourage the rule of law. The Kosovan government also dedicated a budget to repair damaged religious property – millions of Kosovo taxpayer funds were spent in the subsequent years repairing the damage done by the March riots.

Thaçi understood that the riots had handed him a strategic advantage. An eruption of Kosovo Albanian anger could be used as a veto against any end-status option that he disapproved of. The international community was growing tired of its expensive deployment in Kosovo; it needed a semblance of stability before it could wind down.

What better way of sedating Kosovo than to introduce yet another Scandinavian administrator. UNMIK signed up the former chief of police of Copenhagen – and expert on crowd control who knew how to manoeuvre around police bureaucracies – to overhaul policing in Kosovo. Kai Vittrup's starting point: local Kosovan police, not international units, had to be in the frontline of communal clashes.

The internationals were retreating inside Kfor's fortified bubbles, cut off from most useful intelligence and blind to potential flashpoints. Vittrup's aim was community policing – crime prevention councils in all municipalities – and faster response to trouble. He raised police salaries and, by the autumn of 2005, all thirty-two police stations in the province were firmly in the charge of the local constabularies, rather than foreign officers who needed interpreters to read road signs.

Vittrup understood that when the internationals eventually left the province, some of the Kosovan policemen – however well trained – would fall under the spell of their clans. But this was an inevitable pitfall of erecting new Western-style institutions in a largely unreformed polity. Nation-building was the task of a generation and most Western administrators calculated that Kosovo would be a relatively short-term mission, unable to compete for major resources from abroad at a time when the US and its allies were facing a financially ruinous war in Iraq.

Jessen-Petersen made a point when he arrived in Pristina of paying courtesy calls, not only on government officials, Rugova and Rexhepi, but also on Hashem Thaçi at PDK headquarters and Ramush Haradinaj. He lectured all of them on the dangers of endemic corruption and how, in his view, it was holding back the political and economic development of Kosovo. Thaçi took the criticism on board but knew that there was no serious way Scandinavian standards of probity could be applied or enforced in the Balkans, least of all to a society that was in limbo. The economy needs to work to the benefit of all, that was for sure – and that had to go hand in hand with the shaping of a sense of nationhood.

For Thaçi, none of the other political players seemed to fully grasp how to galvanise the nation. The feud with Rugova was beyond healing. Rugova had declared that Thaçi would never become Prime Minister as long as he was alive – an unfortunate ultimatum that was to run its course faster than anyone expected. By January 2006, the chain-smoking, heavy-drinking professor was dead of lung cancer. As for Ramush Haradinaj – a former KLA commander restlessly seeking a new post-war role – he had founded his AAK party as a counterweight to Thaçi, though he never managed to grow the AAK beyond the region of Dukagjini. The man known as Rambo could not stand the fact that Thaçi, always more of a politician than a frontline fighter, was recognised by many in the US establishment as the face of Kosovo's future.

Both were confident political operators. Thaçi derived his authority from his upbringing in the Drenica Valley, the seat of Kosovo's historic resistance to the Ottomans and the Serbs. Haradinaj came from a more traditional background in the Peja region but had worked for many years as a doorman in bars in Switzerland. Yet the force of Haradinaj's resentment at Thaçi's political slickness, and Thaçi's frustration at not being the leader of the nation, ensured that they would be trapped in a venomous arch-rivalry.

Thaçi was furious when, after the election in October 2004, Haradinaj proposed to Rugova that they put together a government excluding the PDK. It was conceived as an anti-Thaçi coalition, a bond born out of personal antipathy to a man they both viewed as dangerous. Thaçi protested to Jessen-Petersen but the Dane must have known that Haradinaj's tenure would be short. He was about to land in court for alleged war crimes. So Jessen-Petersen told Thaçi that the election had been free and fair and that Haradinaj and Rugova could form a credible majority. Thaçi respected the decision, calmed down and realised that the coalition was a back-handed compliment: it was recognition that he was the most powerful man on the stage.

Despite Haradinaj's personal ambition and thirst for recognition, his short time as Prime Minister was purposeful and energetic. Together with the UN, he worked out a programme of what could realistically be achieved in terms of building a modern infrastructure in the fledgling state. The priority was schools for the rapidly expanding population and the modernisation of the roads. 'A lot of it was bluster, stamping his foot to establish authority,' recalls a former colleague of Haradinaj. But it was a welcome contrast to Rugova's vagueness and lack of concentration. Those who had been in the KLA understood the approach – he was trying to run government as if he were motivating troops. 'He's a bit of a performer,' said a former minister. 'But the message was not unreasonable

– he was telling us that we had to start showing concrete results for ourselves if we were going to accelerate progress towards independence.'

The government lasted barely three months before the indictment arrived from the International Criminal Tribunal for the former Yugoslavia in The Hague. In March 2005, Jessen-Petersen called him in for an early-morning meeting to tell him about the charges. It was a tense meeting since none of those present – among them the local NATO commander, General Yves de Kermabon – could be sure that he would give himself up voluntarily. Would he resist arrest, mobilise his supporters? In the event, Haradinaj went quietly, promising to resign after briefing his Cabinet.

The next morning, German Kfor troops sent a plane to pick him up and fly him to The Hague. No handcuffs were needed. And while Haradinaj settled into his cell, Jessen-Petersen was singing his praises to the Kosovars in the hope that this would defuse any angry protests against UNMIK. After a couple of months, spent mainly in the prison gym, Haradinaj was provisionally released and allowed to return to Kosovo providing he did not play a role in Kosovo's political life.

The problem for the prosecutors was, predictably, the lack of witnesses to testify against him. Prosecutor Carla Del Ponte said Haradinaj's allies were scaring people away from travelling to The Hague. 'If I have no witnesses appearing in court,' she said, 'I will be obliged to withdraw this indictment.' Sure enough, by February 2008, Haradinaj was acquitted on all thirty-seven charges. A former Western prosecutor with the ICTY stated that the 'cases against Haradinaj and other Kosovo Albanians were weak; they were launched as a quid pro quo for the Serbian delivery of Milošević to the Hague tribunal.

The court case neutered Haradinaj; illness neutered Rugova. But Thaçi did not make a power grab. Rather, he decided that setting up an organised, structured opposition would serve him better. 'The Americans had come to me', says Thaçi, 'and urged me to join a grand coalition. I told them no – I want to stay in opposition.'

On a personal level, Thaçi had to answer the question: why am I not being universally seen as a credible leader? Why is it Rugova who is seen as a natural leader, the man for peace, while I'm the man people call in if there's war? Thaçi had been reading Churchill's works and had taken on board that there were times when it was better to resist the Balkan urge to chase after power whenever it was offered.

> We had to be able to win on the basis of strong ideas. So I organised a shadow Cabinet, on the basis of how the British opposition works, with each member of the team taking up a departmental portfolio. We needed to govern differently, to prevent constructive alternatives. There had to be a daily agenda, a weekly meeting of the shadow Cabinet.

Kosovo was beginning slowly to turn round, to display some of its potential. No surprise, perhaps, given the sheer volume of Western assistance. But it needed more, thought Thaçi: a concrete, detailed perspective of independence if investment was to flow in; a legal system that would not collapse when the international community eventually withdrew. And leadership at all levels of society. Those were the tasks Thaçi set himself. He had plunged into politics as a young man fighting dictatorship. He was still callow when he negotiated with some of the world's heavyweights at Rambouillet. 'Now was the time', he recalls, 'to step back and study the art of strategic patience.'

CHAPTER 10

OUT OF THE TWILIGHT ZONE

On the screen of Martti Ahtisaari's mobile phone, the caller's name jumped out: Kofi Annan. The former Finnish President assumed the UN chief was ringing for information about a peace deal he was shaping between Indonesia and the breakaway province of Aceh. Ahtisaari, perhaps one of the world's most experienced peace brokers, had spent the balmy Finnish summer of 2005 working out the details of a settlement. It was about to be signed. But, for Annan, a deal struck simply meant that the formidable Finn was now available for a new task. And the priority was now status talks on Kosovo.

'I replied that I was indeed available but that, as he knew, I wasn't really seeking any new work,' says Ahtisaari. 'The implementation of the Aceh peace agreement was only just beginning.' Indeed, Ahtisaari's desk was covered with folders designated Aceh, Horn of Africa, Namibia. He had started his working life as a provincial school teacher in Finland, and that's what his study resembled now – a teacher's table strewn with the unmarked homework of his pupils.

For Ahtisaari, though, Kosovo was unfinished business, and Annan knew as much.

In the final days of the 1999 bombing of Serbia, Ahtisaari had firmly faced down Slobodan Milošević. Although the Finn had formed a firm bond with the Russian negotiator Viktor Chernomyrdin, he had an acute sense of how Serbian nationalists and their Russian backers could stamp on Kosovar freedom once NATO lost interest. He had watched as the Russians spread out their maps of the Balkans on the tables of the Finnish presidential palace, in the Hall of Mirrors, the former throne room of the Czar. It looked to Ahtisaari as if the Russians might have forged a secret bargain with the Serbs to create a Russian sector in northern Kosovo. Perhaps they were ready to partition the province. Thanks to Ahtisaari's smooth-talking, Moscow had accepted the idea of a Kfor presence. But nothing was certain: nationalists in the Russian Duma had turned on Chernomyrdin and, by the beginning of 2000, a former KGB officer called Vladimir Putin had been installed in the Kremlin.

Five years on, it was clear to Ahtisaari that Putin still regarded Kosovan independence as a humiliating setback. It showed the world that Moscow was too feeble to support its allies. Ahtisaari's view was that it would have been better to push for full independence earlier, rather than let the issue fester.

Annan had commissioned the Norwegian diplomat Kai Eide to compile a new report into whether the time was right to start political talks on the status of Kosovo. Although the report wasn't officially presented to the UN Security Council until October 2005, Annan already knew which direction it was going to take when he rang Ahtisaari. The analysis wasn't all doom and gloom. Progress was being made, it said, in health and education, but there was little reconciliation between Kosovo's communities with the rule of law and the independence of

LEFT Most of Hashim Thaçi's family photos were burned when Serbian police torched his old family home. Here he is as a sixteen-year-old, with an old family hunting gun, in his family home in Burojë. Behind him are portraits of medieval Albanian hero Gjergj Kastrioti Skanderbeg, Shote and Azem Galica as well as Ismail Qemali and Isa Boletini. *Hashim Thaçi archive*

BELOW Hashim Thaçi in a KLA uniform, 1998. After years as a student leader and a member of a clandestine guerrilla group, in 1999 Thaçi was named as the political director of the Kosovo Liberation Army. He wore the uniform of the KLA during his time in Kosovo.

Hashim Thaçi archive

ABOVE LEFT Serbian arrest warrant, 1997. During the Milošević years, Serbia issued several arrest warrants for Thaçi, accusing him of various acts of subversion towards the Serbian state. These warrants are still active today. *Hashim Thaçi archive*

ABOVE RIGHT Signing ceremony of peace accords in Paris, 1999. The Kosovo delegation signed the Rambouillet Agreement after weeks of negotiations with Serbia and the international community. The Serbs, however, refused to sign the peace deal, which prompted NATO intervention in Kosovo and the bombing of Serbia. Hashim Thaçi, then thirty years old, led the Kosovo delegation during the talks and was one of the principal signatories of the treaty. *© AP Photo/Pool, John Schults*

Meeting Prime Minister Tony Blair, 1999. Britain's Prime Minister Tony Blair met Hashim Thaçi, the political leader of the Kosovan Liberation Army, during the European Union summit in Cologne, Germany, on 3 June 1999, days after Serbia accepted full withdrawal of forces from Kosovo.
© AP Photo/Adam Butler

With President Clinton in Kosovo, 2009. Thaçi met President Clinton for the first time in 1999 during the war in Kosovo; the two would later meet again many times. President Clinton remained a steadfast supporter of NATO bombing as well as of an independent Kosovo. In 2009, President Clinton visited Pristina, where he and Prime Minister Thaçi unveiled a statue of Clinton on a boulevard bearing the former US President's name. *© Astrit Ibrahimi*

With President Shimon Peres, 2006. Hashim Thaçi met the leaders of Israel several times. His first visit was in 2006, as head of the Kosovan opposition, when he met President Shimon Peres as well as defence and foreign ministers. *Hashim Thaçi archive*

Declaring Kosovan independence. On 17 February 2008, three months after winning his first national elections and becoming Prime Minister, Hashim Thaçi declared Kosovo an independent and sovereign state. The declaration was approved by the representatives of the people, though most Serb local MPs boycotted the session of the Kosovo Parliament. Independence was declared a full decade after the fateful Rambouillet Agreement collapsed, which propelled Thaçi onto the international stage. Ten years later, most UN members now recognise Kosovo as an independent republic.
© Astrit Ibrahimi

Unveiling the new nation, 2008. The EU's foreign policy chief, the Spaniard Javier Solana, was among the first to visit Kosovo after independence. Hashim Thaçi unveiled the new flag, which was designed not to offend any ethnicity and thus used the colours of the European Union and the outline of Kosovan territory. © Astrit Ibrahimi

Visiting President Bush and President Sarkozy, 2008. In the year following Kosovo's declaration of independence, Thaçi launched a tour of bilateral visits to key capitals to push for international recognition of the newly independent Kosovo. In July 2008, President George W. Bush hosted both the then President of Kosovo Fatmir Sejdiu and Prime Minister Thaçi. Months later, President Sarkozy also hosted Prime Minister Thaçi in the Élysée Palace. *Élysée Palace press service/Hashim Thaçi archive*

Thaçi in a trilateral meeting with Turkey's Prime Minister Recep Tayyip Erdoğan and Albania's Prime Minister Edi Rama in Kosovo, 2013. As Prime Minister, Thaçi hosted his Turkish and Albanian counterparts in the ancient Kosovan city of Prizren, which has a sizeable Turkish minority. Thaçi has developed a close relationship with Erdoğan, now Turkey's President, while Turkey became one of key supporters of Kosovo's independence and its quest for international recognition. © *Astrit Ibrahimi*

In 2010, Prime Minister Thaçi visited New York and Washington DC. In New York, he spoke at the UN Security Council on the need to allow Kosovo to become a UN member. In Washington, Thaçi was hosted by Vice-President Joe Biden. During a tour at the White House, Biden remarked to the media pool that Prime Minister Thaçi 'is Kosovo's George Washington'.

© *Astrit Ibrahimi*

Hosting Chancellor Merkel in Kosovo, 2011. Germany was one of the strongest supporters of Kosovo's independence, though their relationship with the former KLA leaders was sometimes more fraught. Chancellor Merkel visited Kosovo in 2011 to support efforts by Prime Minister Thaçi for an agreement with Serbia. © *Astrit Ibrahimi*

Thaçi's presidential inauguration, 2016. Hashim Thaçi became Kosovo's fifth democratically elected President in 2016. He took over the position from Atifete Jahjaga, who was the first female President in the Western Balkans. The inauguration attracted delegations from over fifty countries, including heads of states, as well as the Vatican and the Organisation of Islamic Cooperation. The festivities were also marked by protests from the opposition, who disapproved of Thaçi's agreements with Serbia. © *Astrit Ibrahimi*

President Thaçi and Pope Francis. Thaçi met Pope Francis several times for private audiences, amid rumours that behind the scenes the Holy See was supporting the dialogue between Kosovo and Serbia. Kosovo recently played an active part in the promotion of global interfaith dialogue through the Interfaith Kosovo initiative supported by Thaçi, which brought together hundreds of faith leaders in Kosovo as well as Nobel Peace laureates. Thaçi has stated that he 'remains dedicated to the process of reconciliation with Serbia'. © *Astrit Ibrahimi*

In 2014, Thaçi's PDK was trailing badly in the polls and he launched a whirlwind tour and started using Facebook to attract young voters. In the end, the PDK overwhelmingly won their third mandate, and Kosovans got used to seeing more of Thaçi's closest family. © *Astrit Ibrahimi*

the judiciary. None of this came as a shock to those in the international community who had been keeping an eye on the province. It was Eide's conclusion, though, that rattled them out of hibernation: 'There is never any ideal moment for starting the process of future status, but I believe the time has come.'

The core of Eide's analysis was that Kosovo, if denied the prospect of moving forward more quickly, would slip backwards. Ahtisaari not only agreed, he went further. A stagnant Kosovo would end up, he thought, as a frozen conflict – the kind that Vladimir Putin would favour to block the West from gaining an advantage – and he didn't believe in them. 'There's not a single conflict in this world that can't be solved,' says Ahtisaari, who after his term as Finnish President went on to establish a highly effective mediation centre.

So Ahtisaari accepted Annan's offer – on two conditions. First, he was not prepared to be a neutral mediator. There was no moral equivalence between the Milošević regime and the Kosovars. 'What Milošević did to the Kosovars simply cannot be ignored. And it was not just a question of Milošević – he had been supported by the whole state apparatus,' argued Ahtisaari. 'The whole of Serbia was responsible.' To deny this, he said, to attempt to please both parties, would have meant abandoning Western values. 'Then, a solution would never be found.'

Annan thus had to realise that the Finn's destination was full independence for Kosovo. 'The essential thing,' he said later, 'was to be able to create an agreement that was so good that the Serbs too felt they could live with it.'

The second condition was that he could hand-pick his own team, starting with a very able Austrian diplomat called Albert Rohan who was to become his deputy. Ahtisaari's first question to Rohan was whether the Austrian was in favour of full Kosovan independence.

'I replied that I was. It was typical Martti – he wanted to know for certain that we were singing from the same hymn sheet.'[20]

The core team was put together – two Finns, Kai Sauer and Anna Elfring, the UN communications chief Hua Jiang – and a set of rooms was found in the heart of Vienna. In November 2005, Ahtisaari met the Contact Group for dinner at Nora's in Washington, and it was plain that the US would be watching his back. The ex-NATO ambassador Nicholas Burns, newly appointed under-secretary of state for political affairs, would deal with the UN and with Russia. Frank Wisner, a veteran ambassador who had worked together with the Finn on Namibia, came into the mix and immediately brought him up to date. Britain was onside, he explained, Germany was nervous about accelerating towards independence, France was historically pro-Serb. Russia, according to Wisner, 'did not oppose and did not indicate that it would oppose the outcome of a negotiation properly conducted'.

Moscow, however, was concerned that an independent Kosovo would set a precedent for many disputed territories on its borders, including Nagorno-Karabakh.

China, meanwhile, saw Kosovo as a purely European problem, but one which, if settled with too much triumphalism, could stir up Tibetan separatists. Neither Russia nor China, then, were in a hurry. What everyone could agree on were three principles for the conduct of the talks: Kosovo should not be partitioned, borders should not be redrawn in a way that would encourage the emergence of a Greater Albania and the present unstable status quo could not be accepted.

As far as the Americans were concerned, there was one stand-out Kosovan politician in terms of resisting moves towards a Greater

---

20 Katri Merikallio and Tapani Ruokanen, *The Mediator: A Biography of Martti Ahtisaari* (2015), p. 332

Albania that would take in not only the Albanian republic but also the Kosovars and the Albanians of Macedonia. That man was Thaçi. Six months after the ending of the NATO bombing campaign, violence had erupted between the Slavs and the Albanians in Macedonia. The Albanians there claimed that they were almost as badly persecuted as the Albanians of Kosovo: they represented a quarter of the Macedonian population yet they were discriminated against in the civil service and their schools and hospitals were under-funded. There was a privately funded Albanian-language university in Tetovo, but no state-funded access to higher education. This resentment was channelled into the so-called National Liberation Army, made up of radicalised Macedonian Albanians and KLA veterans. Guns were smuggled across the border by the victorious KLA. Macedonian state forces started to crack down. The aim of the rebels was to make common cause with the Albanians in the Preševo Valley and break away, join forces with a free Kosovo and perhaps enter a union with the Albanian state.

Thaçi, however, saw that the redrawing of the Balkans' borders would bring chaos, a Serb counter-attack, and would ultimately cost Kosovo all of its international support. He had been told as much by the Americans. Despite his own close ties to the Albanian state, he understood that a Greater Albania was 'a romantic dream – not a practical way of dealing with the world'. NATO had gone to war to free the Kosovo Albanians, he told the Macedonian rebels on a fire-fighting mission, 'from a discredited and destabilising Serb dictatorship. It would not go to war to sort out domestic discrimination. We could not expect that NATO would intervene every time an Albanian in the Balkans raised an AK-47.'

That was a political risk for Thaçi and it was recalled by Contact Group members as they weighed up who could lead Kosovo into independence. His standing during the bombing campaign had been measured against his ability to make the KLA look like credible allies. But his efforts in Macedonia showed another dimension to the man. 'For some of us, the penny dropped,' recalls a Western diplomat involved in Balkan politics at the time. 'He helped defuse tensions in the neighbouring countries and then eased the way towards the ceasefire and amnesty deal with the Albanian rebels in Macedonia. That earned him respect.'

Known as the Ohrid Agreement, the Macedonian state agreed to open up to their Albanian citizens and give them more security. The accord narrowly sidestepped what could have been a vicious civil war and a new regional flare-up. It was a big, if under-sung, achievement in the early days of the Bush administration at a time when it was keen to move on to bigger geopolitical issues and leave behind what they saw as Clinton's messy Balkan legacy. The fact that Thaçi played his role in reining in the rebels was remembered by the Bush team when it returned to Kosovan dilemmas four years later.

Although some Europeans were sceptical about Thaçi – unsure whether he was merely a good war leader and too divisive at home – the Americans had him marked as someone who could work with the international community. This became particularly clear when Ibrahim Rugova died in January 2006. The Bush team had not thought much of him; there was too much of the Parisian Left Bank intellectual about him. 'Stubborn, docile and ultimately irrelevant' was one harsh judgement from a US official. The Bush administration sent only the US Secretary of the Department of Housing to the funeral, Alphonso Jackson, and his main contribution to the ceremony was to mispronounce Rugova's name during a short tribute.

Hundreds of thousands had gathered to see the President's body carried on a gun carriage to his resting place on Pristina's Martyrs' Hill. Some KLA veterans had objected to him sharing space with the main guerrilla fighters buried there: they remembered a different Rugova. Not the mild-mannered professor-statesman but someone who, in their recall, had ducked out of critical moments on the road to independence. His nervous, smiling encounter with Milošević, his comfortable exile in Rome during the final weeks of the NATO bombardment, his slow return to the homeland after the bombing stopped.

The duel with Thaçi had become a constant feature of the Kosovan political scene. Rugova had returned to power in 2002, elected by Parliament, and again in 2005, while Thaçi, who considered himself the province's true liberator, stayed in the cold. In his funeral tribute to Rugova, the head of European Union diplomacy Javier Solana declared: 'It is a cruel irony of history that he left at the moment when he was most needed, the very moment when he was expected to provide leadership in helping to decide the future status of Kosovo.' It was the week that the status talks were supposed to begin.

Thaçi had visited Rugova the previous October; the last moment that he saw his arch-rival up close before his death. Rugova had lost his hair after gruelling chemotherapy for his lung cancer, the therapy administered by US military doctors. He could manage barely a croak. If Rugova had any residual political power, it was ebbing away fast.

Thaçi understood the symbolic significance of Rugova's approaching death. He would soon be the leader of an independent state, one that would have to project strength not infirmity. It took the funeral to convince the West that Thaçi was no longer the young firebrand of the Rambouillet conference. Then, he had been politically gauche and had allowed his self-doubt to show. True, he had ultimately persuaded the West that it should deploy the world's strongest alliance to back a small rebel army; the result had been a good one for Thaçi but it had been a close-run thing.

Now Thaçi's challenge was even more complex – he had to make the international community understand that the long-term peace and stability of the Balkans hinged on a Kosovo that was fully sovereign, rather than a limbo-state.

Ahtisaari looked askance at the Kosovo unity team. He didn't see much unity. There was Fatmir Sejdiu, who had replaced Rugova, Agim Çeku, the former KLA chief who was now Prime Minister, Assembly speaker Kolë Berisha, the publisher Veton Surroi, and Thaçi. It was as close to a ruling class as Kosovo could muster. They were bound by an absolute conviction that they would never accept 'autonomy', a return to Serbia's constantly rolled-out offer of limited self-rule, rather than sovereignty. They wanted nothing less than full-blooded independence. Otherwise, though, they were not a coherent team; their negotiating expertise had improved since Rambouillet, but they were a collection of strong-willed and very different individuals.

'They hated each other's guts,' concedes Ahtisaari, 'and at the end they hated mine too.' The Finn remained baffled by Thaçi: 'Sometimes I didn't know what to make of him.'[21] But out of the unity team, it was Thaçi who had learned most about the ways of the world, the geopolitical game. Everything that had happened since Rambouillet had been a crash course in Realpolitik. He understood that the US was in a hurry – Kosovo was a distraction from the fires in the Middle East – and that the Serbs (this time without the lurking presence of Milošević) had to be presented as the obstructer. The Serbian tactics were predictable: they would spread fear among those European countries with separatist problems of their own. And Belgrade would do what it could to make the Serbs of northern Kosovo look as if they were being persecuted by ex-KLA hoodlums. 'It was inevitable that I would become the butt of

---

21 David L. Phillips, *Liberating Kosovo*, p. 166

Serb propaganda as the process wore on,' says Thaçi. 'Destroying my reputation has been part of their plan all along.'

Ahtisaari reckoned that since the two sides were so far apart, he should concentrate on the end result and work backwards. So, irrespective of the final status of Kosovo, the two sides should at least agree on the rights of minorities, on local self-government and the protection of cultural sites – all matters that touched directly on the lives of Kosovan Serbs. The endgame had to be a secure, multi-ethnic Kosovo in which democracy, human rights and the rule of law would be internationally guaranteed. This was not an outcome with which Russia, as a Contact Group member, or Serbia could disagree. There were other areas of common ground among the Contact Group and Ahtisaari tried to build on those too. On these, both the Kosovo Albanians and the Serbs had to be ready for compromise.

The Kosovar leadership would have to create the right conditions for the return of refugees; those Serbs who remained in the province had to be given a large degree of self-governance in their municipalities. The Serbian language would become official, despite being spoken by only 5 per cent of the population in Kosovo. Ahtisaari was in effect asking Thaçi and his colleagues to break with the Balkan tradition of winner-takes-all. In order to win the greater prize of independence, it had to be ready to share its state with non-Albanians. In return, the international community would keep a strong civilian and military presence to make sure the eventual deal would be properly implemented. And all sides should be ready to cooperate with the International Criminal Tribunal for the former Yugoslavia.

Serbia, in other words, should be shown that cooperation was in its interests; it might end up losing Kosovo, but it would secure a Serbian cultural presence within it. Ahtisaari's fellow Finn, the EU commissioner for enlargement Olli Rehn, held out the prospect of the West Balkans – including Kosovo and Serbia – treading the path towards European membership. If Serbia could turn away from the likes of its ultra-nationalist Radical Party – which still revered Slobodan Milošević, even as he sat in a Hague prison cell awaiting trial – then it could become part of the modern world.

It wasn't ever going to be easy. It was just a question, calculated Ahtisaari, of spelling out to Belgrade and to Moscow that there was no choice. The Finn knew what he was up against. His visit to Serbian Prime Minister Vojislav Koštunica was almost as frosty as his encounter with Milošević six years earlier. Koštunica's office was a short walk from the Defence Ministry and the state broadcasting centre hit by the NATO bombardment of Belgrade in 1999. The buildings were still scorched ruins, a statement of Serbian contempt for the actions of the Western alliance. Koštunica was direct with Ahtisaari: he was ready to offer Kosovo 'more than autonomy' but never independence. The Finnish mediator matched the premier's bluntness. 'You have lost Kosovo,' he said, 'now the question is how best to clean up the mess left by Milošević. In my opinion it would succeed best under your management.' The meeting came to an abrupt end.

'He wanted to be the hero who fought bravely for a united father-land until the very end,' recalled Ahtisaari later. For Koštunica, as for Milošević, Kosovo was above all a way of consolidating his own leader-ship. The grievances of Kosovo Serbs were more useful to him than their contentment. Serbian politics had become more encrusted after Milošević (he died in custody in 2006), not more open to change.

Ahtisaari had higher hopes of the Serb President Boris Tadić. Koštunica was born in 1944, Tadić in 1958. It was reasonable to count on generational change in dealing with Kosovo. But even though Tadić was keen for Serbia to join the EU, Tadić too stressed that Kosovo belonged to Serbia and the Serbs.

Under the circumstances, Ahtisaari thought it was better to wait until after the over-heated Serbian election in January 2007 before unrolling his plan. Before the election it would have been electoral suicide for a Serb politician to admit that Kosovo was lost. After the election, there might be some wiggle room. Thaçi thought this was a naive hope – 'things had gone too far along the nationalist path in Belgrade' – and sure enough the clear winner of the election was the stubbornly chauvinist Radical Party of Tomislav Nikolić. The key positions in government continued to be held by loyalists of Koštunica and Tadić – but nothing was going to move without the say-so of the Radicals, least of all concessions on Kosovo.

Ahtisaari flew to Belgrade in February 2007 and handed over the 100-page plan, his road map that would turn Kosovo into a European society. It didn't mention 'independence', but every page made it clear that, after a transitional phase supervised by the international community, Kosovo would gain statehood. Ahtisaari did not expect to be hugged in a warm embrace. Belgrade had been the lion's den under Milošević; it was still hostile terrain. When his car stopped in front of the presidential palace, the Finn was told to stay seated while three dark armoured screens were lowered around the limo. Support for a free Kosovo was still reason enough to be assassinated. Only four years earlier, Zoran Đinđić, the Serbian Prime Minister, had been assassinated by members of Serbian special police forces who considered Đinđić a traitor for being too weak on Kosovo and delivering so-called Serbian heroes to the Hague tribunal. Tadić did not even glance at the bag containing the Ahtisaari plan. 'As long as I'm President', he said gruffly, 'Serbia will never accept an independent Kosovo.'

The plan had been a year in the making. Ahtisaari had not just commuted between Western capitals and Moscow. In Pristina, typically, he would stay with the Finnish army battalion at Camp Ville, sleeping in a shipping container. 'What was especially pleasant was the fact that next to it there was a sauna, which I could go to wearing only a towel,' said the down-to-earth mediator. Immediately after his abrupt meeting with Tadić, Ahtisaari flew to Pristina to hand the report over to local leaders. He knew there would be problems there too – it demanded sacrifice and depended heavily on the goodwill of Belgrade. Around Pristina, graffiti had been smeared denouncing it as a betrayal. Rubbish bins had been plastered with the words Ahtisaari Plan. The newly established radical political group Vetëvendosje was objecting to any degree of centralised power for the local Serbian community. 'The Kosovo Albanians didn't much like it,' admitted Ahtisaari. 'But it was genuinely a compromise. Of course they would have preferred faster independence, not to be bound by conditions set by local governments and their minority politicians.'

The Finn had three more meetings with the parties before handing the draft to the United Nations Security Council. Thaçi shared the concerns of other members of the unity team; it left open too many loopholes that could be exploited by Belgrade. How many Serbian municipalities were to be allowed in Kosovo? Where should their borders be set? What would be the limits to the power of the international administration before independence?

Yet there was no serious comparison between the outright obstruct-ionism of the Serbs and the scepticism of the Kosovo Albanians. Belgrade saw any movement towards compromise as in the realm of treason. The Kosovar position was born rather out of the conviction that Belgrade, signature or no signature, was determined to sabotage their path to freedom. Ahtisaari seemed even-handed when he announced the results of his talks: 'There was no will from the parties to move away from their previously stated positions ... I had hoped, and very much preferred, that this process would lead to a negotiated agreement.'

But it was actually a call to the West to carry through diplomatically the situation it had helped to create with its military offensive; to simply give up because Belgrade didn't want to accept the new realities was no way to anchor peace in the Balkans.

The plan was formally submitted to the UNSC in April 2007. It was endorsed by the Secretary-General of the United Nations, Ban Ki-moon, the United States and the European Union members. Sergey Lavrov, the Russian foreign minister, said Moscow would not agree to a resolution unacceptable to Belgrade and called for the sacking of Ahtisaari. New drafts were circulated aimed at reassuring Moscow that the plan did not erode the principle of state sovereignty. The Kremlin insisted on another review with the obvious aim of delaying any decision until, eventually, the proposals died a quiet death. Angela Merkel, the German Chancellor, and Solana seemed to agree that Russia should be kept happy. 'Don't go wobbly on me,' Ahtisaari told them. The West, at least, had to be firm about the end-goal of full independence. Otherwise, the post-Cold War architecture of peace would start to cave in. What was the point of limited military intervention against those who transgressed global rules if there was no follow-through, no attempt to construct structures that would prevent abuse happening again?

The Russian position had shifted from being a more or less cooperative member of the Contact Group to being both an open and a covert opponent to any move that could weaken Serbia's hold over Kosovo. That was partly down to a sense that Serbia was its natural ally in the Balkans, partly fear of a legal precedent that could encourage separatist movements in Russia, but chiefly it was down to Vladimir Putin. In 2000–2001, fresh in office, he had been a tentative leader, apparently open to new forms of cooperation with the West. In February 2007, however, he demonstrated how much had changed.

At the annual security conference in Munich, Putin had launched a thunderous attack on the US, on its supposed attempts to create a unipolar world, and at the expansion of NATO membership. 'We have a right to ask against whom this expansion is directed!' exclaimed Putin. The Russian leader seemed to have come to the conclusion that his country was being deliberately encircled, with nuclear missile defence bases planned in Poland and the Czech Republic. NATO membership action plans were being offered to Russia's neighbours to encourage them to standardise and coordinate with the Western alliance. Former members of the Warsaw Pact were being taken into the European Union.

Seen from the Kremlin, Kosovo was the original sin – a piece of NATO expansionism that was intended to create a Western springboard in the Balkans. A rebel group had been supported by US firepower. The US and its allies now treated Kosovo as a friendly garrison state. It was the first step in Cold War 2.0 and Putin was furious with himself for having let it happen. Now he was determined to throw rocks in Kosovo's path.

Ahtisaari had really believed that Russia would end up acting rationally. 'I couldn't bring myself to believe that Russia wanted to send the message out to the world that a dictator like Milošević could act as he liked without feeling the consequences,' he said. The whole thrust of the Ahtisaari plan had been to construct a long-term peace in which it would be impossible for its Serbian allies to accuse Moscow of having abandoned its friends.

Once Putin understood that Ahtisaari was not (as one US diplomat termed it) a 'vodka buddy', the growling propaganda offensive against the Finn began in earnest. Ahtisaari's family had been thrown out of their home by the Russians during the Second World War. Perhaps, Russian propagandists calculated, the Finn was pushing Kosovan independence as an act of personal revenge. The attacks were channelled through the Serbian media but the original source seemed to have been the disinformation department of one of the Russian intelligence services. According to one report, Ahtisaari's father had served as an SS officer. The report was bunkum. So too was an elaborate report in a Bosnian Serb newspaper that Albanians had paid €2 billion into a Swiss bank account in return for Ahtisaari backing Kosovan independence. Supposedly German intelligence had taped incriminating evidence and the new UN Secretary-General Ban Ki-moon was worried.

These crude attempts at 'fake news' were denied and brushed aside as the work of politically motivated conspiracy theorists. Similar attacks were mounted against anyone who seemed to challenge Moscow or Serbia's position in the Balkans. 'Thaçi in particular has become the butt of crazy fabrications,' says one Pristina analyst. 'It's perversely flattering – it shows that Belgrade and Moscow consider you a real danger.'

The black propaganda against Ahtisaari reflected a concern in Russia that momentum was shifting away from Moscow. George W. Bush came to Tirana in July 2007 after a session of the G8, where he had sensed that France, Italy and Spain were reluctant to see a sovereign Kosovo. European governments were hostile enough to the Bush administration without him forcing the pace on Kosovo. The newly minted French President Nicolas Sarkozy seemed to be counting on a breakthrough in talks between Belgrade and Pristina. So President Bush, who had bought into the argument of his staff that Kosovan independence should be pushed harder, reluctantly decided to hold off for six months. An independent Kosovo would need the full support of Europe, Bush advisors calculated, so a tactical delay was a price worth paying. It would show the EU that Washington was not simply trying to bulldoze Kosovo into statehood. After the bad blood caused by the Iraq invasion,

Bush had to at least simulate the involvement of the EU and the UN, and show that he respected multilateral solutions.

Kosovo therefore became a test case, not only for the efficacy of limited military intervention, but also for how the US administration could work together with Europe. Bush thus travelled to Albania to soften the blow of a delay in the Kosovo decision and to reassure the Albanians – many Kosovars had crossed the border for the visit – that he wasn't going to let them down. Six months meant six months. And to drive home the point, he put his weight behind Albanian membership of NATO. The crowds gave him a more enthusiastic response than anywhere else in Europe. Even the theft of his watch, a star-spangled Timex, did not dull their zeal, or his. There's a bronze statue of him now in the village that he visited, while one of the main avenues in Pristina was named after George W. Bush. And the promise was kept: Albania did indeed join NATO not long afterwards, in 2009.

The question, though, that hung over 2007 in the wake of the blocked Ahtisaari report was when, rather than if, Kosovo would be allowed to declare itself independent. Throughout the late summer, Thaçi and the unity team had jumped through hoops. They had proposed setting up a bilateral dialogue with the Serbs, an institutional channel that would smooth the way after independence. The Serbs rejected the idea, as they did many others. There was a real head of steam building up. In that year's election campaign, Thaçi presented himself as the standard-bearer of a new, about-to-be state. Rugova was gone, Thaçi's domestic competition was enfeebled, the province wanted to move on. US advisors helped Thaçi professionalise his campaign and he embarked on town hill meetings. On the side of his campaign bus was emblazoned: 'Be Proud of Kosovo!' Thaçi recalls: 'People would come up and say, "What's there to be proud about?" But there was plenty to be proud of in a society that was so willing to embrace change. And it worked.' In November,

Thaçi's PDK won a commanding chunk of the vote. Back in 2001, Thaçi says, 'Dick Holbrooke told me straight – if US voters were voting, you would win. But I'm telling you that this time you should step aside.' Six years later, Thaçi understood Holbrooke's message: you had to win elections on the basis of persuasion, not entitlement.

Thaçi was thus in the starting blocks when George Bush's six-month delay was up. It was 7 December and it was plain to all and sundry in the EU that neither Serbia nor Russia would ever agree to a variant of the Ahtisaari plan. Kosovo had to make its way without the blessing of the Serbs. Condoleezza Rice told her fellow NATO foreign ministers: 'The process is at an end. That means we have to move on to the next step. It is not going to help to put off decisions that need to be taken.'

The plug had been pulled. The US was ready and braced for the diplomatic, perhaps even military, consequences of independence. Thaçi's hour had come.

CHAPTER 11

INDEPENDENCE DAY

F rank G. Wisner's Manhattan apartment looked improbably large and opulent to Thaçi. Outside it was cold and New York was still moving at half speed, the slumber days of January. Inside, though, the atmosphere was electric. Wisner had brought together a trusted group of Kosovo enthusiasts from within the US establishment, including growling, booming Dick Holbrooke, with the aim of pinpointing a suitable date for Kosovan independence. If it had been up to Thaçi, he would have declared independence on the day after the so-called troika – the EU, the US and Russia – had formally given up on finding a consensual exit for Kosovo. But Thaçi had dutifully listened to advice to hang on for a little longer. The US, he was told, need time to line up the allies. And it was good tactics to wait at least until the UN Secretary-General had issued a report. Thaçi saw the sense in that. 'We promised not to do anything without the support of Washington, Brussels and NATO,' he says. 'It was the best – and actually, the only – way forward to have a coordinated declaration of independence.' Thaçi was also remembering the words of Condoleezza Rice, from an earlier meeting in 2007. 'You can declare independence now if you want but it's not enough for you to be recognised only by the US, Turkey and Albania.'

That was a measure of Thaçi's growing self-confidence; he understood that while the West might not be wholly united on Kosovo, there was at least serious momentum. And it was a testament to his trust in the American pro-Kosovo lobby, which included such people as Bob Dole and John McCain, the US Republican senators, Chuck Schumer, the Democrat senator, and Tom Lantos and Eliot Engel, the Congressmen, as well as Frank Wisner himself. No US foreign policy specialist was better positioned to accompany Kosovo on its final sprint to statehood. Condoleezza Rice had appointed the businessman and former ambassador – India was his last post – as her special envoy to Kosovo. For the past six months, he had been the US part of the troika (the German diplomat Wolfgang Ischinger was his EU counterpart) and he grasped that there really was no other option than a unilateral declaration of independence (UDI). 'You can't put Humpty Dumpty back together again,' he said. The diplomatic challenge would come in the management of UDI and the inevitable repercussions. Russians and Serbs would consider the independence declaration to be unilateral, which is why it was so important for Western allies to be on the same page.

Wisner was in fact Frank G. Wisner Jr. Wisner Sr had been one of the founding fathers of the CIA, a member of the Office of Strategic Services that had organised covert operations, sabotage missions and underground resistance groups in Eastern Europe. Wisner Sr's territory was the Balkans and he became CIA station chief in Albania, tasked with the mission of toppling the communist dictator Enver Hoxha. That backfired, but he remained doggedly committed to the politics of Eastern Europe. In 1956, when the West looked helplessly on as Soviet tanks crushed the Hungarian uprising, he realised that the whole idea of rolling back communism was over. He suffered a mental breakdown and, on recovery, was made station chief in London. His depression grew darker, however, and in 1965 he killed himself with a shotgun.

In happier times, however, Wisner Sr had been a great socialiser, using New York dinner parties to float new ideas and plans. His son inherited not only an interest in Albania and its environs but also his father's ease of manner and ready wit. 'If Frank's got your back, you're going to be OK,' says a former professional friend of his. And he had Thaçi's back. After retiring from the State Department, Frank Jr became a successful businessman and consultant, drawing partly on his early training as an Arabist. His flat, furnished largely by his French wife, became a salon for diplomats, lawyers and former spooks trying to make sense of the fast-changing post-Cold War order. It bustled with European (his wife had once been married to Nicolas Sarkozy's father) and Middle Eastern guests. Indeed, it was President Sarkozy who became the first European President to acknowledge the forthcoming independence of Kosovo. Weeks before Kosovo declared its independence, Sarkozy visited a French primary school and, pointing towards a map of Europe, said: 'The borders will soon change as Kosovo will become the newest state.'

Back in Wisner's apartment, plans were being drafted on the chronology of steps leading to the independence of Kosovo. 'As far as I know he never had a guerrilla leader round before Thaçi,' said his friend. 'But with Frank you never could tell.' As late as 2011, Secretary of State Hillary Clinton was calling on him to go to Cairo and deliver a message to Hosni Mubarak, who was grimly hanging on to power in Egypt.

But it was Albania and Kosovo that engaged him most, his father's intriguing old stamping ground. The US sense of purpose about what should now unfold in the Balkans came from him. The informal axis between Thaçi, Wisner and Holbrooke was based on a shared understanding about the role and responsibilities of limited military intervention. The US had intervened in Bosnia, but hadn't included Kosovo in the Dayton Agreement. It had backed and helped engineer military intervention in Serbia, but had failed to grasp its complexity or guess the consequences. They had tried to prevent as best they could brutal outrages against civilians and thus uphold the credibility of the alliance. Yet the Kosovars had read the US military action as more than a humanitarian gesture. For them, the message was clear: the US bombing was intended to support the KLA in its attempts to slip the grip of Milošević. The force of Kosovar expectations thus bore down on those members of the US establishment who had not been completely swallowed up by the confusions of the 2003 Iraq War.

Kosovo had been a good intervention and needed to be defended as such, lest the whole business of projecting US power abroad be brought into discredit. Since the post-intervention administration by the UN was failing, it was clear that the Kosovars themselves had to build their own state. The perspective of that fledgling state joining the European Union – the journey towards that goal – should be sufficient to ensure that a Kosovo government would respect the rights of the Serb minority. All this should have been set out in 1999. But rather than risk a row – splitting Europe between those who favoured independence and those who thought there was an obligation to keep Serbia intact – it fudged.

Now was the time to put things right. Wisner and Holbrooke knew that the Kosovo problem could be wished away as many Western states wanted. And it fell to Thaçi to keep the issue alive, to turn inter-communal instability into a catalyst for change. John Sawers, Britain's representative at the UN (who would continue to meet Thaçi after he went on to become head of the secret service), had set out a few weeks before how the debate was shifting decisively in Kosovo's favour and against Serbia. 'You have the principle of territorial integrity,' he told reporters, 'and you also have the principle of self-determination. There are times when those principles are in tension with one another, and the principle of territorial integrity has to be qualified by the principle of self-determination.'

Serbia, such was the emerging majority view in the West, had to be cajoled into surrendering Kosovo and both states had to find a way of living at peace alongside each other. But no one was trying to establish a universal doctrine that would encourage the break-up of other Balkan states or other sovereign entities around the world. Kosovo's independence had to be carefully managed and was considered to be *sui generis*, a product of very specific historic circumstances.

All that remained, it was agreed in the Manhattan apartment, was the question of timing. The crucial factor was the Serbian presidential election, the two rounds of which were scheduled for 20 January and 3 February. Declaring unilateral independence before then, or even letting the intention leak out, could have robbed the initiative from Boris Tadić, who, despite opposing a breakaway Kosovo, did at least favour the Europeanisation of Serbia. The advantage would then have shifted to his ultra-nationalist rival Tomislav Nikolić.

There were no exaggerated Western hopes for either candidate. Belgrade was a long way from publicly conceding that the abuses of the Milošević era had forfeited Serbia's right to rule over Kosovo. But it did count on Belgrade eventually taking the chance of championing the minority rights being offered to Kosovar Serbs under the constitution. If it could do so without turning every flare-up into an existential struggle, or an excuse to threaten Pristina, that would be progress of sorts. The point of the Ahtisaari plan had been to put some distance between Serbia proper and the Kosovar Serbs, for Belgrade to see them as cousins whose welfare should be spoken up for, rather than as blood brothers. The sense of the plan was that an independent Kosovo would be generous to the Serb minority, holding out the possibility of them running their own courts, hospitals and schools and collecting their own taxes.

The European Commission too was engaged to help reach a Tadić victory. Weeks before the vote it granted Serbian citizens easier access to EU visas. The divisions in the EU over Kosovo were still entrenched: Spain, Greece, Cyprus, Romania and Slovakia were all in outright opposition to independence. Spain feared a precedent for Catalonia, Slovaks and Romanians worried over irredentism of their own Hungarian minority, while Greece was more open to Kosovo but had to keep an eye on Cyprus, which had its own dispute with the Turkish-populated part of the island.

But, as Thaçi heard, perched on one of Frank Wisner's tasteful sofas, the stars were aligned. Slovenia – which had always been sympathetic to Thaçi – had just taken over the rotating presidency of the European Union and would keep the position until June. Croatia had just become an elected member of the UN Security Council. Neither state, both formerly part of Yugoslavia, were friends of Serbia. They remembered all too well that Milošević had attacked both these countries at the onset of the Yugoslav crisis.

'There's never going to be a good time for Europe,' said Holbrooke. 'No point in hanging around.'

'Let's just do it,' said Wisner. 'Second or third week of February.'

The period was entered into diaries and Thaçi swore to keep the date secret until the very last moment in order to reduce the chances of Serbian or Russian sabotage and to provide the time needed to organise a schedule among Kosovo-friendly countries. Rather than them all announcing recognition on Independence Day, it would be better to stagger announcements. 'A rolling avalanche of approval,' in the words of one US diplomat, 'smothering the critics.'

Thaçi had impressed at the NY meeting; he was a leader, they agreed, who could actually deliver. That was important not just for the future of the Balkans but also for the doctrine of US military intervention after the smarting setbacks of Iraq. Somehow, thanks to Thaçi, they had got a fair number of Europeans working together again with the Bush administration – even though, as in Iraq, they were operating without a UN Security Council resolution.

'Hashim, he sure scrubbed up nice,' said Wisner to a friend.

Coordinating closely with Tina Kaidanow, the US envoy in Pristina, was Vlora Çitaku, one of Thaçi's most trusted advisors. Çitaku worked with Western media during the 1999 war but she joined Thaçi's party soon after liberation and became one of the most prominent Kosovar voices in the Western media, representing Kosovo in half a dozen sessions of the UN Security Council. She was a representative of a new generation of Kosovo experts who joined Thaçi's team and was promptly tasked to work on the choreography of Independence Day and the management of the security situation. A flag had been designed under Thaçi's supervision – a blue, Euro-friendly background, an outline map of Kosovo with six stars representing the six main communities in the new state. The Independence Declaration would be handwritten in complete secrecy by a professor of calligraphy from Pristina University, while a printing shop in Turkey had to print flags under strict control. A national anthem was in the works. It would not have any lyrics, so as not to provoke the Serbian community with overly patriotic declarations of love towards the newly established republic. The national symbol – the two-headed eagle – would have to be ditched.

The eagle was a nod to the main icon of Albanian nationhood. According to legend, an Albanian youth, having saved a baby eagle from a snake, is rewarded with the protection of eagles, sharp-eyed and ready to strike at his enemies. As Independence Day loomed in Pristina, plenty of red-and-black Albanian flags appeared in shops and on the streets; at the banner's centre was the double-headed Albanian eagle facing both north and south. It is still favoured over the politically correct European design.

Independence Day itself was freezing. 'Ambassadors complain to me all the time – why do we have the coldest Independence Day in the diplomatic calendar?' says Petrit Selimi, a young associate of Thaçi who became deputy foreign minister. Thaçi seemed not to notice. The Western diplomats who paid him a courtesy call on the day found him sombre and distracted. He was going to read part of the speech in the Serbian language – a big gesture of conciliation – and he was weighed down by the sense of historical moment. It had been what he had fought for, but he was only halfway up the mountain. The United Nations mission in Kosovo would stay neutral. UNMIK was now led by Joachim Rücker, the German diplomat, who understood that the time had come for UNMIK to take a back seat in Kosovo's history.

The acceleration of the past few weeks since he had sat in Wisner's apartment in New York had been almost overwhelming. It was the culmination of a struggle that had begun in the 1980s in his student protest days and now, despite all the impending pomp, it was unclear precisely what this independence would add up to. For a politician who constantly tested the limits of his power, who carefully calculated risk, it was disconcerting to know so little about how far the international community would run his country. A day before UDI, the European Union endorsed EULEX, the European Union Rule of Law Mission in Kosovo. This EU-run body was set up to 'monitor, mentor and advise in all areas related to the rule of law in Kosovo.' It was given the authority to investigate and prosecute organised crime, fraud and war crimes. That was of course intended as reassurance to the West that a new Kosovo state would not end up as a corrupt banana republic with crooked judges.

Thaçi was at ease with anything that smoothed the path to statehood. But it gave the agency extraordinary powers and the potential to dig into Kosovo's tangled domestic politics. Could he rule effectively with such a large surrender of sovereignty? He would have to see, have to react. Yet every one of his instincts told him to personally shape the new Kosovo, to make Kosovars feel as confident about their country as he felt confident in himself. The crucial relationship would thus have to be with the so-called International Civilian Representative (ICR), a job roughly equivalent to the High Representative in Bosnia and Herzegovina. That post was tantamount to a Western governor-generalship and had an echo of colonial rule about it.

Kosovo's ICR, its top foreigner, was Pieter Feith, a Dutch diplomat who had worked together with Ahtisaari since the 1970s, not only in the Balkans but in Namibia and the Indonesian province of Aceh. He intended to follow the guidelines set out in the Ahtisaari plan – he wouldn't be directly involved in the running of Kosovo but would have 'strong corrective powers'. In theory, he would have the right to annul decisions made by the Kosovo administration and sack public officials. Was that the kind of independence that Thaçi wanted for Kosovo? Almost certainly not. How comfortable could the idea of 'supervised independence' really be for an ambitious politician?

But as Feith arrived and set out his stall, it became clear to Thaçi that they agreed at least on some fundamentals. Young Kosovars – and indeed young Kosovo Serbs – needed to be given a strong sense that it was worth staying in the new state. The EU was about to put in place the biggest civilian crisis management in its history to construct a credible system of justice within controlled borders. It was important that this should not be projected by Thaçi or any senior Kosovo politician as a kind of neo-colonial regime; the foreigners were there not to undermine or diminish Kosovar independence but rather to ensure that the state was not pushed off course. Thaçi agreed with Feith: the worst that could happen to Kosovo now was probably not an act of open warfare from Belgrade (although that could never be entirely ruled out) but rather that it could become one of the world's many 'frozen conflicts', inhabiting a geopolitical limbo.

The Declaration of Independence that Thaçi proclaimed to Parliament at 3.38 p.m. on 17 February was naturally a model of political caution. The wording had been guided with US advice and it gave more than a passing nod to the importance of the European Union. And it was a calculated answer to governments around the world who were hesitating about extending recognition. He did indeed say some words in Serbian, although the small contingent of Serb MPs stayed away from the session. Thaçi recalls that some Serb MPs visited him to congratulate him on independence but that they would not attend for fear of the reaction from Belgrade. He did not celebrate Albanian identity; this was not going to be a piece of Balkan triumphalism, rather a conscious attempt to align Kosovo with Europe and European values.

'We declare Kosovo to be a democratic, secular and multi-ethnic republic,' read the charter, 'guided by the principles of non-discrimination and equal protection under the law.' To drive the point home, it went on: 'We shall protect and promote the rights of all communities in Kosovo and create the conditions necessary for their effective participation in political and decision-making processes.' The declaration was passed unanimously, with deputies raising their hands and declaring: 'Po! Yes!'

In Pristina, the celebrations lasted for days. A huge cake was sliced up outside Parliament – replaced soon after being guzzled by another, this time in the geographic shape of Kosovo. Flags, still chiefly the Albanian standard, fluttered in the biting wind. Fireworks lit up the night. There were house parties, the dancing only interrupted by relatives phoning from abroad. Remarkably, not a single incident of violence was reported in the main cities, despite so much champagne and raki being guzzled. Some Western allies feared that the declaration of independence would cause local Serbs to flee en masse. They did not. Costa Rica and Afghanistan were the first countries to recognise Kosovo as a sovereign state. US recognition came soon after. Bush wrote to President Fatmir Sejdiu promising a 'deepening and strengthening special friendship'. Britain and France recognised Kosovo shortly afterwards, followed by Germany, Turkey, Australia, Denmark and Poland. As the recognitions rolled in, almost all from the West, it became obvious that the sequencing had been planned. EU foreign ministers 'acknowledged' Kosovo's new status but left it up to member states to make their own decisions. To make it easier for doubters, their statement stressed that recognition of Kosovo would not set a precedent. Even so, by the autumn of 2008, five EU states – Spain, Greece, Romania, Slovakia and Cyprus – were still refusing to recognise Kosovo. Thaçi guessed that winning them over would become a major diplomatic task over the coming years.

First, though, he had to ride out the inevitable backlash from Serbia and Russia. In the week after the parliamentary vote, rioters besieged nine foreign embassies in Belgrade, torching the US building. Police looked away or found other pressing tasks. Shops were looted, McDonald's restaurants were wrecked and stones were hurled at the headquarters of the pro-Western opposition Liberal Democratic Party. Independent journalists were beaten. 'They have broken our state,' said Velimir Ilić,

Prime Minister Koštunica's infrastructure minister. 'But we only broke a few windows.' The nationalist daily *Večernje Novosti* said the US embassy had not been set ablaze by Serb nationalists but 'by US policy and contemporary fascism'. One violent rally followed another. In the Serbian enclaves of northern Mitrovica, protestors seized the courthouse and held it for three days before UN police and Kfor troops took it back. UN chief Ban Ki-moon called for calm, NATO threatened firm action. Belgrade, for its part, warned that it would cut off electricity supplies to Kosovo. Orders came down to local Kosovar Serbs from Belgrade that they shouldn't take flight – prompting fears that Serbia could be ready to move in and formally annex the territory. The US had gamed such a possibility and Kfor was on alert; Thaçi was briefed continually.

While Kosovo pledged to open embassies in key Western capitals, Serbia said it would be withdrawing its ambassadors from all countries that recognised Kosovo. As for Vladimir Putin, he demanded that the declaration of independence be declared null and void since it was 'immoral and illegal'.

The Serb rioting died down but the anger continued to inform Belgrade's policies. The long-standing coordination between Belgrade and Moscow was shaping up to be a real working axis aimed at derailing the international acceptance of Kosovo. The initial tactic was to use all possible legal avenues to reverse UDI or at the very least to create such an atmosphere of uncertainty that Kosovo would be shunned by investors. Russia's ambassador to the UN, Vitaly Churkin, ensured that Boris Tadić was given a hearing at the UN Security Council. There, he asked the members why – while Milošević was still in power – a settlement was imposed which left Kosovo a legal part of Serbia. Yet, when Serbia overthrew Milošević, and obeyed the rules set by the international community, it found itself punished with the loss of nearly 20 per cent of its territory. That, he said, was not just.

Backed by Moscow, Serbia then asked the UN General Assembly to refer the legality of Kosovo's independence declaration to the International Court of Justice. The calculation: it would take the court at least a year to come to a decision and in the meantime the Russians and the Serbs could slow down the momentum of recognition, sow doubt about Kosovo. This was intended to be a blockade across broad fronts. The Kremlin and Belgrade would exploit the splits in Europe to bar Kosovo from joining international organisations, from FIFA to UN agencies. Moscow calculated that Kosovo would become a state adrift, unsuitable for NATO membership. And, to make the message even clearer, it marched into the Russian enclaves in Georgia, a country that had shown interest in joining NATO and the EU. A short war ensued in the summer of 2008 and few doubted that one of Putin's motives had been to show its fury at Kosovo being, as he saw it, recruited into the Western alliance.

There was no serious Western response to Putin's behaviour in the Caucasus; it had taken the alliance by surprise. The Kremlin seemed to be assuming that Georgia, as a former member of the Soviet Union, should be regarded as part of the Russian sphere of interest. Yet where did this 'national interest' end? With its ancient Orthodox ally Serbia in the Balkans? With (as the West began belatedly to ask in 2014) Ukraine, a country that bordered not only Russia but many EU states? Russia ended up freezing South Ossetia and Abkhazia in Georgia, seizing Crimea as its own and making sure that the Ukrainian government could not spread its power into Donetsk and Luhansk. It cannot entirely freeze Kosovo – not as long as there is a firm US commitment to its future – but it can intimidate those who want to be its friends.

Not all these issues were understood or even properly monitored. Western hopes for a Kosovo breakthrough were pinned largely on the hope that ultra-nationalist rule in Belgrade was gradually coming to an end. Elections seemed to show that young voters for the post-Milošević Socialists and even the Radical Party were keen on 'Europe', that they were more concerned about becoming a backwater in the Balkans than they were about the exact legal status of Kosovo.

The EU analysis put its bets on the emergence of a self-interested reform movement within Serbian parties. Promote the cause of the pro-Europeans in the Serb government in the expectation that generational change would open them up to some kind of working relationship with Brussels. Bring Serbia out of the cold, and Kosovo will prosper. That was not entirely unreasonable but the idea that it would happen at anything like the required pace to secure Kosovo's future was naive. Thaçi knew better. Ivica Dačić, regarded by EU optimists as being the bright new face of Serbian socialism? He was in fact the former spokesman of Milošević, a man who had sought to justify his master's conquests. They used to call him Little Slobo.[22] As for Aleksandar Vučić, he had been information minister under Milošević and had defended the ethnic cleansing of Albanians from Kosovo. Indeed, it was Vučić who, days after the Srebrenica genocide in 1995, had threatened Bosnian Muslims in the Serbian Parliament by declaring: 'For each Serb you kill, we shall kill one hundred Muslims.' And Tomislav Nikolić, now President of Serbia? He used to say that Milošević had been too soft in his drive for a Greater Serbia.

These were no friends of Kosovo. And so Thaçi, while wanting the best for Kosovo, was deeply sceptical of an improvement that depended on a new-look reformist Belgrade. Serbia, he said, would find a way of

---

22 'Serb prime minister's battle to rehabilitate the "Leper" of Europe', *Daily Telegraph*, 1 June 2013, accessed 5 September 2017 at: http://www.telegraph.co.uk/news/worldnews/europe/serbia/10093578/Serb-prime-ministers-battle-to-rehabilitate-the-Leper-of-Europe.html

talking European while doing its best to do down the Kosovars. With Russia guarding its back and Europe divided, Thaçi felt that Kosovo was still trapped in the dark game of Balkan power. Thaçi would soon encounter that in a very personal way.

CHAPTER 12

THE MARTY REPORT

12 **December 2010** would mark one of the darkest days of Hashim Thaçi's career.

The same day that Thaçi was re-elected as Prime Minister, a report appeared in *The Guardian* newspaper in the UK that would rock Thaçi's world.

The Guardian had been leaked a report compiled by Dick Marty, a Swiss senator, who was the human rights rapporteur for the Council of Europe.

In it, Marty named Thaçi as the 'most dangerous' of a network of organised crime leaders in Kosovo who engaged in assassinations, drug dealing, weapons smuggling and prostitution. But the worst – and by far the most dramatic – of Marty's allegations was that Thaçi led a network of criminals who took captive Serbs over the Kosovan border into Albania and removed their organs. Testimonies in the report alleged that prisoners had pleaded for their lives and begged not to be 'chopped into pieces'.

The 31-page report, entitled 'Inhuman treatment of people and illicit trafficking in human organs in Kosovo', was a bombshell.

Marty claimed to have had sight of 'confidential reports spanning more than a decade' in which 'at least five countries have named Hashim Thaçi and other members of the former KLA as having exerted violent control over the trade in heroin and other narcotics'.

The Swiss senator – who asserted that Thaçi was at the centre of 'mafia-like structures' – said that he felt a 'sense of moral outrage'.

Marty added that he had undertaken the investigation because a former chief war crimes prosecutor in The Hague had been blocked from doing so herself, evoking the stench of a cover-up.

Unsurprisingly, the media ran with it. It had all the ingredients of a fantastic news story. Horror, secrecy, claims that Western governments, including that led by Tony Blair, were complicit, and all within the existing narrative of a dark and dirty war in the Balkans.

It was also an easy story to write without fear of being sued: all the allegations and testimonies were contained in a public document which could be cited at length in a news story. For the laziest and most legally averse journalists, all that was required was a quick call into Thaçi's office for a denial. Which is what they got. Thaçi's office denied the allegations immediately and he threatened to sue Marty.

> Today, *The Guardian* published an article that referred to a report from a member of the Parliamentary Assembly of the Council of Europe, Dick Marty, which follows up on past reports published over the last twelve years aiming at maligning the war record of the Kosovo Liberation Army and its leaders.
>
> It is clear that someone wants to place obstacles in the way of Prime Minister Hashim Thaçi after the general election, in which the people of Kosovo placed their clear and significant trust in him to deliver the development programme and governance of our country.

> Such despicable and bizarre actions, by people with no moral credibility, serve the ends of only those specific circles that do not wish well to Kosovo and its people.

While Thaçi said he would sue the Swiss senator, he never did. Marty had immunity, writing the report on behalf of the Council of Europe. But even before the years of investigations that would follow, none of which culminated in a single conviction, the damage was irreparable.

Newspapers whose readers had had little interest in the Yugoslavian war ran the story at length, not least because it was pitched as a story about one of Tony Blair's allies. One story in the *Daily Mail* ran: 'Mr Blair has some very bizarre friends, but a monster who traded in body parts beats the lot.'

The allegations threatened to undermine the whole rationale of NATO intervention in Kosovo.

Tim Judah, the respected journalist and expert on the Balkans, wrote in the *Daily Telegraph*: 'If ever it is proved that the KLA leader [Thaçi] Blair backed was really a mafia boss, a murderer, and traded in human organs, then the history of that campaign will have to be rewritten – and the gloss put on it by Mr Blair will vanish.'

Thaçi was wounded publicly, politically and personally by the Marty report.

In an interview with the authors in early 2016, Thaçi claimed that he felt deeply insulted by the allegations. He was worried that he would never be able to look his son Endrit, then just ten years old, in the eye.

However, the Marty report – as explosive as it was in December 2010 – had been a long time in the making.

Allegations about Balkan organ trafficking had been circulating in the Serbian media from as early as 1991. News stories appeared claiming that Croatian and Bosnian fighters had been engaged in taking organs from Serbs and selling them. Such stories which evolved over years to become Kosovars stealing Serb organs has led some to suspect that the organ story was conveniently horrific to work as Belgrade war propaganda. It led one war crimes lawyer, who declined to be named, to quip that he wondered what it was about Serb kidneys that were so much better than any other nationality.

As the war drew to a close in June 1999, the process of trying to find the missing, and ascertain what had happened to them, began. There were many convictions against Serbs but rumours began to circulate about members of the KLA kidnapping Serbs, smuggling them to Albania and murdering them.

One experienced investigative radio and print journalist – Michael Montgomery – travelled to Kosovo in the summer of 1999 to work on a documentary entitled *Massacre at Cuska*, where a number of Kosovar Albanians were murdered by Serbs. It was while gathering material for his investigation that he began hearing other tales of the KLA kidnapping Serbs and Albanians.

Recalling 1999, Montgomery said at a Balkans conference in 2015:

> At that time we heard that there were people – Serbs, Roma, some Kosovo Albanians – killed by the Kosovo Liberation Army, and they simply vanished, and it was very strange and we started looking into that. And because of our work in Cuska, we got very good sources on the Kosovo Albanian side and we started talking with low levels of the KLA and they started telling us these stories of captured civilians being moved across the border to Albania. My sources were low-level KLA guys who were drivers or were in vehicles when these people were driven. But as these were the low-level guys they didn't know the whole picture.

Montgomery said that even though he was worried he did not have enough material to produce a story, he felt that he should write down what he did have and send it to a UN mission in Kosovo. He said:

> We had multiple sources but not everything lined up. We had people who heard that people have been taken away for their kidneys. There were a couple of houses we were able to locate where these things allegedly happened, but we decided we didn't have enough information to publish and that at the time our evidence didn't support the allegations.

While Montgomery, who had been the Belgrade correspondent for the *Daily Telegraph*, had worries about what information he had, he did have something. He found three people who claimed be witnesses to the KLA abducting around 300 Serbs in 1999. Those three said the kidnap victims had been captured inside Kosovo and taken to a house over the border in Albania that was painted yellow on the outside. He wrote down the accounts from the three, who claimed that the Serbs had been murdered and then their kidneys trafficked, by flying the organs out of the country. They accused the then Kosovo Prime Minister Ramush Haradinaj and his brother of being behind the atrocities.

Montgomery sent those witness statements to the International Criminal Tribunal for the former Yugoslavia in The Hague.

At the time, the chief prosecutor of the ICTY was Carla Del Ponte, a former Swiss attorney general who would later order an inquiry into the Montgomery allegations.

The result was a report compiled by Eamonn Smyth, Head of Mission in Skopje and Pristina, which was sent to Patrick Lopez-Terres, Chief of Investigations at the UN's ICTY, in October 2003.

The report was structured around eight witnesses, none named.

By the admission of Paul Coffey, on secondment from the US Department of Justice to Kosovo, the credibility of the eight was 'untested'.

All eight of them were ethnic Albanians from Kosovo or Montenegro and all had claimed to have served in the Kosovo Liberation Army. Of them, four said that they had helped transport at least ninety ethnic Serbs to detention facilities in Albania and one said that he had helped take body parts and organs to Rinas airport, near Tirana. None of them witnessed a medical operation.

While unnamed and untested, some of their testimonies are detailed, recalling dates and routes to and from detention centres and graves. The sources also helped the ICTY compile a list of ten victims. Their testimonies make gruesome reading.

Source 2 recalled 23 July 1999:

> The same two KLA men who drove in the cab on the first trip. The same route, the same truck. This time we drove further from the previous place on the road to Suva Reka [...] This time I saw corpses wrapped in grey army blankets. I felt the smell of blood so I knew they were fresh. Both sexes though mostly men. Around fifteen holes were already dug when we came. Two corpses into one hole. It took us one hour and a half to finish off.

A number of the sources claim that in the period between mid-1999 and the following summer, trips over the Kosovan border into Albania were relatively easy because of the chaos that ensued at the end of the war in June 1999.

Source 1 told the investigators about two trips he had made, one at the end of 1999 and another in the spring of 2000:

> I was driving a different vehicle, a Mercedes van. They put four

Serbian men in the van. They were young and in good shape. We had two people to escort and drove to a house south of Burrel [town north of Tirana]. About twenty minutes from Burrel you cross a bridge and turn onto a dirt road. The road follows a river. We drove to the end of the road where there was a light yellow house. It was old and had eaves. At the house were several men and two doctors (the men were referred to as doctors). One was an Arab and the other was an Albanian called Dr Admir. The men (Serbs) were really nervous. The Serbs were taken out of the van and led to a building (a shack or barn) behind the main house.

The third trip was in spring 2000. I was again in Burrel and took one Serbian man and a Serbian woman. She was young and they spoke Serbian. The Serbs were frantic. At one point the man asked us to kill them immediately, 'we don't want to be cut into pieces,' he said. We drove them to the same house south of Burrel in the early evening.

While none of the sources witnessed any medical procedures, one account describes the inside of the now infamous yellow house in Burrel and of overhearing talk among others of organ smuggling.

Source 1 continued:

When I made the first delivery in Burrel I thought they were testing them, taking blood samples. I had heard earlier that they were taking blood samples from captives. But this confused me, why?

But after the third trip I knew something was happening. I had gone into the first room of the house south of Burrel to get a drink of water. It was clean and there was a very strong smell of medicine. It reminded me of a hospital, you know, sickly sweet, and made me sick. I wanted to get out of there. I thought this was the only house where I brought people but never picked anyone up. It was around this time that I heard other guys talking about organs, kidneys and trips from the house to the airport. […] I heard from a friend who was also a driver that […] two girls from Mirdite were also taken to the house (house/clinic) and were used for 'spare parts'. I remember being very unhappy because these were Albanian girls. And they were young. The first time I didn't know what was going on, the second time I thought it was all about prostitution, but the third time when I realised what was going on I was horrified and just wanted to hide. These were good soldiers but they really disappointed me. I thought they were fighting a war but this was something entirely different.

So where did the 2003 report go? It begot another report. In February the following year, Del Ponte appointed Matti Raatikainen, a former Finnish policeman, to head up a new investigation in his capacity as head of the war crimes unit of EULEX, the European Law and Justice Mission in Kosovo. His team included UN and ICTY investigators, a few bodyguards and an Albanian public prosecutor. His remit was to ascertain what had happened at the so-called yellow house.

They arrived at the so-called yellow house on 4 February, much to the surprise of its owner, an elderly farmer called Abdulla Katuci. In an interview with Katuci and his family four years later in *Der Spiegel*, the weekly German news magazine, he revealed how he had been looking after his sheep when his wife ran over to him in the hills to say that a group of men had arrived at their home.

'For two days they turned our house upside down, rummaging through our clothing and collecting the garbage, even the cigarette butts,' he told *Der Spiegel.*

What they were concentrating on, however, was one room in the house on the ground floor which was different from the other rooms in the property. This one had a black polished floor with a number of cracks in it.

According to the *Der Spiegel* interview: 'The investigators had wanted to break it open, the old man recalls, but he told them: "Only if you compensate me for it." Then the men and women, as Katuci says, [...] changed their minds and left.'

Raatikainen's team sprayed the room with chemicals and found traces of blood, but could not determine after at least four years after the alleged killings whether the blood was animal or human. They also found traces of what they said could have been urine. Most significantly, however, were piles of discarded stuff outside the Katuci house and their rubbish. In it, the team found medical gloves and empty packets of muscle relaxant drugs. There were also bandages and syringes found in the rubbish, some dumped at the bottom of the river near the house.

When *Der Spiegel* interviewed Katuci's family and asked them to account for the bandages, traces of blood and syringes, one member of the family said that in remote areas of Albania it was normal for people to administer their own medicine. The blood, another family member claimed, could have come from a woman who had given birth there, and also animals were killed in that room for Muslim holidays.

The family had denied to Raatikainen's team that the house had been painted yellow during the years 1999 to 2000 – as described by a number of witnesses in the 2003 report. When Raatikainen arrived, the team discovered yellow paint under a white painted coat.

The other major blow to Raatikainen's inquiry was that Montgomery's original three witnesses had disappeared, two had vanished and the third was dead in an apparently unrelated row over money and unpaid debts.

Raatikainen returned to The Hague and said that he had found insufficient evidence to back up the witness accusations and he had also been unable to re-interview the original three and take legal testimonies from them.

Six years later, Raatikainen would declare: 'The fact is that there is no evidence whatsoever in this case. No bodies, no witnesses.'

In an interview with the BBC's Nick Thorpe, the Finn investigator said that the media attention over the original and sensational organ allegations 'have not been helpful to us. In fact, they have not been helpful to anyone.'

He explained that the alleged scandal and the attention it attracted had only served to distract EULEX's job in tracking down the bodies of 1,861 who were missing after the war and finding their killers – Kosovo Serbs and Albanians alike.

After Raatikainen's conversation with Del Ponte, the organs report was abandoned.

Far from seeing an end to the alleged organs scandal, it marked only the beginning for Thaçi.

The original Montgomery witnesses had claimed that Ramush Haradinaj, who became the Kosovar Prime Minister in December 2004, was responsible for the alleged Serb donor killings and the subsequent organ trafficking. But the allegations that had been dropped against Haradinaj would years later be reheated and this time, directed at Thaçi.

While the UN investigators had dropped the organ report citing insufficient evidence, Haradinaj was indicted the following year in 2005 on thirty-seven counts of war crimes and crimes against humanity. None of these included allegations connected with killing for organs or trafficking them.

According to Sir Geoffrey Nice, the lead prosecutor at the ICTY trial of Milošević from start to finish, and later legal advisor to Thaçi, the indictment was drawn up in an irregular and unusual manner. Apart from the fact that it was not drawn up by the usual teams, the indictment itself was not subject to the checks and balances of a peer review where teams of lawyers analyse the document before it is issued. Sir Geoffrey also wrote a report on Kosovo's accession to the Council of Europe.

As soon as the indictment was issued, Haradinaj resigned, having served exactly 100 days as Prime Minister. Three years later, after a snail-pace trial, he was found not guilty in April 2008, having served much of the intervening period in jail.

Del Ponte took much flak for her failed Haradinaj indictment. Søren Jessen-Petersen, head of the UN mission in Kosovo, said that Haradinaj had 'demonstrated respect for the process and institutions of international justice' but that Del Ponte had 'failed to live up to the same high ideals'. Haradinaj was retried in 2012 and acquitted for the second time.

Del Ponte left the ICTY in 2007. Just after Kosovo declared independence in February 2008, she published a book called *The Hunt: Me and the War Criminals*, effectively her memoirs during her tenure as a war crimes prosecutor. In the book, she included information supplied to her by Montgomery regarding organ trafficking and the alleged involvement of the KLA.

The book had four main consequences: it repeated the same claims that were dropped for lack of evidence four years before; it placed Thaçi in the frame for the first time; thirdly, it raised questions as to why she had not ordered an investigation when she was the chief prosecutor; fourthly, it triggered another report into the allegations – but this time by the Council of Europe.

Del Ponte was a high-profile figure and at the time was the world's best known war crimes prosecutor. Elegantly dressed, 5ft tall and a chain-smoker, Del Ponte divided opinion. To her supporters, she was perceived as a ballsy and highly experienced lawyer with a track record for taking on organised crime cartels. To her critics, she was seen as an egotistical, impulsive battle-tank with an appetite for the public eye.[23]

Having served in private practice in Switzerland in the 1970s, she then switched sides to become an investigative magistrate and then public prosecutor. She soon made drug trafficking, fraud, money-laundering and racketeering her patch. By the 1980s, she and the anti-Mafia magistrate Giovanni Falcone worked on the famous 'pizza connection case' that established the link between the Mafia and Swiss money launderers. She tracked down the Swiss bank accounts of the Cosa Nostra and tried to promote transparency in the Swiss banking sector, such as it is. She began to attract nicknames – the Mafia called her La Puttana (the whore). Falcone was blown up by a car bomb and she was the subject of at least two death threats, making her the first Swiss official to be granted round-the-clock security, armed bodyguards and a bullet-proof Mercedes.

In 1999, Del Ponte was appointed chief prosecutor to the International Criminal Tribunal for the former Yugoslavia, based in The Hague. She had worked as the chief prosecutor for Rwandan war crimes before being appointed to investigate the same for the Yugoslav wars.

But the publication of her memoirs created a stir. Like the 2003 UN report, the book contained gruesome details. She wrote: 'The victims, deprived of a kidney, were then locked up again, inside the barracks, until the moment they were killed for other vital organs. In this way, the other prisoners were aware of the fate that awaited them, and according to the source, pleaded, terrified, to be killed immediately.'

---

23 http://www.b92.net/eng/insight/opinions.php?nav_id=52057, accessed 5 September 2017

She also revealed in her book that evidence taken by the ICTY team from the notorious yellow house had been destroyed allowing former KLA members to assert that there was no evidence against them.

Her book drew the ire of Serbs who had lost members of their own families, who threatened to sue for failing to pursue the alleged war criminals while she was in the chief prosecutor's role. She argued that the reason she had not was because she faced so much resistance from Serbia, Albania and NATO that she was thwarted in her job.

The following year, in 2009, Dick Marty volunteered to launch an inquiry into Del Ponte's allegations on behalf of the Council of Europe.

While Raatikainen had said that his investigation had found no witnesses, Marty said that he had in the course of his inquiry.

By the summer of 2010, Marty said that he had managed to track down witnesses and requested an extension on the delivery deadline for his report. Instead of handing it in in the summer of that year, it would now be Christmas.

His report was leaked to *The Guardian* newspaper the same day that Thaçi was re-elected as Prime Minister. Only a few months earlier, US Vice-President Joe Biden had hailed Thaçi during a visit to the White House, calling him the George Washington of Kosovo. It is difficult to not draw the conclusion that the timing of the leak was deliberate rather than coincidental.

In common with Montgomery's information, the Marty report also alleged that there had been organ harvesting. It argued that the harvesting had allegedly taken place during and after the Kosovo War and that victims had been taken over the border into Albania to be killed and have their kidneys removed and sold. However, Marty's report was by no means consistent with the claims made by Montgomery. While Montgomery's witnesses had held Haradinaj responsible for the alleged crimes, this time round, it was Thaçi who was fingered.

In addition, the Marty report argued that alleged organ removal had not happened at the so-called yellow house, but somewhere else, which would mean that either or both witnesses relied on by Marty had not been rigorously interviewed, and/or that Montgomery's witnesses were mistaken.

No witnesses were named in the Marty report because he said that they feared for their safety if identified: 'Some of the sources who provided these testimonies have not been able to meet with us in person.' This included some key witnesses – especially those raising claims of organ harvesting. Moreover, no names of victims or of their alleged killers were referred to in the report. There was no evidence in the report – or even names – of those around Thaçi who were accused of doing his bidding. Nor were there any dates.

The Marty report was devoid of any hard evidence; instead, the Swiss senator referred to 'numerous concrete and convergent indications' of criminal activity.

By any legal measure the Marty report was a lousy document.

Sir Geoffrey Nice QC first condemned the Marty report in an article commissioned by the *London Review of Books*, who had asked him to consider the report and other allegations being made at the time.

Sir Geoffrey was subsequently hired by Thaçi to advise on how to respond to the Marty allegations and how best to prepare for Kosovo's application for membership of the Council of Europe. As a lawyer now acting for Kosovo, he compiled a report to the Council of Europe in which he railed that allegations made in the Marty report were 'unsupported by any identified evidence', and that Marty had linked two cases 'in entirely disingenuous ways'. Those cases were the original 1999 allegations – which dated back to Montgomery's witness statements alleging organ harvesting and murder – and a separate case in 2008 of a clinic that illegally paid poor donors from Turkey, Russia, Moldova and Kazakhstan for their kidneys. The case of the Medicus clinic saw its owner, his son and the lead anaesthetist convicted and jailed for organised crime in connection with people trafficking. The key difference, which Marty failed to point out, was that illegal kidney transplants associated with Kosovo's Medicus clinic involved paying poor 'donors' with their agreement, not illegal organ harvesting and murder.

Nice's report notes that 'we record with our complete astonishment that your Council should have allowed this connection to be made in a public document'.

Nice also attacked Marty's claim that he had found it difficult to find evidence in Kosovo because the clan culture among Kosovar Albanians meant effectively that they clammed up to outsiders. Nice argued that such an attack on an entire culture constituted ethnic prejudice, that it was naive, and served 'as a camouflage for the emptiness of that report'. He accused Marty of using 'the blur of generalisation' to obscure the fact that he had found no evidence of organ harvesting and as such would never have been able to produce a proper, police-style report.

Whatever the shortcomings of the Marty report, the Council of Europe recommended that a new investigation be opened by an independent body – this time to be headed by Clint Williamson, a Department of Justice director who had worked for the UN mission in Kosovo in 2002. By August 2015, Kosovo established special chambers to be working under Kosovo law but based in The Hague, to address the Marty allegations. As of January 2018, no indictments had been issued. Thaçi and the US, the great ally of Kosovo, both understood that the Marty allegations had to be tested in court. The Kosovo public saw the establishment of a so-called special court in The Hague to be unfair and one-sided. In a speech in the Kosovo Parliament, Thaçi called on MPs to vote for the special chambers: 'I know it's a historic injustice to establish this court, but for the sake of our partnership with the US, NATO and the EU, I call upon all to vote for the court.' In the end, the court dealing with the Marty allegations was established by a two-thirds majority in the Parliament.

Two years after the vote, Thaçi stated: 'I know how deeply unpopular was the decision to grant the Marty allegations legal credence in an international court, but it was the only just decision as we really had nothing to hide. It was the right decision for the country. It is a necessary evil for the country.'

While the chronology of allegations, witness statements, investigations and lack of any convictions for organ harvesting tells its own compelling story, the timings of leaks of various investigators and source statements carry their own narrative.

The leaking of the Marty report on the same day that Thaçi was re-elected as Prime Minister raises questions about whether Marty and his team were politically motivated – in favour of Serbia and the Russian camp.

While the Marty report failed to produce any convictions, it did create one enduring legacy – it rattled the Americans in the extreme.

Whether there was anything true in the allegations or not, it brought into question the judgement of the Clinton administration, who pushed for NATO bombardment, who supported Kosovo independence and who personally endorsed Thaçi. The Americans were embarrassed.

CHAPTER 13

DEALING WITH THE ENEMY

The atmosphere crackled. Hashim Thaçi and Ivo Dačić had walked into the room and sat down with the most cursory of handshakes. Dačić had been a True Believer; young, over-eager and a professional Socialist spin doctor for Milošević. Thaçi had hated Milošević until his death in 2006 and saw no reason why he should extend anything more than the bare minimum of courtesy to the Serb. Baroness Ashton, the EU foreign policy chief, shuffled her papers, cleared her throat and invited the Serb and the Kosovar to speak.

Dačić, not in the most relaxed mood, spoke first.

'I wanted to kill you in the past,' Dačić told Thaçi. 'Now I have to meet you.'

That was not a light-hearted way of breaking the ice. Belgrade had been out to get Thaçi for decades, and not just during the Milošević era. 'Let's put it this way,' recalls Thaçi, 'I wasn't their most beloved person.' Seven arrest warrants had been opened against the Kosovar since 1993 – membership of an illegal organisation, subversion. In 1997, he was sentenced in absentia by a Serb court. After independence in 2008, another charge was added to the docket: breaching the constitutional order of Serbia. Little wonder that he has never shown his face in Belgrade.

'I remember on a flight home from Vienna, the flight attendant announced that due to dense fog over Pristina the plane might have to divert to Belgrade or Skopje,' remembers Thaçi. 'I called her over and said: "You may not have enough jet fuel but it had better not be Belgrade, otherwise there will be an international incident!"' The pilot found another landing spot. 'Even so it was a nasty moment.' Until Thaçi became President, Serb customs officers used to have photographs of him on their watch lists.

Thaçi had dodged the Serb police, seen Serb soldiers up close, but he didn't know them very well. He certainly hadn't grown up with them; there were very few Serbs in the Drenica Valley and none at all in his village.

> My first contact with a Serb was when I was seventeen in high school. And since I didn't do military service, I didn't have the opportunity to meet them in the army. True, when I started as a student there were Bosnian Muslims and Serbs in our hostel dormitory. We hung out in an awkward sort of way. Then Milošević imposed his apartheid system and pulled apart Serbs from Albanians in Kosovo.

The encounter with Dačić in Brussels was thus a novelty. At Rambouillet, the Serb delegation with its late-night carousing and loud piano-plonking had confirmed for him a stereotype of an arrogant ruling class incapable of showing respect to their colonial underlings. The arrest warrant issued during the Rambouillet conference wanted Thaçi 'dead or alive'. This time, under the auspices of Catherine Ashton, it was different. Dačić, despite his past, was a serious politician, a Machiavellian moderniser who had been elected to take over the chairmanship of the Serbian Socialist Party after the death of Milošević. As Prime Minister, he now formed part of a ruling triad with deputy premier Aleksandar Vučić and President Tomislav Nikolić. In early 2012, Nikolić was still claiming that the Srebrenica massacre was an invention of the French secret service, and that he regretted nothing about serving with Serb militias in their bloody fights against the Croats in the 1990s. He still swore by the idea of a Greater Serbia. The Serb leadership, in other words, was not exactly raring to bury the hatchet with Thaçi.

It fell to Ashton to discover common ground. She knew she would never be able to force the Serb leadership to rewrite its national history. Instead, she wanted Belgrade to acknowledge a simple truth: that as long as the relationship between Serbia and Kosovo was unstable, a new explosion was inevitable.

Ashton's authority was not great. The Serbs saw the former Labour activist as too closely connected with Tony Blair – the man who had been so instrumental in the bombing of Serbia in 1999. To some in the EU, Ashton seemed to have been chosen for her weakness, not her strength. Nation states were reluctant to surrender sovereign powers in the name of a common EU foreign policy. And since five EU states actively refused to recognise Kosovo, she seemed to carry little clout. The best that she could do was to sniff out signs of a changing mood on the Balkans and exploit whatever openings offered themselves. The US government supported the dialogue and sent Phil Reeker, an experienced diplomat, to attend the dialogue rounds in Brussels. A few months later, both Hillary Clinton, then US Secretary of State, and Baroness Ashton paid a visit to both Pristina and Belgrade to provide personal support for both sides of the process.

According to the former US ambassador to Serbia, Cameron Munter, the Kosovan declaration of independence had, despite Serbia's public outrage, also set a thought process in motion among the Belgrade elite. 'It became clear to me that the post-Milošević Socialists [Dačić, in other words] and the post-Šešelj Radicals [Nikolić and Vučić] sensed that their constituencies wanted "Europe", or the kind of prosperity and ease that the prospect of EU membership seemed to offer.'

Serbia's economy, after all, was floundering. Unemployment was at around 28 per cent and the jobless rate among young people was even higher. The European Union, buffeted by a euro crisis, might have seemed spectacularly damaged but to young Serbs it still held some promise. Croatia, only recently at war with Serbia, was going to join the EU in July 2013 and the mere prospect of this was boosting its economy. Its per capita GDP was 70 per cent higher than that of Serbia.

The Serbian negotiating mission, then, was to find a way of clinging on to Kosovo while putting itself on track for EU membership. To Robert Cooper, a shrewd British diplomat who had become a senior advisor to the EU foreign service, there was enough wiggle room in Serb politics and Serb expectations to find a path to a deal. The planets, it seemed, were correctly aligned. After Kosovo's declaration of independence in 2008, the United Nations General Assembly had voted to test its legality at the International Court of Justice. That was Belgrade's way of deterring states from recognising Kosovo. But, by July 2010, the court had advised that the declaration 'did not violate general international law because international law contains no prohibitions on declarations of independence'. There was, in other words, no apparent legal impediment to countries around the world acknowledging Kosovo as a sovereign state. An important weapon in Belgrade's strategy of isolating Kosovo had thus been removed.

Meanwhile the then Serbian President Boris Tadić had applied to join the EU and had thus made his country open to some external pressure to make concessions on Kosovo. 'This application was being blocked by two or three member states who said they wanted to see a more forthcoming, positive attitude from Serbia on the question of Kosovo,' recalls Cooper. 'So we put these two things together and it looked like an opportunity.' Two months after the court ruling, Serbia was pressed to agree to an EU- and US-sponsored UN resolution calling for 'normalisation' of links with Kosovo.

The prize of possible EU membership began to shape Belgrade's behaviour. Under German and Dutch pressure, it set about seriously tracking down Ratko Mladić, the general who had presided over so many massacres in the Bosnian war. He had been on the run for sixteen years – actually hiding in plain sight to the north of Belgrade – and he was arrested pending extradition to The Hague.

Under Robert Cooper's supervision, the first high-level 'technical dialogue' between Serbia and Kosovo got under way in Brussels. The Mladić arrest encouraged the EU optimists to believe that Serbia was starting to change faster than anyone could have predicted. This was a rash assumption; there was movement, but it was very hesitant. Opinion polls showed that 40 per cent of Serbs still considered Mladić to be a hero; 78 per cent said they would never have betrayed the general's whereabouts, even for the €10 million reward. There was a long way to go.

Cooper understood the scope of the challenge. Allowing relations to fester would have nudged the Serb-dominated north of Kosovo into the clutches of Belgrade, which would have either been a prelude to the partitioning of Kosovo or created a permanently destabilising Serb presence in Kosovo akin to the Republika Srpska in Bosnia and Herzegovina. Peace-brokers work by analogy. Cooper had served as a diplomat in Bonn before the capital of united Germany moved to

Berlin. He thus had a detailed memory of how West and East German states had moved closer, despite high levels of enmity. For decades, the West German government had refused to recognise the communist East, but the Ostpolitik of Willy Brandt found a dozen different ways to make the Berlin Wall more porous. 'Technical' talks on seemingly minor points of friction had helped sidestep major flare-ups but also kept a dialogue going. The end result of the German crisis – reunification – was plainly not a model for the Kosovars. But Thaçi saw clearly that he had to tackle the unresolved problems of the Serb minority in north Kosovo; neglecting them risked disabling the state of Kosovo before it had even found its feet.

Between March and May 2011, talks were thus focused on freedom of movement over the bridge in ethnically divided Mitrovica. More: the birth registers that had been removed from the north by Serb forces in the 1999 war had to be restored to Kosovo so that Thaçi's government could get a proper overview of the size and location of the Serb community. University diplomas from Kosovo and Serbia had to be mutually recognised. Kosovo was represented at this stage by Edita Tahiri, the Deputy Prime Minister, and on the Serb side by the political directors of its foreign ministry, Borislav (Borko) Stefanović.

What brought them together was the carrot, in Serbia's case, of becoming a candidate member of the EU, and for Kosovo the prospect of a Stabilisation and Association Agreement, an even lower rung of the ladder. 'Maybe "leverage" isn't a very nice term,' says Cooper, 'but there we are. We are trying to get people to do things which are actually good for them.'

It should have been easy. Indeed, the game plan was that life would be made more manageable for ordinary people, building up a basic consensus for later top-level political talks between Thaçi and whoever emerged as the victors in the May 2012 Serbian elections. In fact, even the most straightforward issues stumbled on the problem of diplomatic non-recognition. After months of horse-trading, Serbia agreed to grant citizens of Kosovo entry into Serbia proper using documents issued in Pristina bearing the stamp of the Republic of Kosovo. This seemed like quite a breakthrough at first – and tantalisingly close to diplomatic recognition. Tahiri said citizens of Kosovo should simply be allowed to use their passports to enter Serbia. Stefanović said Serbia was not a foreign country, so no passports. It was agreed eventually that Kosovo citizens could use their ID cards until they reached the administrative border of Serbia, when they would be issued special passes by the Serb police. Using those passes they could then travel, for example, to Belgrade airport and then use a Kosovo passport to fly to a third country providing the destination had recognised Kosovo as a state.

Any Kosovar driving into Serbia would be required to exchange their RKS (Republic of Kosovo) number plates for temporary Serbian plates. Alternatively, they could travel with KS plates issued by Kosovan authorities but without the insignia of the Kosovan republic. These plates are favoured by Kosovan Serbs.

These measures were designed to bring the communities together in Kosovo; instead, they often underlined the gulf between ethnic Albanians and Serbs. They also drove a wedge between those ethnic Serbs living in the north of Kosovo – who essentially followed the rules and rhythms set by Belgrade – and the ethnic Serbs living south of the Ibar river, who found themselves reluctantly pushed into accepting the new realities of living in an independent Kosovan state.

These agreements were agreed orally. Nothing was written down because the Serb side said this would imply recognition of a separate Kosovo. 'Belgrade has an interest [in securing a neighbourly relationship] because these are Serbs. Belgrade has an interest in them being allowed to lead their lives without undue interference and without security problems,' says Cooper. 'Pristina has an interest in them being brought formally under Kosovo law as part of the Kosovo state. That was the basis of agreement.'

The switch to a political dialogue – with Dačić, Thaçi and Ashton – came in November 2011. It was prickly and awkward. Ashton's tactic was simple: she let the two Prime Ministers talk, guiding them a bit like a therapist. Cooper was full of praise for her approach, knowing from his experience earlier in the year how easy it was for the two sides to become petrified by the need to stick to a written commitment.

'I thought that Catherine approached it very well, in a very political way, very different from the way in which we had done the first part of the dialogue,' says Cooper.

> I suggested to put forward a 'take-it-or-leave-it' agreement on north Kosovo. She very wisely didn't do that. Instead, after the first six or seven dinners, she said: 'Well, I think we're beginning to reach an understanding on this. Maybe we can start writing it down.' That's how it was done.[24]

Thaçi, too, admired Ashton's subtlety. It demanded time and patience but it was not the usual way of doing business in the Balkans. 'I really admired her ability to ease tension, her skill in calling breaks, judging when it was best to have a *tête-à-tête* and when to leave us alone together.' The format of the meetings was tight. Thaçi was accompanied by his advisor Bekim Çollaku, who played an important role in framing the final texts of agreements, while Dačić was accompanied by his interpreter.

---

24 'The Brussels Agreement "generated by conversations, not by relentless pressure"', LSE blog, accessed 21 August 2017 at: http://blogs.lse.ac.uk/lsee/2015/02/06/robert-cooper-interview/. The film *The Agreement* gives a vivid account of the talks.

There was certainly plenty at stake. Plainly the parallel Serbian power structure in north Kosovo was a problem. Angela Merkel, the German Chancellor, had already made clear that Serbia could not count on EU candidate status as long as they continued to operate. In July 2011, Thaçi had ordered Kosovo's special police units to control the border posts in the north of Kosovo. Local Serbs rebelled and started attacking Kfor units, mostly composed of German soldiers. Merkel was furious. Brussels was unhappy with Thaçi's unilateral move in the north, which threatened to wreck the dialogue. But the violent reactions by Serbian paramilitaries in the north helped European capitals move fast to dismantle the parallel structures in north Kosovo. Thaçi recalls this tense period:

> Before I decided to send special units to the northern border posts, I informed NATO and the US embassy in Pristina. Both told me that I had a right to use all constitutional means to control my own borders. Unfortunately, a Kosovo policeman was shot dead by the Serbian paramilitaries. I didn't quite manage to control both border posts in the north of the country, but I got NATO helicopters to carry our police forces to the north. This was an important signal that nationalist insurgency in the north would not be tolerated. Kosovo was united. Belgrade understood the message.

The dialogue became a way to solve the essential riddle: how could the Kosovan Serbs be given a large degree of municipal power while remaining inside the state of Kosovo? At the moment it was operating on a makeshift basis with interim municipal councils appointed and funded by Belgrade – and often controlled by the ultra-nationalist Progressive party. At the same time, many representatives were also receiving a salary from Kosovo. Prosecutors, the courts, police commanders were all serving two masters. The result: an often lawless space in which the main commercial activity was cross-border smuggling in and out of Serbia.

Thaçi, watching his counterpart closely as the negotiations started to narrow on these issues, understood that Serbia was more interested in controlling the territory of northern Kosovo than in the welfare of the Serbs living there. Every interview he gave on the sidelines of the talks tried to expose the weakness of Belgrade's position. He told *NIN*, the Serb weekly: 'The difference between me and the leaders of Belgrade is that I'm committed to creative solutions in improving the living conditions for Serbs in the north, and to providing greater security so that they can be integrated into local and central government.' Whether the readers of *NIN* believed that was largely irrelevant. The main aim was to sap the ties between Belgrade and the Kosovan Serbs, and convince the community that they would ultimately be better off being loyal and law-abiding Kosovars than the pawns of Milošević's heirs.

Thaçi sensed that the Serb side was increasingly on the back foot. 'Serbia's current leaders should do no more and no less than accept reality and tell the truth about Kosovo to their citizens,' said Thaçi. 'The battle of Kosovo was won by the Kosovars in June 1999 and it was Slobodan Milošević who lost that.' Although Serbia was stronger, better industrialised and more prosperous than its former province, it was also a hostage to the past. The pro-Europeans in Serbia – including those ultra-nationalists who had changed their spots – were scrambling for a coherent narrative to offer their disillusioned and resentful voters. Kosovo knew it had only one road to the future: the European Union. Serbia, by contrast, was still confused by its choices – between striving to be a regional leader, getting closer to Russia or membership of the European club.

The strain was telling on Dačić. 'He was sweating a lot, maybe because of the political pressure,' remembers Thaçi.

He really didn't look well, letting out loud sighs. He would leave Catherine's office to study text messages from Belgrade, then punch out a reply. On his cigar breaks he would phone Vučić who was technically his deputy. So I told him when we were alone together, 'Look, you're the Prime Minister, why don't you just summon Vučić here to Brussels?'

The knottiest problem was about the nature of the power that should be enjoyed in the future by the so-called Association of Serb Municipalities. From the Pristina point of view, it made sense for Serb communities in Kosovo to form a network and a coherent platform. This was agreed even during President Ahtisaari's negotiations back in 2007. That way they could make Kosovo stronger, not undermine it. Belgrade, however, wanted to make something grander out of the Association, a kind of alternative government whose loyalty to Serbia would always be more pronounced than to Kosovo.

Vučić came and went. 'He was tougher,' remembers Thaçi, 'but more productive.' But not productive enough.

The negotiations with Dačić dragged on and Thaçi began to lose his composure, banging his fist on the table so hard that the coffee cups jumped from their saucers. Sessions could last from nine o'clock in the morning through to 2 a.m. Often the time was gnawed away by Dačić's need to consult Belgrade.

'Once, close to midnight, I agreed to sign a paragraph, in fact sign the whole document,' says Thaçi. 'Dačić said he had to consult with the President. I waited and I waited. After an hour the Prime Minister came back and announced: "Nikolić says: 'Don't sign, but don't turn it down either.'"'

After a total of 250 hours of face-to-face negotiation, both Thaçi and Dačić decided that no deal was possible. It was April 2013 and they had both been going round in circles for months. A day earlier than the scheduled conclusion of the talks, they headed for home. Thaçi was supposed to fly via Ljubljana in Slovenia to Pristina; Dačić to Belgrade.

'Brussels was angry, Washington was upset, Cathy Ashton distressed – but we had done everything we could possibly do.' But before Thaçi could make his connecting flight to Pristina, Thaçi received a message from Ashton. She thought she had found a way round the final obstacles – and Thaçi should return to Brussels immediately. Dačić received a similar message. Within hours they were back in Ashton's office for an all-night session, the last.

The way Ashton saw it was that a properly anchored framework deal between Serbs and Kosovo Albanians could transform the Balkans. Macedonia was edging westwards only slowly because of a seemingly endless row with Greece over how to name the country. Bosnia could not move on because of the malign influence of Belgrade on the Bosnian Serbs. A settlement on Kosovo would demonstrate that Europe still had clout in the region, and could bring order to its borders.

Ashton's optimism was not entirely irrational. Some progress had been made. One flashpoint was the Kosovo border posts in the north. Untaxed goods passed massively into the north of Kosovo from Serbia; the contraband flow was huge. Thaçi was adamant that a sovereign state should be in control of its borders; Dačić insisted there was no such border. The Ashton talks had edged the two leaders towards a practical, stopgap solution. EULEX officials could act as go-between ensuring that there would be no direct contact – and potential confrontations – between Serbs and Kosovars. The EU would fund joint border crossings to ensure cooperation between the customs officials from both countries.

But these small concessions were focused more on conflict avoidance than the active establishment of good relations. And it was taking

months to deal with each controversial item. At this pace, a compre-
hensive settlement could take many years. The walkout of Thaçi and
Dačić was thus particularly complicated for Ashton. If the talks did
not come to an accord by 22 April, she would lose her window of
opportunity. The German election campaign was cranking up before a
vote in September. New European Commission officials were due to be
selected in 2014. The whole process of Serb–Kosovan dialogue could
be delayed by eighteen months or more and the tentatively pro-
European mood of the new Serb government could fizzle out. On top
of which Ashton was deeply involved in trying to broker a deal between
the US, three EU countries, Russia and China that would impose curbs
on Iran's nuclear enrichment programme. To the Obama administration, the Iran dossier was beginning to look more pressing than the
Kosovo dossier.

Her solution, relayed to Thaçi and Dačić, was to draw up a list of fifteen
short paragraphs setting out the principles of future normalisation.
The first six points relate to the main bone of contention, the Association
of Serb majority municipalities in Kosovo; they would be given the right
to coordinate in the running of education, health and rural planning
as well as economic development. Other paragraphs asserted Kosovo's
ultimate control over the police: 'There shall be one police force in
Kosovo called the Kosovo Police. All police in northern Kosovo shall be
integrated in the Kosovo Police framework. Salaries will be paid only by
the Kosovo Police.' That was, in effect, a ban on Serbian security agents
running the neighbourhood. But it did provide for police commanders
to be Kosovan Serbs, chosen by Pristina from a shortlist drawn up by
local mayors.

Crucially, the penultimate paragraph of the deal states baldly: 'It is
agreed that neither side will block, or encourage others to block, the
other side's progress in their respective EU paths.' This, Dačić tried

to spin to his electorate as a significant victory. Thaçi had fought for an explicit ban on Serbia obstructing Kosovo's attempts to join international organisations like the United Nations. 'I think this is the most favourable document for the Serbian side so far,' crowed Dačić. It couldn't interfere with Kosovo's road to Europe, at least not overtly. But it was not barred from campaigning on every possible platform against nation-state status for what was still seen in Belgrade as an upstart Serbian province.

The Brussels agreement, two pages that resembled notes for a student's PowerPoint presentation, could be a breakthrough – but only if it is properly implemented. Documents such as these are usually prefaced with the names, ranks and states of the parties to the agreement. And usually there is an indication as to when the agreement will come into force. All that is missing from the Brussels agreement. When Ashton passed copies to Thaçi and Dačić, neither signed it. Rather, after exchanging a meaningful glance with each other, they just inked their initials.

It was the best Ashton could do to meet her self-imposed deadline. The provisional nature of the agreement, however, suggested that both sides were ready to beat a retreat if necessary. Protests broke out in northern Kosovo. In Pristina, a parliamentary session was raucous but ended up approving the agreement. In Belgrade, a few hundred protestors raised banners declaring, 'Kosovo is Serbia, We Need No EU!'

It could have been worse. For the time being, Thaçi was pleased with the agreement and with the handiwork of his skilled Europe team. He said it 'guaranteed the recognition of Kosovo's international statehood, sovereignty and territorial integrity'. In fact, the deal did not quite do that. It described itself as a 'First Agreement'. That is to say the Brussels agreement would have to be implemented with both sides reaching a common interpretation of principles. Only then would there be a 'normalisation' of relations between the two former enemies. There was still a long way to go before one could honestly say that Serbia was close to recognising Kosovo.

Nor was it really clear what 'normalisation' meant within the cramped confines of the relationship. In an interview, Thaçi said he was striving for a situation where it would be 'normal' for Serbian leaders to visit their counterparts in Pristina, and vice versa. Much as already was happening between Belgrade and Zagreb or Belgrade and Sarajevo. Soon after the Brussels agreement was initialled, Serb President Nikolić caused jaws to drop in Europe when he apologised on Bosnian TV for the 1995 Srebrenica massacre. 'I kneel and ask for forgiveness for Serbia for the crime committed in Srebrenica,' said the former extreme nationalist. True, he couldn't quite mouth the word 'genocide', but it was enough to persuade the European Council that Ashton's diplomacy had started a positive trend.

Would Nikolić ever apologise for crimes committed in Kosovo? How genuine was this normalisation – and how far was it an act to speed the way into the EU? It was one thing to give a sign of remorse to neighbours and trading partners, quite another to accept Kosovo not only as a sovereign state, but as an equal.

In June 2013, the European Council announced a date for starting membership negotiations with Serbia and the start of talks with Kosovo on a Stabilisation and Association Agreement. Ethnic crimes also dramatically decreased in north Kosovo as a result of the dialogue, only five such cases being reported by EULEX police throughout the whole of 2016, whereas before the dialogue, the northern area was full of barricades and local nationalists frequently attacked members of the opposite community.

The implementation of the Belgrade Agreement was regarded as a necessary hurdle before the next EU initiation rites could begin. Yet inevitably the process slowed down. Elections and the EU bureaucratic process had put different people in the driving seat. Federica Mogherini, a relatively inexperienced Italian diplomat, replaced Ashton. Isa Mustafa replaced Thaçi as Prime Minister and Thaçi became foreign minister. The ambitious Vučić was now Serbia's Prime Minister (in 2017 he was elected President of Serbia). After a long pause, some of the building blocks of the Brussels deal were put into place. North Kosovan Serb judges and prosecutors, working within the Kosovan legal system, were given a much greater say in handing out justice. But there were plenty of rows too. Freedom of movement had been guaranteed between the Serbs and the Albanians in the northern town of Mitrovica. Barricades were duly removed from the bridge over the Ibar river – only to be replaced by a Serb-built 'Peace Park' which featured concrete flower bins. Pristina saw this not as urban gentrification but as a stealthy return of the bridge barriers.

Europe is the only sensible destination for Kosovo. It will be a way, say members of the Kosovo government, of disconnecting Kosovo from the Balkan cycle of resurgent nationalisms, of 'Blood and Soil' politics. The closer Kosovo is allowed to approach EU membership, the stronger is the regional motivation to maintain good neighbourly relations and respect for minority rights. Yet Thaçi's dream will only be realised if Serbia stops stoking the discontent of Kosovo Serbs, and accepts that the forced partition of Kosovo, its deliberate destabilisation, will invite chaos back to the region.

When, in early 2017, Serbia sent a train to Kosovo sprayed with slogans reading 'Kosovo is Serbia' in twelve different languages, the two sides were quick to talk of a possible military clash. Calling it a provocation, Kosovo worried that if the train – completely painted in Serbian colours – crossed the border it could be attacked by outraged citizens. 'We do not want war, but we will even send the army if needed to protect Serbs from possible killings,' said President Nikolić in a less-than-subtle attempt to escalate the crisis that his government had created in the first place. In the end, Serbia decided to stop the train before it crossed into Kosovan territory. But the Kosovan government analysis was probably correct: although Serbia had promised not to impede Kosovo's path to the EU, it is still looking for ways to prod Pristina into blotting its Brussels copybook.

Thaçi has been aware since his many hours of verbal wrestling with Dačić that making the concessions demanded by the EU would put strain on his citizens. And that Serbia would try to exploit that impatience. Europe is still far away. And Belgrade and Moscow, in their different ways, are quite happy for Kosovo's EU and NATO ambitions to be pushed well beyond the horizon. 'There is one simple method that Brussels could use to keep alive our country's enthusiasm for Euro-Atlantic values,' says Thaçi: 'Easing visa conditions for travel to Europe. Treating us fairly and equally.'

'The West showed its solidarity by defending us against attack, and then by helping us to build our state institutions,' continues Thaçi.

> Our young people would appreciate these great contributions even more if they could travel freely. They have to see how the West works in practice not just in theory, its weaknesses and its merits. That's how they will come to understand better their own country, and the sacrifices that the older generation made for them.

CHAPTER 14

UNESCO AND GETTING RECOGNITION ON THE WORLD STAGE

The day after Kosovo's independence was declared, Thaçi had to start a global campaign for Kosovo's recognition. The UN Security Council could not endorse Ahtisaari's plan for independence, because Russia blocked the decision. Vladimir Putin, the new Russian President, was keen to project power on the global stage after years of Yeltsin rule, and Kosovo's quest for independence soon became diplomatic trench warfare between Moscow and the Western capitals. This meant that Kosovars had to chase individual recognitions from countries from the Caribbean seas to the Baltic states. All things considered, little Kosovo, helped by London, Washington, Paris, Berlin and Ankara, did well – far more countries recognised Kosovo than other disputed territories such as Taiwan.

This being said, the 2013 deal with Serbia was only the beginning of Thaçi's battle for Kosovar recognition. Thaçi knew that for Kosovo to be able to hold its head up high and for Kosovars to feel a sense of national identity, the country must fight to sit at all the top tables on the world stage and be members of global clubs.

While membership of the United Nations and NATO were the real prizes, Thaçi pursued other, smaller types of recognition – from FIFA and the International Olympic Committee to UNESCO and Facebook.

However, what Thaçi's battle to get worldwide recognition of Kosovo as an independent nation state exposed was the deep thicket of private vendettas of Russian and Serbian leaders, implicit alliances between other countries and domestic anxieties that would be brought into play – all of which would stand in the way of Kosovo's independent journey.

The very act of declaring independence had – as Thaçi had anticipated – created a very public set of two rival international camps: those who needed to curry favour with Washington, Whitehall and Berlin, and those who needed the support of Belgrade and the Kremlin. Thaçi also predicted that any country with secessionist groups – such as Spain, Indonesia and Morocco, would fall in with Serbia for fear of stoking trouble at home.

Thaçi started lobbying for independence even before declaring the formal independence of the country. As a leader of the opposition as well as a recently elected Prime Minister, Thaçi visited several countries to test the mood of foreign interlocutors. In February 2007, he visited and met senior politicians including President Shimon Peres, Defence minister Ehud Barak and the then Leader of the Opposition, Benjamin Netanyahu. Thaçi said: 'Israel had sympathies for Kosovo, stemming from the 1999 war. Israel had accepted Kosovo refugees, while American-Jewish leaders in Congress from Tom Lantos to Eliot Engel were instrumental to ensuring decade-long US support for Kosovo.' This being said, Israel to this date has not yet recognised Kosovo. Israel, Palestine and Iran are the only countries in the Middle East that have not recognised Kosovo.

Thaçi, recalling the intensive lobbying campaign for recognition, remembered a conversation with President Clinton in 2013.

Kosovo's recognition by Russia and allies is an issue that can only be resolved if there is a big deal between Washington and Moscow. The USA is the only country that can convince Russians to allow Kosovo's accession to the UN – not you. Kosovo's recognition is not anymore an issue right versus wrong, but part of a wider dialogue between global powers.'

While Kosovo knew it could rely on American allies, African countries on whom Britain and France could apply old colonial-style pressure, and historic friends such as Turkey to support them to join the top clubs of the global political stage, many countries, for fear of irritating Russia, would side with Serbia.

Kosovo's quest for recognition was dependent on the support of allies, but also sheer luck. After lobbying from Pristina, including personal visits to Cairo by Thaçi, Egypt formally recognised Kosovo in June 2013. Only a few days later, the government of Mohammed Morsi was overthrown. Although the new military leaders overturned most of the decisions made by Morsi, Kosovo recognition remained intact. Erdoğan made many personal calls to countries to lobby for recognition. Thaçi claims several heads of states managed to persuade several Muslim-majority countries:

Many of the countries from the Organisation of Islamic Co-operation belonged to the old world of non-aligned nations and still had nostalgia for Belgrade, stemming from Tito's old Yugoslavia. They did not understand that Yugoslavia was dead – and Milošević was the one who pulled the trigger. So it was important that leaders such as King Abdullah of Jordan and President Erdoğan got involved to offset Serbia's lobbying.

When Thaçi had declared independence, he confidently said that 'a hundred' nations would acknowledge Kosovar statehood within weeks. Kosovo is now recognised as a sovereign nation by 115 countries – soon approaching two-thirds of the UN membership. Thaçi visited half of them and met over 150 world leaders in the margins of United Nations sessions in New York. Thaçi credited four post-independence foreign ministers with persuading so many countries to recognise Kosovo – Enver Hoxhaj, Vlora Çitaku, Petrit Selimi and Skënder Hyseni – who, he said, never stopped in search of a new venues for recognition of Kosovo's independence.

This private diplomatic cats' cradle of competing interests – from loyalties to Belgrade, hatred of the US and fear of the Kremlin – was played out very publicly during Kosovo's first bid for membership of UNESCO in November 2015.

Thaçi wanted UNESCO membership badly, not least to promote its membership of the IMF and the World Bank. It would have marked a step towards national recognition on the world stage, albeit in a small way, and attracted millions of dollars' worth of UN money for cultural and educational projects for Kosovo. The values that UNESCO membership promoted – that after two world wars political and economic agreements were not enough to sustain peace and that education and culture were needed to cement a society – would all have been helpful signals for the impoverished and damaged young country.

UNESCO membership would also have given Pristina control of protecting all of the country's heritage sites, including a 700-year-old Serbian Orthodox monastery in the town of Gračanica and three other Christian sites which UNESCO has placed on its endangered world heritage list.

But Thaçi's bid for membership – that Serbia had gained in 2000

(Yugoslavia had been a member since 1950, but Serbia had to re-apply) – would unleash the worst of what Serbian propaganda could use to damage Pristina, deploying the might of its Russian ally and stirring up the paranoia of Serb minorities in Kosovo who long feared that an independent Kosovo meant a takeover and elimination of the Serb way of life.

Serb communities in Kosovo believed they had good reason, however, to be paranoid. In 2004, Serbian monuments and churches were destroyed in violent riots, prompting mass protests and calls for international protection. The Organization for Security and Co-operation in Europe mission in Pristina estimated that around 200 graves were desecrated.

With this backdrop, in September 2015, Albania formally requested that Kosovo be recognised by UNESCO, and was backed by another forty-four members. It marked Kosovo's second attempt. The request immediately drew the ire of Serbia. Aleksandar Vulin, the Serbian Labour minister, threw his weight around: 'I'm sorry that Albania did what it did. That doesn't restore trust in the region and shows there are countries that don't care or only care a little about what Serbia and Serbs feel.' The Serbian ambassador to UNESCO was even more aggressive. In an interview for the Russian Radio Sputnik, Darko Tanasković stated: 'All Christians in the world must unite and reject Kosovo's application.'

But the Albanian bid – accepted by both the UN and UNESCO – set the ball rolling.

Thaçi and Kosovo's fledgling diplomatic team went into lobbying overdrive. In the final day of voting, Kosovo needed a two-thirds majority, at least ninety-five votes. There were the definite 'no's – apart from Serbia and Russia, Kosovo's application made some strange bedfellows, as both Israel and Palestine voted against Kosovo. There were probably 'yes' votes – an anti-Soviet vote – all of Scandinavia and the Baltics. While 111 countries had recognised Kosovo since the declaration of independence in 2008, not all of them had paid their UNESCO membership bills so were only allowed to abstain, including Antigua and the Dominican Republic.

As soon as Russian foreign minister Sergey Lavrov arrived, the Kremlin began pulling delegations. The UNESCO vote for a country of just 1.8 million had spun into a microcosm for the global power play between Russia and the West, with renewed insistence by Serbia that Kosovo had no claims to independence, and that it had failed to care for Serbian heritage sites after the war.

Azerbaijan abstained, along with Romania and Greece. Russia, India, Brazil and South Africa all sought to block Pristina, as did – unexpectedly – Slovakia.

Thaçi insisted that the campaign for UNESCO membership could be considered a success because it was a true 'battle between David and Goliath. Serbia and Russia used all their ammunition to stop us and still had three times less votes than us. Procedures were against Kosovo but the size of the supporting countries was overwhelming. In this respect, one has to recognise the brilliant lobbying efforts by Petrit Selimi.' Selimi, one of Thaçi's close, Western-educated advisors, was able to design an innovative digital campaign that got mentioned on the front page of the *New York Times*.

The night before the UNESCO vote, Thaçi said that the final calculations were made and he knew that Kosovo would either win or lose by two or three votes.

> I was really struggling with a major decision. Should we try for a vote or withdraw the request before the vote happened? Four votes made me worried. Japan and South Korea confirmed abstention from voting, Slovakia and Greece had promised us a positive vote but changed their minds in the very last hours. We

were also handicapped because the Americans could neither vote nor even attend the session. They lost their voting rights after US Congress cut its funding for UNESCO. The American diplomat Hoyt Yee called me close to midnight, hours before the voting session would start. Americans thought we were far from two-thirds and they too were contemplating to advise us to withdraw. Yet, their final advice was 'go ahead'. I knew we were very close but that, with the Americans out of the room, the Russians were using all methods to stop us.

On the day of the ballot, Thaçi's vote calculation was proven correct. Kosovo lost by three votes, with ninety-two in favour, fifty against and twenty-nine abstentions.

But, apart from a bloody nose, and another victory for Serbia, the failed UNESCO application had other consequences.

Egged on by Belgrade and the Kremlin, the UNESCO bid stoked up deep anxieties among the Serb communities in western provinces in Kosovo. Exploiting the paranoia of the 130,000 Serbs who live in Kosovo – outnumbered by the 1.8 million ethnic Albanians – the Serbs panicked that Kosovan membership to UNESCO would see Pristina seize control of Serbian Orthodox Christian sites, already UNESCO-listed. Citing Kosovan desecration of Serb cemeteries and the looting of churches after the 1998 war, Serbia cautioned that the sites would be at risk if Pristina was trusted to protect them. The rhetoric easily prompted memories of incidents such as a Serb Orthodox cemetery desecrated by Albanian extremists near Peć in October 2001.

Thaçi was acutely aware of Belgrade's attempt to paint the dispute over Kosovo's independence as a religious issue and set about trying to show the multi-faith identity of the tiny republic. He opened a memorial to Kosovo Jews who lost their lives in the Holocaust, and developed relations witht the Vatican. He was received by Pope Francis soon after he became President of Kosovo. Thaçi said:

> Pope Francis supported our efforts for dialogue and reconciliation between Albanians and Serbs. He was keenly aware of the issue of Kosovo's recognition by the Vatican and told me that the Holy See missed the opportunity to recognise Kosovo in the first wave together with other Western nations. He said, however, that Vatican recognition would be forthcoming sooner or later.

And Russia was only too happy to stir up Serbian paranoia, using its global media channels such as Radio Sputnik and Russia Today. The Kremlin tried, unsuccessfully, to delay the vote and Russian foreign minister Sergey Lavrov insisted in his address to UNESCO that Kosovo's membership bid was 'very dangerous'.

The failure to win UNESCO membership – and the raw wounds it exposed among Kosovo's Serbian minorities – could not have come at a more sensitive time for Thaçi. Only the month before the UNESCO rejection, opposition MPs had begun protests in the Pristina parliament building, flinging tear gas canisters, to express fury over Thaçi's plan to give more autonomy to Serb communities. The opposition in Kosovo parliament argued that the EU-brokered deal to help Kosovar Serbs set up an association of Serbian municipalities – as it was agreed in the Ahtisaari Plan – would simply boost Belgrade's influence in the country.

In an interview in late 2015, Thaçi revealed that he had three missions in life.

The first was to establish liberty for Kosovo. 'I achieved that in the summer of '99,' he said.

The second was Kosovan independence: 'We declared independence in February 2008.'

But a third remained: that Kosovo first become a member of NATO and then, ultimately, a member of the European Union.

Thaçi predicted that Kosovo would be admitted to NATO by 2025, and would achieve EU accession by 2030 – 'if there is any European Union to join by then,' he added cautiously.

What the Rambouillet peace talks and subsequent NATO bombing proved was that Thaçi is a wily and stubborn negotiator with a quiet flair on the world stage next to Western leaders with far more experience, clout and power than him. Privately, Thaçi admits that he still pinches himself that he was able to convince the West to bring all their force to eject Serbia from Kosovo and back his tiny country's bid for independence.

But the tedious, painstaking bureaucracy to gain recognition from the world's most important clubs – the UN, the Council of Europe, NATO and the EU – is far from Thaçi's forte.

One of his oldest and trusted friends – Bekim Çollaku – explained how Thaçi despises detail, the mundanity of bureaucracy and of paperwork.

It was for this reason that Thaçi appointed Çollaku as his chief of staff throughout his time as Prime Minister and then Minister of European Integration, tasked with managing the Kosovan membership process for the UN, NATO and, ultimately, the EU.

Çollaku said: 'Hashim was not born to be a technocrat. He hates office work – he was born to be a leader. He does not go into details, but he is the man who makes the decisions. He doesn't like routine and hates having to waste time on minor things.'

Thaçi does not even own a mobile phone. He is not the type of politician who manically checks emails or – like Angela Merkel – a fanatical texter. Given that Thaçi is rarely alone, he is contactable by the small, elite circle around him, of whom Çollaku is a part.

Çollaku, a slight, erudite, affable academic, first met Thaçi in 1996 in a rented student flat in Pristina. He had no idea that the tall, skinny 28-year-old was the leader of the KLA, and had missed him at university, being six years younger than Thaçi.

> In those student days, Hashim never revealed what he did. I just thought he was a good guy. I remember him turning up at my flat, with Kadri Veseli [who became Speaker of Parliament]. They turned up with a cake. There was certainly no sense that they had come to recruit me.
>
> It wasn't until the war that I realised what role he had come to have in the KLA.

Çollaku recalls that all the students who came to his digs at that time became members of the KLA.

'Most of us knew that peaceful policy [against Serbia] would not work. Serbia was just too strong. We came to the conclusion that something radical had to happen.'

With a friendship forged over twenty years, a decade in hiding and a war, it is no surprise that the young advisors such as Bekim Çollaku and Vlora Çitaku have been entrusted to handle the legwork and painstaking detail of Kosovo's interaction with Washington and Brussels.

While accession to the EU is Thaçi's ultimate goal, and what he hopes will form a large part of his legacy, for most Kosovars it is visa liberalisation which is paramount.

Kosovars cannot travel across the EU without a visa, and the process for applying for one – through a host nation's embassy – is protracted and onerous. Çollaku once described the amount of paperwork needed to obtain an EU visa as sufficient to 'cover the floor of a good-sized room'. Kosovars also need to prove they have funds to pay their way while abroad.

Kosovo got its roadmap for visa liberalisation from the European Commission in 2012 and signed up to a range of reforms, which included beefing up document security, control of the country's borders and the handling of illegal migrants. But, five years on, Federica Mogherini, the High Representative for EU Foreign Affairs, said that Kosovo had still made no progress on other issues such as a border deal with Montenegro.

Visa-free travel would allow Kosovars to travel across the EU and to stay for a maximum of ninety days in a 180-day period, for family visits, medical treatment, tourism, short business trips and courses. Effectively, citizens who no longer need a visa to travel in the EU are granted membership to the so-called White Schengen list, allowing them to travel across the border-free Schengen area of the twenty-two EU member states and also Iceland, Norway, Switzerland and Liechtenstein. Britain and Ireland opted out.

But, while countries such as Colombia were granted visa-free travel to and across the EU in December 2015, prompting President Santos to brag that his country had been given back some 'dignity', Brussels heaped more obstacles on Pristina.

According to Çollaku, other countries had to meet fifty requirements, whereas Kosovo had ninety-six.

While Pristina railed against the unfairness of its treatment over visas and accused the EU of political bias, Brussels had clearly been rattled by a surge in illegal Kosovars in late 2014 being trafficked into Austria, Hungary and Germany looking for work in the EU.

At its height, Dimitris Avramopoulos, the EU Commissioner for Migration, Home Affairs and Citizenship, reckoned that 1,400 Kosovars were leaving the country a day, trying to smuggle themselves into the EU. That was on top of record migration numbers in early 2015 which reached post-1990 war levels.

In February 2015 alone, 30,000 Kosovars requested asylum in Hungary and another 13,000 the following month asked for the same status in Germany.

Unemployment rates vary for the Kosovar economy – not least because such a large chunk of the country operates through a cash black market. The IMF claims that the official Kosovar unemployment rate – as of January 2016 – was 30 per cent. American federal agency Millennium Challenge Corporation measured unemployment at 17 per cent in 2017. But, with the youngest population in Europe – half of all Kosovars are under the age of twenty-five – youth unemployment is estimated to be far higher.

While Kosovo grumbled about the unfairness of the protracted visa liberalisation process, Brussels clearly wanted assurances that Pristina had a means and incentives to take rejected migrants back.

On the long road to Kosovan recognition on the world stage, Çollaku reckons that admission to NATO will be by far the country's easiest of hurdles. He pointed out that NATO desperation to limit the reach and influence of Russia in the Balkans would make it far more amenable to new entrants from the region.

After the Kremlin's annexation of Crimea in March 2014 and Russia's slow creep into eastern Ukraine, the West grew ever more paranoid about President Putin's ambitions on Europe's doorstep. The emergence of a new Russian military base in Serbia did little to allay NATO fears.

Hoyt Yee, the US diplomat, in a recent tour of Balkans expressed deep concerns about Russia's role in the Balkans:

Our message to Serbia is that it needs to be vigilant and understand what Russia is attempting to do, why it, for example, wants to create a so-called humanitarian centre in Niš. I think it is not obvious what Russia is up to and I can't tell you what its strategy is. But what we see though are recent attempts by Russia to prevent countries from pursuing their own national strategies whether it is integration with the EU or integration with NATO or simply to have independence.

What stands in the way of Kosovan membership of NATO are final reforms of its armed forces. What NATO will want to see is the completion of the transformation process of Kosovo's soldiers – a few thousand of whom date back to rebel fighters in the KLA. What Thaçi will have to be able to prove is that the process that he started in 1999 – of the disbanding of the KLA – has been completed.

As we saw earlier, Thaçi has recalled how persuading Kosovars to abandon their arms was far harder than persuading them to take them up in the first place.

But NATO acceptance will hinge on how successful Thaçi is seen to have been in transforming the country's Kosovo Security Force into a new army, built from scratch with NATO vetting of applicants. While the official Kosovar line is that NATO vetting was essential to produce an armed force of suitable age, education and training, it was also necessary to weed out criminal elements and remnants of a guerrilla movement.

———————

While Pristina has regularly played the victim card in its dealings with the EU, insisting that progress towards recognition and EU candidacy is at every stage stymied by Serbia, the European Commission 2015 report into Kosovo made grim reading. Tackling corruption – from people trafficking, drug smuggling, money laundering to dodgy procurement methods for government contracts – is high on Brussels anxiety list, and the 2015 report would do little to allay their concerns.

Kosovo, the EC report concluded diplomatically, was at an 'early stage' in developing a judicial system that even resembled being independent, let alone one that could be defined as efficient. 'Judicial structures are still prone to political interference,' the report argued. 'The number of judges dealing with serious crimes remains low' and forty cases had been brought against judges on 'disciplinary and ethical grounds'.

The fight against corruption was, it found, also 'at an early stage'. Kosovo had not yet 'established a track record of investigations, prosecutions and convictions in corruption cases'. Financial investigations could not be conducted properly because of 'undue political influence'. The rate of convictions against human trafficking 'remains low despite Kosovo being a source and transit country for trafficked women and children'. Kosovo's 9,000 policemen did not fare much better in gathering evidence against drug dealers either. In short, Brussels – albeit in a polite way – concluded that corruption remained rife across Kosovo.

One line of defence by Thaçi and his inner circle is not that the corruption does not exist but that the country is subject to more scrutiny because of the EULEX mission based full time in Pristina. 'I would like to see how Italy would fare if they had such a mission scrutinising them in Rome,' one minister pointed out. However, by March 2017, Mogherini did issue a statement saying that some progress had been made in the battle to crack down on corruption.

The biggest obstacle to EU accession, however, beyond stemming corruption and limiting the flow of asylum seekers trying to leave Kosovo, is relations with Belgrade.

The thorny issue was whether Serbia – about five years ahead of Kosovo in its journey towards EU membership – would use its new status to block Pristina's later bid for accession, all the while lobbying the other five European states who do not recognise Kosovan statehood – namely, Cyprus, Greece, Romania, Slovakia and Spain.

Even as late as February 2016, Brussels had still not decided whether a key criteria of Serbian membership should be Belgrade's recognition of Kosovan statehood. In an attempt to wheedle round a confrontation with Serbia, Thaçi and Çollaku examined other scenarios such as an undertaking from Belgrade that it would not try to block Kosovan membership of international bodies, including the UN and the EU.

'If Serbia does this,' Thaçi said, 'it's more than the recognition of Kosovo. We can live without the recognition of Serbia.' Thaçi believed he could secure such a deal within a five-month timeframe.

Mired in Serbian opposition and Brussels bureaucracy, Thaçi did manage one important step on the road to EU accession: on 27 October 2015, Kosovo signed its first agreement as an independent nation with the EU. Thaçi dubbed it Kosovo's Europe Day. It was a long time in the making. The signing of the Stabilisation and Association Agreement (SAA) had taken two and a half years to seal after Cathy Ashton brokered a deal to normalise relations between Kosovo and Serbia. The Ashton deal had been predicated on Serbia being allowed to become a candidate for EU membership and Kosovo getting a SAA deal with the EU. The SAA established a free trade area between the EU and Kosovo and saw Pristina agree to adopt – albeit slowly – the EU's *acquis communautaire* – the principles of the European Union that govern trade, education, employment and the judiciary.

Critically, the SAA demanded that Kosovo set up a special court in The Hague to investigate alleged war crimes during the war – a move that puzzled international prosecutors given that it was far and away more of an onerous requirement than that subjected to other post-conflict countries.

But such attempts by Thaçi at formal bridge-building with Belgrade faced no bigger opposition than from within his own country. In 2015, members of opposition parties threw tear gas into the Pristina parliament building in protest over a Brussels-brokered deal in August of that year to allow Serb majority municipalities to form an association to protect their interests in Kosovo. The attacks – which culminated in a mass protest and part of the Pristina parliament building set on fire – prompted Johannes Hahn, the Brussels Commissioner for EU Enlargement – to offer to convene talks between Thaçi and the opposition.

Despite the protests, Thaçi, with the support of advisors from Rambouillet days like Blerim Shala and Edita Tahiri, plodded on with pursuing so-called technical agreements between Pristina and Belgrade. On top of the August 2015 Serb municipalities deal, Kosovo managed to get agreement to have its own international dialling code and Serbian and Kosovan police began cooperating over checks at the six crossing points on the border they share. According to an interview with Agence Europe, the head of Kosovo's border police said the two forces also shared intelligence on trafficking – albeit through EULEX.

If Thaçi is able to get an agreement with Serbia that beckoned full normalisation of relations with Belgrade, it is likely that UN membership for Kosovo would follow. According to Thaçi, such an agreement would mark 'the end of all our struggles'.

At the beginning of 2016, Kosovo had a mixed bag of results to show for its ambition to be members of clubs on the world stage. Apart from the International Monetary Fund and the World Bank, they had just a few memberships to regional bodies. Kosovo became part of

FIFA in 2016 – it was granted membership of UEFA and FIFA since May of that year. It joined cultural organisations such as Organisation internationale de la Francophonie and it managed to obtain votes to become a member of a several European bodies as a sovereign nation – such as European Bank for Reconstruction and Development as well as Venice Commission of the Council of Europe.

Thaçi hopes to get EU candidacy status by 2023 and be on course for NATO and EU accession before 2030. In the meantime, he wants to become a member of other regional bodies and UN agencies such as the Commonwealth, the WHO or the council of Europe.

But with Thaçi's first five-year presidency due to run until 2021, he faces the prospect of being out of the picture by the time Kosovo EU membership would even be possible. It is a notion that Thaçi has mulled over. Just two months before he was elected President by the Parliament, Thaçi said that he was considering whether he would change the country's constitution so that he could run for President for a second term – but, this time, elected by the public rather than MPs. Such a move, if successful, could see him secure EU membership while head of state.

CHAPTER 15

INAUGURATION AND
THAÇI'S FAMILY

When Thaçi clambered out of a NATO helicopter at the height of the three-month bombardment in the Drenica Valley, it was not, this time, to offer intelligence about Serb positions for Western targeting.

As he landed in a field near the village of Burojë, in spring 1999, it was to see if his parents were still alive. Both parents had been hiding in the nearby hills throughout the entire bombing campaign, with little possibility of communicating with the outside world.

His father Haxhi, then sixty-one, and his mother Hyra, a year older, still lived in the house where Thaçi had been born, and where they had raised their nine children, of whom Hashim was their seventh.

But Burojë, a rural hamlet with fewer than 300 houses, lay in the heart of the Drenica Valley, the hotbed of Albanian insurgence, where the seeds of the uprising against Serb domination had been sown, and from where the cream of the Kosovan Liberation Army had been recruited. The entire region became a focal point of Serbian 'slash and burn' warfare against civilians. What the Serbs failed to destroy was finished off by NATO. The Serbs, knowing that their time was up and facing the might of NATO, began a series of horrific reprisal massacres to avenge the Kosovar uprising.

Thaçi knew better than any that his parents would be prized murder targets: he was a key KLA leader and two of his brothers – Gani and Blerim – were also KLA soldiers. Only a year before, his friend Adam Jashari, a founder of the KLA and – like Thaçi – a son of the Drenica Valley, had been murdered along with fifty-eight members of his family.

What confronted Thaçi on that cold March day was not the two-storey family home, surrounded by outbuildings, farming equipment and livestock, but a piece of land and a charred wreck smouldering on top of it. He was too late; his family home had been razed to the ground by the Serbs. It had once been a four-roomed house built on a hillside – where all of the seven boys had at different times shared one bedroom growing up – surrounded by sheep and cows, arable crops and apple trees. It was now a charred wreck.

But, as Thaçi looked around, he saw his parents sitting alone underneath a cherry tree for shelter. They may have lost their home, but Thaçi's parents were lucky to have escaped with their lives.

It was the third time that Thaçi's family home had been raided by the Serbs since he had become a student leader in 1993. It had been burned to the ground twice. On the first two occasions, the raids had been to intimidate him and his brother, through his family, but this time it was revenge for NATO bombardment.

The 1999 Serb raid, however, was far darker than the others. In the days before the Serbs burned down their home, they perpetrated one of the worst massacres of the war – in the village that could be seen from Thaçi's dining room window.

As Thaçi approached his parents, his father confirmed to him what KLA sources on the ground had learned days before. It was a massacre that his father had managed to flee from by hiding in the surrounding Rezalle mountains in the village of Tushilë.

On 28 March, just four days after the beginning of NATO airstrikes, Serb forces stormed the nearby village of Izbica.

Serb soldiers and policemen, some with balaclavas, others with their faces painted, came with knives and guns. They separated the men, many of them elderly, from the women and small children, then ordered them to form two groups. The troops demanded money and valuables from them, and then shot them dead. Numbers of fatalities vary, but the Serbs are believed to have killed between 127 and 154 people that day. So brutal was the massacre, it would form part of the indictment brought against Milošević and four cohorts just three months later.

According to an Albanian doctor called Liri Loshi, who managed to smuggle a video tape of the aftermath of the killings to CNN, he was 'shocked' by what he saw – namely the three groups of dead men, some lying next to their walking sticks. Dr Loshi said that among them he recognised the body of his cousin, who had been knifed in the head.

While the footage was never verified, it appeared to chime with aerial photographs obtained by NATO, which they believed showed forty-three mass graves in Kosovo.

Seventeen years on, the elderly couple have rebuilt the home that the Serbs destroyed just yards from their old property, and have rebuilt their lives. They are philosophical about the attacks on them. 'We were never afraid of the reprisals,' Haxhi recalls, 'but we were all fully aware that such a scenario was likely. We were realistic.'

Speaking from his newly built dining room on wooden stilts, he points to Izbica, now filled with outhouses and farming equipment.

'We would never have given into oppressors. Whether it was the Serbs or during the Second World War. It is in our blood.'

The large room – empty but for a wood-burning stove and cushioned window benches around the sides – is adorned with framed front pages of magazines adorned with Thaçi's face, declaring him to be the new face of the Kosovan peace process. There is another older photograph, however, of Thaçi's grandfather, who fought in the Second World War against units of Serb Chetniks, the paramilitary quisling groups who became notorious for their massacres of Muslim populations in Bosnia and Kosovo. Nowhere is the blood of the Kosovars more obvious than Thaçi's family home. Outside the house is a road sign – '3 *deshmoret*', or '3 martyrs' – referring to local deaths during the last Kosovo war.

Haxhi's long-held pragmatism about Serb reprisals against his family – and the Drenica community – had proved to be prescient.

'The first time we were raided was in 1993,' Haxhi said.

> At the time the Serb secret services had been monitoring the group – called People's Movement for Kosovo – of which Hashim was a part. Some of the members were imprisoned in Pristina jails. But they also targeted us.
>
> I remember the first raid very clearly. It was brutal. They broke down the door around about noon. There must have been sixty Serbian police, fully armed. It took them three and a quarter hours [to search the house].

'There was not a single corner, not a single spot that they didn't turn upside down,' he added, describing how he and his wife waited outside the house during the raid.

> We were not physically hurt, but the insults… It was all about applying psychological pressure on Hashim. Some of them were hoping to find him here, but they didn't. And Idriz [a brother,

six years older than Hashim] received a tip-off at the last minute
that they were coming. They found Idriz's passport and his driving
licence and confiscated them.

What had saved Thaçi's brother, and the lives of other KLA members
from Serb raids, however, was, paradoxically, the very reason they were
a target. The Drenica Valley, while 700 square kilometres wide and home
to around 100,000 people, was, and remains, intensely tightly knit.

Even now, but certainly at the height of the war, few outsiders can
enter the Drenica Valley without attracting attention. It is still impossible
to find the Thaçi family home without the help of locals – and while the
property is now a large house with metal gates and a balcony overseeing
the valley, in style it is still no more distinct than those of its neighbours.
Inside, the house is modern, comfortable and modest. There is certainly
no plaque to commemorate the birthplace of a President.

In 1993, only farm tracks led visitors to the Thaçi family home – and
there were few road signs in the area.

Then, in the villages around Burojë, many adult men had either been
to primary school in Turiqcec with Thaçi or one of his brothers, or
attended the same high school in Skenderaj. Neighbours of different
generations had grown up and been educated together.

Older men had also fought alongside Hashim's grandfather, Sinam,
in 1944 in the battle for Kolasin, in Montenegro, against the Serbian-
led Chetniks.

All seven of the Thaçi boys knew the 5km radius of the family home
– and those who lived there – because they had hunted the terrain for
rabbits and wild pigs with their father as teenagers.

Just before the 1993 raid of Thaçi's family home, villagers before Burojë
had seen the Serbs coming and sent word on. Even with no telephone
landline in the house, Thaçi's brother Idriz was alerted and he fled.

It had been a close call for Idriz. His father said:

> The Serbs were well informed. Idriz had been living in Austria,
> but he had recently been back in Kosovo to take part in street
> demonstrations. The Serbs had monitored him in major
> protests in Vienna too, and had alerted them back in Belgrade.
> He had been photographed outside a UN building in Vienna,
> demonstrating against the Serbs. They wanted to harm him, not
> just because he was protesting, and not just because of his role
> in the KLA, but because he was helping to fund Hashim back
> in Kosovo.

The next raid on Thaçi's family came in September 1997, at the height
of open warfare between the KLA and Serb police that was so intense
it prompted NATO to deliver an ultimatum to Milošević. This second
raid would prove far more serious and violent than the first. According
to Idriz, he and his elder brother Gani had been driving to Skenderaj,
when they noticed a car behind them and suspected they were being
followed. 'Gani told me he thought they were Serbs because he did not
recognise anyone in the car. Skenderaj is a small place but we knew no
one in the vehicle.' The car also had no number plates, a sure sign of
Serbian intelligence services.

Idriz, who is six years older than Hashim, said: 'We would later
find out that they were from the elite unit of the Yugoslav intelligence
service in Belgrade, top-level spies from federal-level intelligence.'

Gani, ten years older than Hashim, was still living in Kosovo as
a KLA commander, unlike Idriz, who had fled to Austria and was
planning to stay with his family for just a fortnight. The elder of the
brothers knew they were in trouble and that the Serbs were about to
detain both of them.

'Stop the car,' Gani recalls telling Idriz. 'You drive on, you continue. I'll take my chances,' Idriz said. 'He risked his life for me that day.'

Gani got out of the car and Idriz continued for a few hundred metres, before stopping to look back to see what had become of his brother:

> From the distance, I saw them bundle him into the boot of their car with a bag over his head. Not detained: kidnapped. We would not see him for another eighteen days. Eighteen days with no news, no information, not even a sense of where he was being held. Looking back, I suspect he was spirited over the border and held in Serbia, where they tortured him.

In the hours after his brother's kidnap, Idriz scoured the area and asked locals if they knew where the car with no number plates had gone, but to no avail.

'I didn't go to the police station because I was afraid it would make Gani's predicament even worse,' he added.

The following day, Haxhi, Hashim's father, went to the police station in Skenderaj, demanding information about the whereabouts and welfare of his son. There he was told to go to see the authorities in the nearby city of Mitrovica. For nearly three weeks, Haxhi was sent between the two towns and the main police station in Pristina, hiring Albanian lawyers, but no information on his son was given.

'The Serb policemen told me that my son had been kidnapped by Albanian gangs – they were saying that his disappearance had nothing to do with ethnic issues,' Haxhi said.

In desperation, Haxhi approached the Americans – at the time, the US had an office in Pristina, which would become the American embassy once Kosovo declared independence.

'Idriz and I both realised that the Americans were our last hope.

This period was one of absolute terror and chaos, and they were among the few whom we could trust. They told me that they would do their utmost to help us.'

On the eighteenth day after Gani's disappearance, a large Serbian convoy arrived at the Thaçi home in Burojë with tanks, a number of police cars and a helicopter. Among them was Gani.

According to Haxhi, the Serb police pulled him and his wife into a small room in the house along with Gani's infant son, who had been sleeping.

'Once the raid was over, one of the Serb police came to me and said: "Look what we have found. You Albanians, you even keep hand grenades under a child's bed." We all knew that they had planted them there,' said Haxhi.

Once the raid was over, Gani was released into the farm track outside the house, handcuffed. According to Haxhi, their 41-year-old son could barely stand up. While his face was not bruised, they would later discover he had been beaten and electrocuted.

Rather than remove his handcuffs, what followed was a bizarre torturous pantomime. The Serb police made Gani get into the family tractor still with his wrists bound, and try to steer the vehicle to show them where the Thaçi brothers had hidden arms and weaponry. They suspected that arms caches were buried in the nearby cornfields, farmed by the Thaçi family. Sitting on either side of him was a Serb police officer, both to guard him and to help him drive the vehicle.

After finding nothing, the police took Gani away, this time to a prison in the northern Kosovan city of Mitrovica.

'They discovered no armaments, except the two hand grenades, which I knew they had planted,' said Haxhi. 'We didn't hide grenades under a child's bed. But this time, even though Gani had been taken away again, at least we knew where he was going.'

Haxhi was able to see Gani a week later in Mitrovica jail. Gani told his father that he did not know where he had been held for the eighteen days but that it seemed to him to be a private house and he suspected that it was owned by the Yugoslav secret service – the UDBA.

It would be another three months before Gani would actually appear in court. According to his father, the main charge against him was the illegal possession of two hand grenades, with another six lesser charges.

'I will never forget the moment I saw him first enter the court room,' Haxhi recalled. 'Gani could not stand on his own feet. Those people who presented themselves as judges, they were everything but judges.'

There were three court appearances – in one, Gani told Serb officials present: 'You planted the grenades in the house, not me.' His father and brother believe that Gani never succumbed to the torture meted out by the Serbs, and admitted to nothing. 'The UDBA – they were very careful. They didn't hit him in the face, they wanted to make sure that the beatings and torture were not visible. But they electrocuted him. He still suffers the trauma of what they did to him, all these years later,' Idriz said.

After the third court hearing, the judges agreed to release Gani temporarily, and he was allowed to go home. The family house was surrounded by journalists from the likes of Voice of America and Radio Free Europe, waiting to interview Gani, where, broken and battered, he predicted that a NATO bombardment would happen very soon because 'we just cannot live like this any more'.

Gani was right. By the time of his next scheduled court appearance, the war had begun. He never returned to the court house and was sentenced to seven years in prison in his absence. If he crosses the border, even now, into Serbia, he believes he would be arrested and forced to serve his term.

Gani was not just a target for the Serbs because he was Thaçi's elder brother. Both Gani and Idriz were part of extensive networks outside Kosovo that raised funds for armaments for the KLA and smuggled money through the Albanian diaspora back home. While Idriz refuses to be drawn on details of who helped move the money, he does says that 'the Albanian diaspora helped in an enormous way, financing the war greatly'.

———————

Eighteen years on, sitting in the back garden of Thaçi's family home, his parents and two of his brothers are philosophical. They have a right to be. Thaçi's vision has paid off, albeit at a terrible price.

Each member of Thaçi's close family has paid that price. Of Thaçi's seven surviving siblings – an elder sister died in 1964, aged three – only one lives in Kosovo: his youngest sister Kumuije, who is forty. His five brothers fled Kosovo and claimed asylum with the Kosovar diaspora in Austria. His elder sister Miradije also fled Kosovo and now lives in France. Gani was tortured by the Serb security authorities, and Thaçi's father, now seventy-eight, lost the sight in one eye during the NATO bombardment. Both of his parents watched as their sons were pursued and lived in fear of them being either 'disappeared' by the Serb secret police or simply murdered.

Thaçi's wife Lumnije was forced to live in exile in Zürich, in the canton of Dietikon, and their marriage was punctuated with Hashim away for long periods after he finished his studies and set about in earnest building a rebel fighting force. Their son Endrit was born in Zürich, during the NATO bombing campaign, and did not go to Kosovo until he was six months old. Even then, time was sacrificed with his father – having spent a short, miserable stint at an expensive boarding school in London.

Now, surrounded by his carefully tended apple trees, in an immaculate garden with outhouses and large roofed barbeque area, Haxhi chain-smokes as he drinks thick black coffee and reflects on his son's journey.

> Hashim was always a good student. I always knew he would turn into someone, into a successful person. His great interest at school, his great interest in education, paved his way to having this successful career although we couldn't have known that he would become Prime Minister and then President. He was always very studious.

Haxhi had encouraged his children to discuss politics from an early age. After walking home from school in Skenderaj and hunting the woods around their home, over the dinner table Thaçi and his brothers and sisters fiercely debated Serb dominance, Belgrade apartheid against the Kosovars and where the fate of the region lay. By Thaçi's own admission, his own sense of nationhood was forged over his mother Hyra's Albanian meals.

As a postgraduate in Zürich, one of his professors would later point out that Thaçi was the only student he had lectured whose own life would change the very text of the history books that were being taught at the university.

While Haxhi and his wife had no home telephone until peacetime, they did have a television, and he recalls his wife and children crowding around the set watching Thaçi filmed at rallies and latterly at the Rambouillet peace talks. His father watched with a sickening mixture of fear for his young son's life, anxieties for reprisals against the rest of his family and a sense of overwhelming pride.

Almost twenty years on from watching their young son brief reporters outside the Rambouillet château for peace talks that would change the course of his own life and that of Kosovo, Thaçi stood before the cameras again – this time for his inauguration speech as President.

In the front row sat his parents – his father wearing the traditional white kufi, the brimless white cap worn by elders across different world religions. On that freezing April day in 2016, Haxhi had to pinch himself as he watched his son – now the fourth President of an independent Kosovo.

From the podium on the Skanderbeg Square in Pristina, in front of a thousand dignitaries, television crews and hundreds of Kosovars watching from the office blocks and apartment buildings that over-looked him, Thaçi began his address.

Thaçi indulged himself briefly, describing how his own journey and struggles matched that of the birth of an independent Kosovo. He explained the sacrifices that he and the people of Kosovo had made to reach his inauguration, and, as one would expect, made a plea for unity, tolerance and solidarity.

> Today, we start building a new tradition. This is another stone in building a joint history as a multi-ethnic, secular state that embraces the values of the Euro-Atlantic family. This ceremony is a new chapter in our book of joint successes, where elections, ceremonies, national holidays, slowly enrich the delicate story of our state. These are ornaments of the statehood that we are jointly engraving.

However, far from being a celebration of his achievements, both Thaçi's speech and the ceremony itself marked the difficult predicament he found himself in and the extraordinary challenges he now faces.

At the beginning of the ceremony, political opponents managed to tear-gas some of the delegates. They were angry that Thaçi – whom they refused to accept as President – had signed a deal the year before giving more rights to Serb minorities. Vetëvendosje, the biggest opposition party in the country, claimed responsibility for the tear-gas attack, which left diplomats and Prime Ministers of neighbouring countries spluttering. One female envoy used her scarf to cover her nose and mouth as a top aide of President Erdoğan, the Turkish leader, was heard to say dryly: 'As a member of the Turkish government, I'm used to tear gas.'

While Thaçi had anticipated trouble – the day before, opposition supporters had thrown stones outside the parliament building – and security was intense, the attack was embarrassing. As the gas spread across the guests, Thaçi declared:

> We must continue dialogue with Serbia. This is an obligation and a national duty that requires us that, even in the most difficult moments [...] and even in the most difficult provocation, we don't despair and we don't give in to hate and don't give up. Kosovo and Serbia must transcend [...] to reconciliation between our two states and two nations.

If his words prove to be true in the future, no one at the ceremony was left in any doubt that he would not have the backing of his opposition party to achieve such reconciliation. And it certainly grated with Thaçi's plea for national unity that would 'enrich the delicate story of our state'.

In his speech, he also vowed to make Kosovo part of the global battle against terror, fresh attacks unleashed by the migrant crisis that saw hundreds of thousands of refugees – including jihadists – arrive in Europe.

However, his promise that 'Kosovo will be a strong link in the anti-terrorist chain' would only months later prove to be challenged by Kosovan extremists. It is now estimated that several hundred former jihadists live in Kosovo, though over 100 of them have been arrested and sentenced after the adoption of a law in the Kosovo Parliament that bans participation in foreign wars. Principal jihadi leaders like Lavdrim Muhaxheri have been killed in Syria, but there are fears that others may have returned to Kosovo. In November 2016, Kosovan intelligence services picked up on online chatter about a possible terror attack at an Israeli football match due to be hosted at a stadium in Albania. What they discovered was a plot by around ten young men from Albania and Kosovo, who planned to bomb the football stadium and thousands of sports fans using an 8kg drone they had bought from Amazon, packed with explosives. Thaçi would later admit how close the extremists had got to completing their attack. The twenty were split into four terror cells, and were guided by a mastermind in Syria. 'I believe it would have been the biggest terror attack on a sporting venue since the Munich Olympics massacre in 1972,' Thaçi said.

The action by the Kosovo intelligence service was well received internationally. Eliot L. Engel, a member of the US House Committee on Foreign Affairs, said:

> I applaud authorities in the Republic of Kosovo for thwarting a planned series of terrorist attacks by ISIS extremists, preventing the massacre of Israel's national soccer team. Kosovo has built an impressive record of confronting violent extremism. No one should doubt the commitment of leaders in Pristina to meet this challenge, and the United States is fortunate to have a partner like Kosovo in this important effort. Given Kosovo's strong record, it's time to speed Kosovo's incorporation into key Euro-Atlantic structures, including NATO and the EU.

Speaking in November 2016, Thaçi was obviously, and justifiably, proud that his own intelligence agencies had foiled such an attack, not least because other strikes on European soil in Paris and Brussels had not been picked up by their own governments. But it also underlined the major threat that Kosovo faces with a jihadist threat – men radicalised in countries such as Syria, returning home to bring terror to mainland Europe.

As Thaçi neared the end of his inaugural address, with ten Kosovan and two EU flags flying by his side, he reiterated his most prized ambition for the country: membership of the EU. 'I will do all that is within my power to support and assist […] Kosovo so that we can move as quickly as we can towards our goal of membership in [*sic*] NATO and in [*sic*] the EU.'

However, his speech left many at the inauguration wondering what state the European Union will find itself in once Kosovo – at least a decade away from membership – is about to join. Today, it is an EU damaged by the Brexit vote just two months after Thaçi's inauguration and battered by the wave of populism and Euroscepticism in France, the Netherlands, Germany, Italy and central European countries such as Hungary.

CHAPTER 16

CONCLUSION

Hashim Thaçi is a puzzle. When we were mulling over whether to write his story, we sat for a few hours in a Pristina café with Enver Hoxhaj, a historian, foreign minister-in-waiting and the man who probably knows Thaçi better than anyone else. Was he a kind of Robin Hood, we asked, an outlaw with ideals? Was he as ruthless as portrayed by Serb commentators? History books are full of revolutionaries (or terrorists, depending on who is in charge of the school curriculum) turning into statesmen. Menachem Begin, Nelson Mandela, Lech Wałęsa, Fidel Castro... Each of these stories is different and we needed to get a fix on Thaçi's. 'You cannot separate Hashim's life from that of the region,' said Hoxhaj. 'You would be better off looking at Hasan Prishtina.'

He had a point. Prishtina was an Albanian hero who had led revolts, attended international conferences, played off empires against each other, led a government.

Like Thaçi, he was born in the Drenica Valley (in 1873) and studied abroad. At the age of twenty-five he was elected to the Ottoman parliament as representative for Pristina. That's when he changed his name from Berisha to Prishtina. Within years, the Ottomans had betrayed the Albanians. Hasan Prishtina organised an uprising, set out demands and steered a rebel army to take over the whole of Kosovo. During the First World War, he drummed up a volunteer army to fight Austria-Hungary which had seized Kosovo. In 1919, he was at the Paris Peace Conference, briefly became Prime Minister of Albania and never stopped fighting for Kosovan rights. He was killed by a Serb assassin in 1933.

What Thaçi and Prishtina have in common is a sense of outrage that the fate of their countrymen should be determined by outside powers. That passion is what has guided Thaçi through from his student years to the present, when, as President, he has to campaign around the clock for recognition. Prishtina, of course, inhabited a different age; Thaçi has had to find modern solutions to age-old problems of independence and survival.

Across the centuries, the Balkans have been regarded as the very fringe of Europe, the region where the East, and the unknown, begins. The break-up of the Cold War order, however, reshuffled the geopolitical cards. It seemed, when the Berlin Wall tumbled, that Western liberal values had won and the old divisions were doomed. First East Germany, then the Soviet Union collapsed as states. Czechoslovakia broke into two. Initial discussions centred on whether East Germany hooked up with West Germany should be 'Finlandised'; that is, declared neutral, westward-looking but retaining strong, even friendly relations with Moscow. The lure of NATO and the increasingly obvious weakness of what was left of the Soviet Union made that option redundant. United, expanded Germany stayed in the Western alliance and inevitably NATO set its sights further east, looking to recruit the likes of Poland and the Baltic republics. The tectonic plates of the continent were shifting and for a while it seemed as if Europe was enjoying a peaceful revolution.

But the Balkans, and in particular the splintering federal Yugoslavia, was never going to make a smooth transition. Its competing nationalisms, its trapped unhappy minorities, its generations of blood feud, had been repressed but not eliminated by Josip Broz Tito. After Tito, those undercurrents surfaced in the 'Serb project', the ambition fuelled by Milošević to assert a Greater Serbia as the pre-dominant regional power. It had the biggest army, the most developed manufacturing base, coupled with a flawed sense of destiny.

Rather than profiting from a 'peace dividend'– an era of prosperity, safety and declining defence budgets – the destructive force of Milošević's plan plunged the neighbourhood into years of bloody warfare and atrocity. And those seemingly robust Western institutions, NATO, the EU and the UN, did not know how to deal with it. Their roles seemed outdated and inappropriate; their processes hollow.

That was the world inherited by Thaçi; a collision between the old snakebite politics of the Balkans, and the sluggish, confused West that was not sure who it was or how to protect Europeans under threat. Hasan Prishtina certainly had to find room for himself, and for Kosovo, amid collapsing empires, but Thaçi's challenge was the greater.

As this book has tried to show, the trouble began in Kosovo, in its crushing repression, and that is where it should end too: with a Serbian acceptance of the rights of the Kosovars to self-determination. In all of these phases Hashim Thaçi has been a significant presence. Sometimes a conspirator, sometimes a fighter, but, since the late 1980s as Europe entered its period of upheaval, always a leader. He outlasted and outwitted Milošević, the man who had declared him to be Serbia's Enemy Number One. He outlived Ibrahim Rugova, the ill-fated President of Kosovo, and won the key arguments about when and how force should be used against tyranny. He has seen Vladimir Putin evolve from a nervous enforcer of Kremlin rule over the breakaway

Chechens to the cynical implementer of Blitzkrieg against Georgia and Ukraine. Now Thaçi watches with alarm as an emboldened Putin spreads his influence through the Balkans.

It was Thaçi who artfully won the support of three US administrations and who is now negotiating with a fourth. He is struggling to make out of his land-locked country a modern, tolerant and vibrant society. And, above all, it is Thaçi who has led Kosovo through turbulent times to independence.

Thaçi is not short of critics. At home his rivals accuse him of selling out to Serbia, of arrogance and of ruling with the help of a tight clique. The critics in the international community say he has been too slow to stamp out corruption. He is often torn between the demands of the EU to reach out more convincingly to the Serb minority and the dark, disruptive deceits emanating from the Belgrade propaganda machine. For some in Kosovo, every concession to Belgrade is a step too far, an act of wilful amnesia that dishonours the dead. Frank G. Wisner, the shrewdest of US negotiators, said of Thaçi after transforming himself from dogged guerrilla leader into a statesman, 'he sure scrubbed up nice'. That was meant as a compliment; to his critics in Kosovo it suggested a chameleon-like politician, one who is trying to please too many people.

Yet it is precisely these qualities that have made him a man of his times. It would have been madness to turn himself into a tinpot, paranoid version of Milošević, another Balkan strongman who chucks his opponents in jail. He understood quickly that Kosovo had to turn its underground civil resistance – its secret classrooms, its clandestine presses – into the germ of an open society.

Most of all, Thaçi will be remembered (and no doubt quietly hated in Belgrade) as the man who persuaded the world's strongest alliance to come to the assistance of his ragtag liberation army; the man who parlayed that war into international support for independence. That took *chutzpah*, but it was only a fraction of what he achieved as he set about reinventing the politics of the Balkans over the past two decades.

When he was a student leader, enraged by the de facto apartheid system imposed by the Serbs on the Kosovo Albanians, he first envied what was happening in central Europe and was then depressed by it. The Velvet Revolution of the Czechs, marching on the Prague Castle with playwright Václav Havel at their head – that would never have worked in Kosovo. Its success depended on the police, uniformed and secret, covertly sympathising with the protestors and allowing them to go unhindered. But the Serb police units were not only paid to uphold the dictatorship, they also believed in it. Like many in Serbia, they were convinced that Kosovo was the very cradle of the Serbian nation. Let it slip away and Serbia would be diminished and weakened. No, Thaçi calculated, the Kosovan struggle was more akin to an uprising against colonial overlords.

And ultimately that would mean some form of armed protest. Ibrahim Rugova admired the Poles with their striking workers and the way that Solidarity intellectuals had pushed an ailing regime into power-sharing talks. But there was not even a narrow segment within the Milošević court ready to sit down and talk on equal terms with Kosovo Albanians. The only expression of power understood by the regime was armed force.

Thaçi helped shape this discussion. There were some guns in the country, chiefly for hunting, but what would they achieve? In his native Drenica Valley, the resistance of family farmsteads, the readiness to use a weapon, had kept Serb police out of their daily lives.

That, however, was no solution for the whole of Kosovo. No Kosovan army would ever be able to beat the Serbs in an outright battle; the heavy artillery and the fighter planes that had made the Yugoslav army a force to be reckoned with now formed the backbone of Milošević's battle-hardened regiments. The Kosovars could create local defence militias to protect farmsteads and run the risk of reprisals. Or they could keep up a low-intensity long-running guerrilla war that would eventually tire out Serbian units. Young urban Serbs had demonstrated against Milošević in Belgrade; if they thought now that they were going to be shot at during conscription, perhaps they would think again about the repression of Kosovo.

That was a bit too far-fetched for Thaçi. Even those Serbs who hated Milošević considered Kosovo to be non-negotiable. And whatever the purpose of a liberation army for Kosovo, it would need a regular supply of weapons and funds. And that would mean reaching out to Kosovars living abroad, creating a kind of global resistance movement. Thaçi's brilliant intuition was this: the accumulation of weapons, the building of a military organisation, was not so much about waging physical battle as capturing attention.

Until Thaçi emerged, Kosovo had been a mere diplomatic footnote. Its leading lights, Rugova and men like his advisor, the surgeon Alush Gashi, flickered on the very margins of global politics. Despite the gross violations of human rights in the province, its representatives found themselves confined to the coffee bar of Geneva's Palais des Nations rather than in the assembly room when the UN human rights committees were meeting. Only member states were given access to meetings. Kosovo was locked out. As a result, even real champions of Pristina's cause such as Austria found it almost impossible to think of Kosovo's future except as a semi-free province of Serbia. Kosovo was not remotely comparable to South Tyrol nor would it ever be susceptible to the kind of power-sharing and autonomy deals that had put an end to the conflict between Italy and Austria. How many times did it have to be explained to Western governments: Kosovo had once enjoyed a degree of autonomy under Tito but it had been extinguished under Milošević. Kosovo needed the confidence that came from statehood.

Kosovo was floundering. Rugova hailed it as a great success when Kosovo was added to the UN Human Rights Commission's statement on eliminating racial discrimination in 1991. The rest of the world didn't notice. Diplomacy for the coming years was trained instead on Belgrade's assault on Croatia and the spread of bloodshed to Bosnia. The plight of Sarajevo in particular made the slow-burning crisis of Kosovo – the targeted killings, the arbitrary arrests, the sacking of Albanian staff – seem like a minor sideshow. Even the Dayton Agreement in 1995, America's attempt to broker peace between Serbia, Croatia and Bosnia, failed to register the needs of the Kosovars. For Thaçi, the lesson was clear: if you don't fight for your country, if you are not seen to be fighting, no one in the West will give a damn about you.

Thaçi, then, was a reluctant guerrilla leader. His intuition – the speed of events would only later provide him with a more solid crash-course in geopolitics – told him that there was no such thing any more as 'Western' or even US opinion. Kosovo staying part of Serbia was the price that US power-brokers had to pay to Milošević to secure a peace with the Bosnians and the Croats. If Kosovars zipped their lips and put up with the indignity of Serb rule, stability would return eventually to the Balkans. Little wonder that Kosovars felt betrayed.

But Thaçi had grasped another strand in US thinking: not just a rush for a deal at any price but also the shame of not having prevented the massacre at Srebrenica, the bombardment of market places, the mass graves. Other interventions such as in Somalia had also ended on a sour note; instances of inaction, such as the genocide of Rwanda, still smarted with Bill Clinton. Thaçi came to understand that the power of shame could nudge the US into action again. It was an important conclusion, one which determined his tactics. Kosovo, and the emerging

KLA, had to keep the pot boiling, openly challenge Milošević's brutality, until the US administration found the will to act independently of the floundering global institutions. The UN was in a logjam, wedded as it was to the principle of non-interference in the internal affairs of member states. And NATO, in flux since the end of the Cold War, could not work out how it should assert itself. The European order, meanwhile, seemed to be crumbling, with hundreds of thousands of Bosnian refugees moving into the core EU states.

And Milošević was still unchained. In 1997–98, he stepped up his campaign of intimidation against Kosovo. He had expected Western rewards after signing up to Dayton but sanctions were suspended, not lifted; the economy was suffering, investors straying away. Milošević had become an international pariah – and his response, typically contrarian, was to launch an offensive against Kosovo. He claimed he was exercising his right to beat down an insurgent force – the KLA – but it became increasingly plain he was going to force out civilians. His troops planted anti-personnel mines in the evacuated villages to make sure the inhabitants would not return. Milošević was reverting to the familiar tactic of ethnic cleansing.

When mutilated corpses of executed civilians were discovered in Račak in central Europe, Thaçi immediately understood its significance. Milošević's men were treading the same path as they had in Bosnia – their crime had made the argument for military intervention. A US envoy was on the spot soon afterwards, declaring it to be a 'crime against humanity'. Thaçi's political talent unfolded in the coming months. First he led the Kosovan delegation to the Rambouillet peace talks – billed by Western participants as a last-ditch attempt at a diplomatic settlement – and risked upsetting his political base at home by reluctantly agreeing with the US that he shouldn't insist on an immediate path to independence. Instead, he won a supplementary letter to the agreement which promised to consider a referendum on independence three years after Rambouillet came into effect.

That seemed to Thaçi's fighters to be pretty lukewarm, but it was a necessary piece of political theatre. If the Kosovars signed up for the deal and Milošević refused, then the US could embark on a military offensive while telling its allies that it had tried every possible diplomatic avenue.

Such was the way of the world and the artifice employed in many US military interventions. Since such campaigns have to be waged as coalitions, often accountable to reluctant governments, the decision to go to war has to be hemmed in with preconditions. The bombing period has to be limited, the targeting agreed by every national government. As a result, the element of surprise is lost. Military orthodoxy – that is, the overwhelming use of firepower – goes out of the window when an intervention is conducted by a coalition of nineteen democracies. None of the coalition considered Kosovo to be a vital national interest.

There was a problem, too, with the legal justification for war against Serbia. Within the Clinton administration, advisors warned against the explicit use of unilateral humanitarian intervention as a legal basis for bombing. If this became doctrine, it would turn the US into a permanent globo-cop. A supportive UN resolution was impossible given the Russian–Serb axis and the Kremlin's reluctance to act.

Clinton thus broadened the US motivation for action beyond the protection of innocent lives and argued that it was needed to prevent a wider war. Two world wars had been sparked in Europe, he argued, and Milošević's use of force – by directly threatening European security – could trigger a third. Thus, if NATO was to remain credible in the post-Cold War age, it had to accept a special alliance responsibility to Europe that went further than its Article 5 commitment to collective defence.

Thaçi thus played a significant role in the intervention debate that was to define military politics for the following two decades. He could not only testify to the persecution of civilians by Milošević's troops, he could also field soldiers of his own, answering any Allied doubts as to whether limited air warfare was enough. On the ground, the KLA relayed targets via bases in Albania to the NATO command. And they would draw hidden Serb units out into the open so that they could be hit by Allied fighter jets. They passed on intelligence and, holed up on Mount Paštrik towards the end of the bombing offensive, they were aided by NATO firepower.

The US administration had more than once vowed never to act as the air force for the KLA. By the middle of 1999, thanks to Thaçi, that was exactly what they had become. The political result was quickly apparent: as de facto NATO allies, the KLA considered itself the victor in a war of liberation and the natural rulers of a soon-to-be independent Kosovo.

That was to bring the KLA trouble as some veterans considered themselves above the law and deserving of Western protection rather than criticism. Every nation state has its founding myth and its founding heroes; statues of KLA soldiers can be seen nowadays across Kosovan territory. Part of Thaçi's post-war passage into institutional politics was to confront and outmanoeuvre domestic rivals. Some of them had been fellow KLA commanders and, though he gained in confidence in dealing with them, he never found it easy to tackle their discontents.

For the Western alliance, meanwhile, Kosovo became a model for successful humanitarian intervention; it gave NATO a new sense of purpose. When the 9/11 attacks shattered the consciousness of America, the Kosovo model informed the US top brass as to how wars could be won from the air, providing the strategic goals were circumscribed and there was no mission creep. In some ways, though, the 2003 invasion of Iraq diminished the achievements of Kosovo. According to the German general Klaus Naumann, the Kosovo campaign had been the most precise air war in modern history, inflicting the least collateral damage. Some 38,000 sorties had been flown and only two aircraft lost. It was a test of newly accurate weapons systems; by the Iraq invasion of 2003, US commanders were glorying in their technological superiority: Shock and Awe became the watchwords.

Yet its political purpose was as imprecise as the weapons were precise. The Kosovo war was far more lucid in its aims: to bring Milošević back to the negotiating table. The coalition had managed to strike a balance between disabling a dictator who had embraced the idea of a full-out war, and an offensive that had to be fought in the full glare of domestic publicity. The war aspired to being limited, transparent and politically accountable. It was wrong, then, to assume that the Iraq War would be fought in a way resembling Kosovo. Starting from the flawed war aim of finding and removing weapons of mass destruction, the war turned out to be infinitely more complex. Its aftermath continues to dog the politics of the Middle East. Milošević was not toppled by the war except in the sense that many Serbs could not forgive him for politicising Kosovo and then losing it. He died not at the end of a noose like Saddam Hussein, but of a heart attack alone in his Hague detention cell.

Thaçi's post-war problems were not comparable to those of post-war Iraq – but they were formidable. He had to win popular trust – many Kosovars seemed to regard him as a wartime rather than peacetime leader – and simultaneously speed the way towards independence. Once he had finally persuaded the international community to allow Kosovo's breakaway from Serbia, he had to win recognition, bang on the doors of global organisations and end Kosovo's limbo status.

There were the conventional challenges of leadership – how to modernise his still-poor country, how to attract investment, how to consolidate national identity, how to find ways for a small fledgling state to project power. All these have made Kosovo into a stimulating place, one that is trying to transcend its difficult geography by embracing the digital age; it is a demographically young country humming with new ideas about statecraft.

Two problems continue to hound Thaçi. The first is a throwback to ancient times: the traditional Russian loyalty to Serbia, its Orthodox ally. The US-led push for Kosovan independence has been met with a Moscow-steered pushback. Russia has been instrumental in closing doors for Kosovo to UNESCO and a whole host of international bodies. To reassure Moscow, NATO had presented its Kosovo campaign as *sui generis*, a one-off response to the brutality of Milošević. But Moscow had seen it rather as an attempt to extend the reach of the Western alliance, to hem in not only Serbia but Russia itself. The West, it said, had violated all international norms with its Kosovo operation. What it meant was: the US was using its military clout to redefine the new post-Cold War world in a way that marginalised Russia. NATO's membership action programme, a kind of extended internship for aspiring alliance members, pressed up hard against the Russian borders. In August 2008, barely seven months after Kosovo declared its statehood, the Russians marched into Georgia for having the temerity to befriend NATO. The pattern continued with the annexation of Crimea and the destabilisation of eastern Ukraine in 2014. Again, the example of NATO conduct in Kosovo was held up as an argument to legitimise Russian aggression. The West, it said, had to respect Russia's sphere of interest.

Today, Thaçi finds himself the target not only of deep-seated Serbian resentment, but also of Russia's determination to undermine his state's independence. It's personal: Thaçi is seen as an Atlanticist, aligned with all those parts of the Washington establishment most hostile to the Kremlin. From Madeleine Albright to Hillary Clinton, Thaçi's political friends in the US have rarely had a good word to say about Putin. Thaçi is seen by Moscow as an evangelist of Western power. They see his hand at work in the rapid enlisting of Albania into NATO. He has explicitly welcomed Montenegro's admission to the Western alliance. Russia is seeing its power shrivel in the Balkans and is duly trying to strengthen Serbia, build it up as a bulwark against NATO expansion.

Thaçi can do little about this wall of hostility, not as long as Putin is in power. He counts on the Trump administration to maintain US support for his state and due vigilance against Putin. Any waning of public support, any US grand bargain with Moscow that curbs NATO's eastward expansion, could sap the defences of Kosovo.

It is part of the Putin plan to split Europe, and Kosovo is a useful instrument. The discrediting of Thaçi as the most prominent US enthusiast in the Balkans has thus been a priority for years. Through their disinformation tactics, Serbia, and its Russian mentor, have attempted to portray Thaçi as a ruthless puppet-master, a comic-book villain who deals in body parts and heads a corrupt business empire. There is nothing, however, in the supposedly incriminating dossier compiled by the European parliamentarian Dick Marty, that holds water. And yet its mere publication served a tactical purpose, giving ammunition and talking points to those EU countries opposed to recognising Kosovo, stiffening their spines.

The actual reason that a small minority of EU countries have withheld their recognition was too shaming and self-serving to be conceded in public. Namely that blockers like Spain and Cyprus were terrified of setting some kind of precedent for the Catalans and the Basques or the Turkish Cypriots. All that was ever required from these obstructionists was an honest recognition that Kosovo was different, that it was separating from Serbia because Belgrade's vicious treatment of Kosovo Albanians meant that staying had become impossible. The mild-mannered mediator Martti Ahtisaari was – like Thaçi himself – most disappointed by Madrid's attitude. 'To me it was astonishing,' said the Finn, 'because they could have taken an entirely different position. They could have said: "We have never treated our minorities so badly that we would find ourselves in such a situation."' This fear, this lack of confidence, has led Madrid to actively discourage South American countries from recognising Kosovo.

Even so, the future for Kosovo must be a growing and deepening alignment with the European Union. It is the EU – in the form of EULEX, its law-and-order arm – that has taken over the lion's share of building a fair and balanced judiciary. Other military interventions, such as Libya in 2011, were let down by failures in nation-building and more specifically by a full EU engagement. Europe, Thaçi believes, could and should do more to stabilise the region. He worries that the appetite for the further enlargement of the EU into the western Balkans will flag; that Brussels will grow tired. That populists in western Europe will use the migrant transit routes from war zones in the Middle East as an excuse to cut off the Balkans and define it again as the continent's wild and lawless outer frontier. The political atmosphere is brittle and the very least the EU could do is to help motivate the younger generation with easier access to visas. Funds are made available, boxes are being ticked – by the Kosovars and the Brussels bureaucracy – but there has been a colossal failure of imagination. Visa freedom for Kosovo is a way of saying to the young future middle and professional classes of Kosovo: we understand that membership of the European Union is still a long way off but we respect your ambition and will reward your efforts so far.

This is Thaçi's great final challenge. The assumption in Brussels has been that Serbia and Kosovo should be allowed to progress towards European membership but only if they accept the necessity to cooperate and respect each other. The start of 2017 showed how far there is still to travel. Belgrade initiated a train line from Serbia towards Pristina by painting the carriages in the Serbian colours and smearing them with 'Kosovo is Serbia' in several languages. It was a deliberately provocative act; not the first and surely not the last. Serbia's cause would be well served if Kosovars attacked such carriages as they rolled into Kosovo. Troops were put on alert on both sides of the border. NATO started to look nervously south. Could it all explode again? The train was halted before approaching the Kosovan border but that didn't stop Serbian newspapers stoking tensions by declaring that the Kosovars, with NATO approval, were about to attack the Serb minority. Thaçi tried to soothe the nerves of the Kosovan Serbs. 'This was old-fashioned Serb propaganda,' he said, 'an attempt to manipulate the feelings of the Serbs living in Kosovo. This is also why I insisted on creating a local truth and reconciliation commission – to establish local mechanisms of reconciliation that are rooted locally, not in the ballrooms of Brussels. I believe in truth. I also believe in reconciliation.'

How to transcend these differences? It took France and Germany until the 1990s before their leaders François Mitterrand and Helmut Kohl were able to hold hands symbolically over the graves of the fallen in Verdun. That reconciliation was more than a photo opportunity; it followed decades of often strained efforts to twin cities, exchange schoolchildren, build common institutions. It demands leaders with strategic patience. Thaçi, we are convinced, possesses this quality. The question is: do the West, Europe and the US have a matching commitment to peace on its borders?

INDEX